MW01194971

Technical Service Manual

FOREWORD

The service procedures contained in this Manual are outlined for Metropolitan Models and Series as listed below:

Model		Series	Starting Serial Number
541	Convertible	A	E-1001
542	Hardtop Sedan	A	
541	Convertible	B	E-11001
542	Hardtop Sedan	B	
561	Convertible	1500	E-21008
562	Hardtop Sedan	1500	

Variations in procedures or specifications are listed under specific Series identification.

INTRODUCTION

Welcome to the world of digital publishing ~ the book you now hold in your hand, while unchanged from the original edition, was printed using the latest state of the art digital technology. The advent of print-on-demand has forever changed the publishing process, never has information been so accessible and it is our hope that this book serves your informational needs for years to come. If this is your first exposure to digital publishing, we hope that you are pleased with the results. Many more titles of interest to the classic automobile and motorcycle enthusiast, collector and restorer are available via our website at www.VelocePress.com. We hope that you find this title as interesting as we do.

NOTE FROM THE PUBLISHER

The information presented is true and complete to the best of our knowledge. All recommendations are made without any guarantees on the part of the author or the publisher, who also disclaim all liability incurred with the use of this information.

TRADEMARKS

We recognize that some words, model names and designations, for example, mentioned herein are the property of the trademark holder. We use them for identification purposes only. This is not an official publication.

INFORMATION ON THE USE OF THIS PUBLICATION

This manual is an invaluable resource for the classic **METROPOLITAN** enthusiast and a "must have" for owners interested in performing their own maintenance. However, in today's information age we are constantly subject to changes in common practice, new technology, availability of improved materials and increased awareness of chemical toxicity. As such, it is advised that the user consult with an experienced professional prior to undertaking any procedure described herein. While every care has been taken to ensure correctness of information, it is obviously not possible to guarantee complete freedom from errors or omissions or to accept liability arising from such errors or omissions. Therefore, any individual that uses the information contained within, or elects to perform or participate in do-it-yourself repairs or modifications acknowledges that there is a risk factor involved and that the publisher or its associates cannot be held responsible for personal injury or property damage resulting from the use of the information or the outcome of such procedures.

It is important that the reader recognizes that any instructions may refer to either the right-hand or left-hand sides of the vehicle or the components and that the directions are followed carefully. One final word of advice, this publication is intended to be used as a reference guide, and when in doubt the reader should consult with a qualified technician.

Technical Service Manual

ENGINE SECTION

Engine

ENGINE SECTION

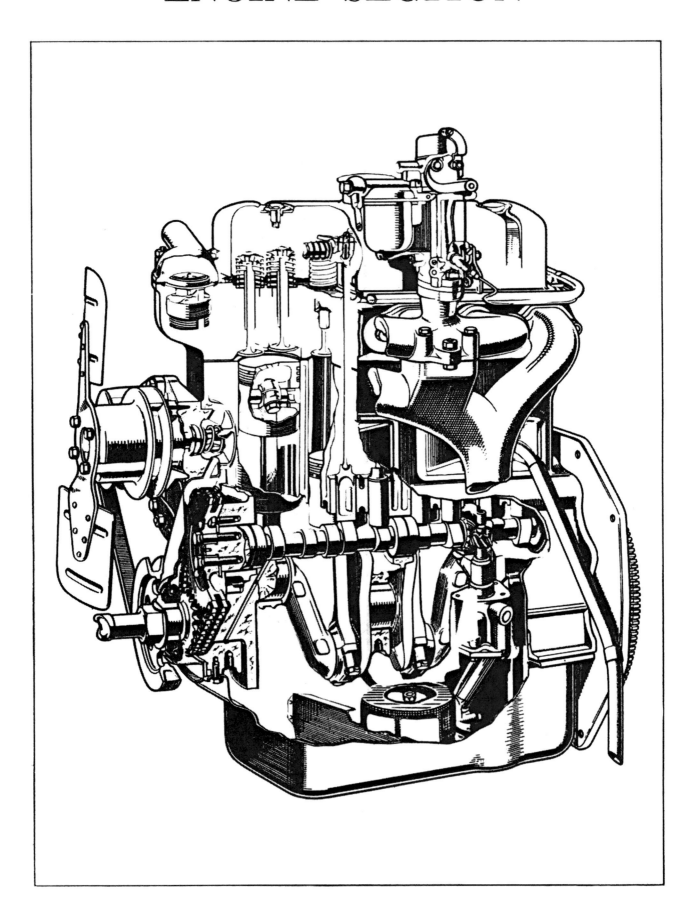

FIGURE 1—*Sectional View of Engine—A and B Series Shown*

1. Connecting Rod and Piston Assembly
2. Push Rod and Tappet
3. Thermostat
4. Cylinder Head Assembly
5. Valve Cover, Breather, and Oil Filler Cap
6. Carburetor
7. Fan and Water Pump Assembly
8. Camshaft and Camshaft Gear
9. Cylinder Block
10. Hot Spot

11. Intake Manifold
12. Exhaust Manifold
13. Fuel Pump
14. Timing Gear Cover and Timing Chain
15. Crankshaft Bearings, and Sprocket
16. Starting Nut, Pulley, Fan and Fan Belt
17. Oil Pan
18. Oil Pump and Strainer Assembly
19. Flywheel

FIGURE 2—*Engine Assembly (Exploded View) A and B Series Shown*

ENGINE IDENTIFICATION

The engine as illustrated in Figures 1 and 2 is of the four cylinder, valve-in-head design.

An engine serial number stamped on a metal tag riveted to the right side of the cylinder block (Fig. 3) is provided for means of identification.

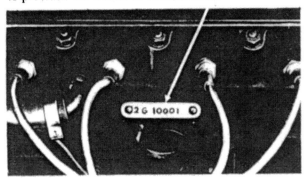

FIGURE 3—*Engine Serial Number Location*

The "A" Series, 1200 c.c. engine became effective at Engine Number IG-880854.

The "B" Series incorporating construction changes in the cylinder block, crankshaft, camshaft, oil pump, rocker arm assembly, and front engine supports became effective at Engine Number 2G-10000.

The "1500" Series engine became effective at Engine Number IH-140001 at which time the piston displacement was increased from 1200 c.c. to 1500 c.c.

At car Serial Number E-43116, the engine serial number prefix was changed to 15 C-N-H designating a higher (8.3 to 1) compression engine in the "1500" Series. A full flow oil filter and lead-indium main and connecting rod bearings were also incorporated at this point.

ENGINE MOUNTING

The engine is mounted on four rubber cushions supported by two crossmembers.

The front support cushions are attached to the engine block, end plate (Fig. 4), and crossmember by suitable brackets.

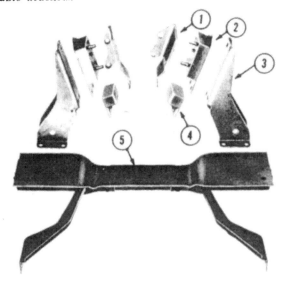

1. **Engine Support Cushion to Engine End Plate Bracket**
2. **Engine Support Cushion**
3. **Engine Support Cushion to Front Crossmember Bracket**
4. **Engine Lower Support Snubber**
5. **Front Engine Support Crossmember**

FIGURE 4—*Front Engine Support Assembly Sequence*

Two support snubbers are used in each front mounting bracket to prevent excessive torque movement of the engine with possibility of interference noise. It is important that a 1/32″ to 1/16″ lower snubber clearance be maintained to prevent engine noise transmitting into the passenger compartment.

It is possible to change the front mounting cushions with the engine weight supported by a chain hoist.

The engine assembly is supported at the rear of the transmission assembly by a crossmember (Fig. 5).

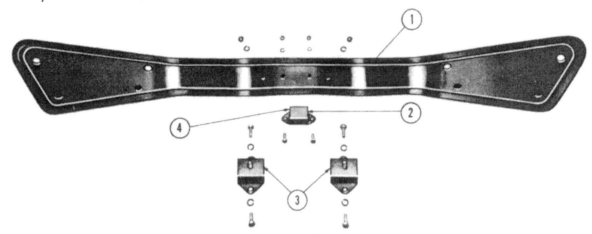

| 1. Rear Crossmember | 3. Engine Rear Support Cushion |
| 2. Engine Rear Support Lower Cushion | 4. Maintain 0 to 1/32″ Maximum Clearance Between Lower Cushion and Transmission Rear Cover |

FIGURE 5—*Rear Engine Support Assembly Sequence*

ENGINE SECTION

ENGINE REMOVAL

There are two methods of engine removal suggested. The first method is used for service engine replacement. The engine is removed for this purpose from the top through the hood opening after separating the engine at the clutch housing. The second suggested removal procedure is used for major engine overhaul services involving main bearing replacement, crankshaft or camshaft removal, and engine end plate gasket replacement.

Engine Removal Procedure for Service Engine Replacement

Drain oil from engine and coolant from cylinder block and radiator core.

Remove hood top and radiator core.

Remove starting motor assembly (from top side).

Remove air cleaner and cylinder head cover.

Disconnect exhaust pipe from manifold.

Disconnect fuel supply line at fuel pump.

Disconnect Weather Eye to engine hoses.

Disconnect all electrical, oil filter, and window washer connections at the engine.

Attach engine lifting fixture (Figs. 9 and 10).

Remove the eight engine support bracket to engine front crossmember attaching bolts.

Remove bolts attaching clutch housing to engine rear plate from engine compartment and from below car.

Move engine forward and upward as illustrated in Figure 6.

Engine Removal Procedure for Major Overhaul Service

Drain oil from engine and transmission units.

Drain coolant from radiator core and cylinder block.

Remove hood top and radiator core.

Remove air cleaner and cylinder head cover.

Disconnect fuel supply line to fuel pump.

Disconnect Weather Eye to engine hoses.

Disconnect and remove the exhaust pipe from the exhaust manifold and front of the muffler. Wire the muffler to left side of underbody.

Disconnect all electrical connections and any other connections, oil filter, window washer, etc.

Attach engine lifting fixture (Figs. 9 and 10).

Remove propeller shaft.

Disconnect speedometer cable from transmission and engine end plate.

Disconnect shift linkage at transmission and wire shift rods to clear engine assembly.

Disconnect clutch linkage.

Support engine weight with lifting fixture and remove all front and rear crossmember to body side sill attaching bolts.

Lower engine assembly from car (Figs. 7 and 8).

FIGURE 6—*Engine Removal for Service Engine Replacement*

FIGURE 7—*Removing Engine Assembly
for Overhaul Service*

ENGINE LIFTING FIXTURE

To simplify the engine removal, as shown in this manual, dimensions of the lifting fixture used are illustrated in Figure 9.

CYLINDER HEAD AND GASKET

Whenever a cylinder head is removed, inspect the studs to make sure they are tight in the engine block. If the studs are removed, they should be sealed with compound upon replacement.

The cylinder head can be removed by removing air cleaner, cylinder head cover, and spark plug wires.

Drain coolant. Disconnect bypass hose from top of water pump. Remove carburetor, exhaust, and intake manifolds. Remove eleven cylinder head to cylinder block stud nuts. Loosen tappet adjustment screws and remove push rods.

The use of a rope sling around the rocker arm shaft will facilitate cylinder head removal from the block.

The replacement of the cylinder head is the reverse of the above. The gasket is marked "Top" on its top side and should be so installed. In all cases of cylinder head gasket replacement, a non-hardening gasket paste should be applied to the gasket. Install cylinder head and tighten stud nuts finger tight. Install push rods.

FIGURE 8—*Lowering Engine Assembly as
Removed for Engine Overhaul*

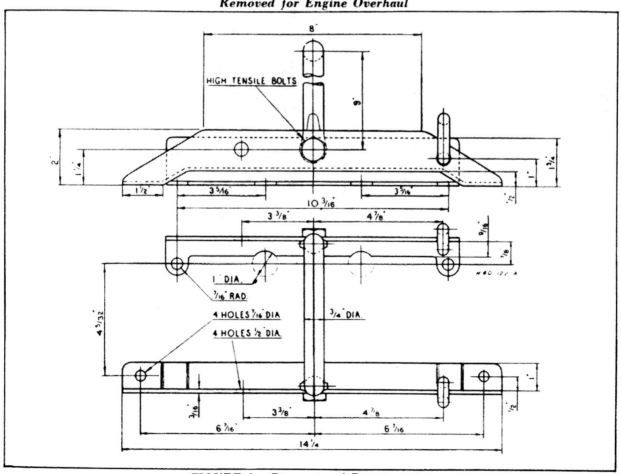

FIGURE 9—*Dimensional Drawing of
Engine Fixture*

FIGURE 10—*Engine Lifting Fixture Assembly*

Tighten cylinder head stud nut to proper torque (40 Ft. Lbs. dry thread) gradually in sequence from the center, outwards, as shown in Figure 12.

NOTE: *Adjust valve clearance to .015".*

Recheck cylinder head nut torque after approximately 100 miles of operation. Re-adjust valves as required.

VALVES

A valve stem oil seal and retainer are located below the upper valve spring retainer. Refer to Figure 13 for valve assembly sequences.

Valve Springs

When removing valve springs for valve operations, it is suggested that the valve spring tension be checked (Fig. 14).

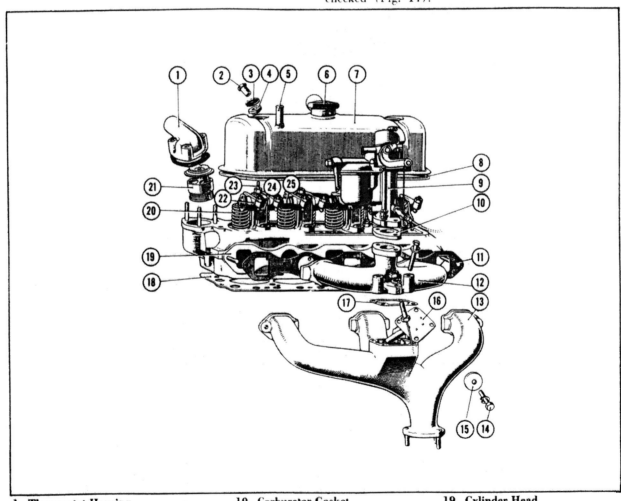

1. Thermostat Housing	10. Carburetor Gasket	19. Cylinder Head
2. Cap Nut for Cylinder Head Cover	11. Manifold Gasket	20. Valve Spring
3. Retaining Washer	12. Intake Manifold	21. Thermostat
4. Oil Seal	13. Exhaust Manifold	22. Rocker Arm
5. Breather Pipe	14. Manifold Attaching Screw	23. Cylinder Head Cover Stud
6. Oil Filler Cap	15. Manifold Attaching Washer	24. Rocker Shaft Support Bracket
7. Cylinder Head Cover	16. Hot Spot	25. Rocker Arm Locating Spring
8. Cylinder Head Cover Gasket	17. Hot Spot Gasket	
9. Carburetor	18. Cylinder Head Gasket	

FIGURE 11—*Cylinder Head Assembly (Exploded View) A and B Series Shown*

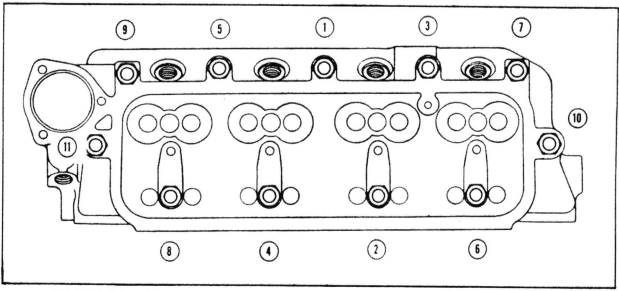

FIGURE 12—*Cylinder Head Tightening Sequence Torque 40 Ft. Lbs. (Dry Threads)*

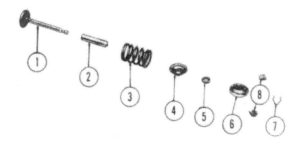

1. Valve
2. Valve Guide
3. Valve Spring
4. Valve Stem Seal Retainer

5. Valve Stem Seal
6. Valve Spring Retainer
7. Valve Lock Safety Pin
8. Valve Locks

FIGURE 13—*Valve Assembly Sequence*

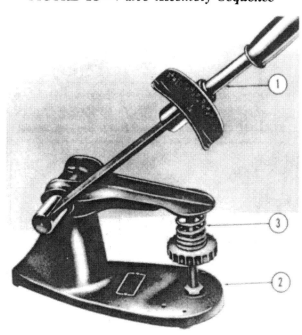

FIGURE 14—*Testing Valve Spring Tension*

It is not necessary to remove the cylinder head to replace a single broken valve spring. By the use of air pressure through the spark plug hole of the affected cylinder, the valve can be held in the closed position while the valve spring is compressed to permit removal of locks, retainer, and broken spring (Fig. 15).

FIGURE 15—*Removing Broken Valve Spring*

Valve Grinding

To reface valve seats and valve faces, the intake and exhaust manifolds should be disconnected prior to removal of the cylinder head. The rocker arm assembly can be removed on the bench as it aids in lifting the cylinder head from the cylinder block.

CAUTION: *Disconnect the oil feed pipe from the cylinder head and rocker arm shaft support prior to removal of the rocker arm shaft assembly on the A Series.*

Tool J-4487, a "C" type valve spring compressor, is used to compress the valve springs for removal of the valve stem locks.

Grind valves and reface seats to a 45 degree angle. The seat width must be ground to 1/16", Plus 1/32", Minus 0" (Fig. 16).

NOTE: *The valve seats may extend beyond the valve head with valve seated.*

New valve stem seals must always be used upon reassembly.

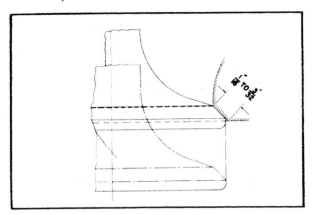

FIGURE 16—*Valve and Seat Matching*

Valve Guides

Check valve guides for excessive wear when valves are removed before grinding valve seats.

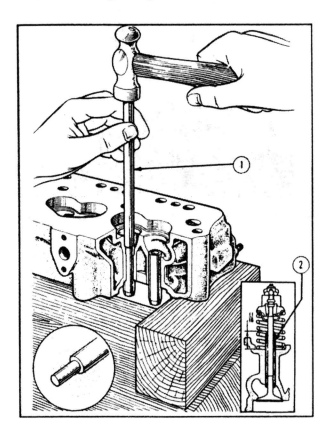

1. Tool J-5564   2. Location of Guide

FIGURE 17—*Replacing Valve Guide*

To replace a worn valve guide, use Tool J-5564 Valve Guide Remover and Installer; drive the guide through the head from the top side.

Use Tool J-5564 to install the new guide. Drive the guide in *from the combustion chamber side toward the top. The guide must protrude 11/16" from the spring seat machined surface as shown in Figure 17.*

Valve guides must be reamed after installation.

Valve Adjustment

The valves are adjusted with engine at room temperature for a lash or clearance of .015".

When cranking the engine during valve adjustment, make the valve adjustment at the point where the push rod for the valve being adjusted ceases to move downward.

Recheck valve clearance after tightening the lock nut (Figs. 18 and 19).

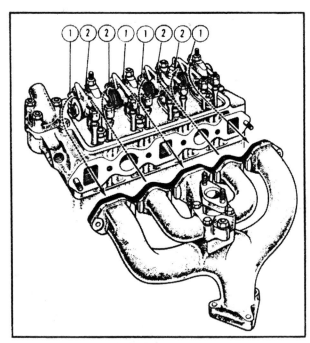

1. Exhaust Valves   2. Intake Valves

FIGURE 18—*Valve and Port Arrangement*

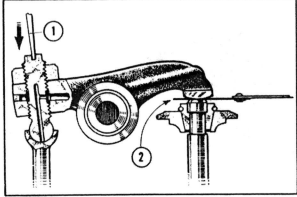

1. Screw Driver   2. .015" Feeler Gauge

FIGURE 19—*Valve Adjustment*

Push Rod Removal

To remove push rods during cylinder head removal, loosen the valve adjustment screws completely. Then depress the valve spring (Fig. 20) until push rod socket end is free of ball part of adjustment screw.

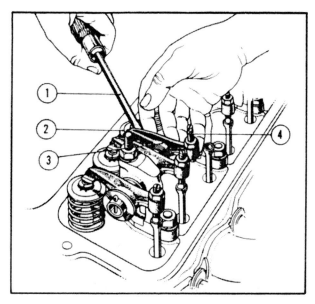

1. Screw Driver   3. Rocker Arm
2. Valve Spring Retainer   4. Valve Adjustment Screw

FIGURE 20—*Removing a Push Rod*

Slide rocker arm to the side and remove push rod while holding side pressure on the push rod so the lower end will snap out of the tappet without pulling the tappet out of its bore.

When removing the end push rods, the end rocker arms must be removed from the rocker arm shaft.

Valve Rocker Arm Assembly

The valve rocker arm shaft assembly is force-fed lubricated throughout its length. Upon engine overhaul, flush out any sludge that may have accumulated.

**FIGURE 21—*Rocker Arm Lubrication Outlet
—B and 1500 Series***

The rocker arms are drilled to permit oil feed to valve adjustment screws and valve stem tips. Valve adjustment screws are drilled to lubricate the sockets on upper end of push rods.

The rocker arm shaft assembly can be removed as a unit after removing cylinder head cover. Also remove the oil feed tube on the A Series. Remove eight attaching nuts and washers from rocker arm support brackets and remove assembly.

Rocker Arm Shaft Diameter	.624″-.625″
Rocker Arm Bushing Inside Diameter	.6255″-.626″
Rocker Arm to Shaft Clearance	.0005″-.004″

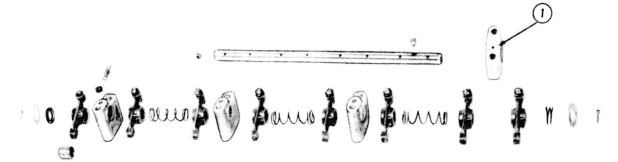

1. Pressure Lubrication Passage

**FIGURE 22—*Rocker Arm and Shaft Assembly
—B and 1500 Series Shown***

Valve Tappets
"A" and "B" Series

Valve tappets are of two-piece construction with the push rod cup being pressed into the main body of the tappet. Oil under pressure is directed to each tappet bore in the cylinder block.

"1500" Series

Prior to Engine Number IH-142719, valve tappets of the two-piece construction were continued in the "1500" Series. At this point, a one-piece design tappet with lubrication provided by oil splash and mist became effective.

All Series

Only tappets of a one-piece design are supplied for service replacement.

The valve tappets can be removed as required after push rod and engine side cover removal (Fig. 23). Tappets must be reinstalled in their original location as they are select fitted at time of assembly.

FIGURE 23—*Valve Tappets Removed*

CAMSHAFT AND BEARINGS

The camshaft is supported in three pressure lubricated replaceable shell type bearings. To remove a camshaft, the engine assembly must be removed from the car.

Camshaft Removal

With the engine on a bench or stand, remove the valve push rods, side cover, and tappets.

Remove generator, fan belt, fan pulley, and blades.

Unlock the crankshaft pulley nut lock plate and remove nut. Then pull crankshaft pulley.

Remove timing cover assembly and oil shedder.

Remove two cap screws holding cam sprocket to camshaft and pull timing gears and chain assembly from the camshaft and crankshaft as a unit on the A and B Series.

Remove the nut after unlocking lock plate on camshaft for sprocket removal on the 1500 Series.

On the 1500 Series remove the timing chain tensioner assembly from the engine front plate section (Figs. 24 and 25).

1. Tensioner Contact Shoe

**FIGURE 24—*Timing Chain Tensioner—
1500 Series***

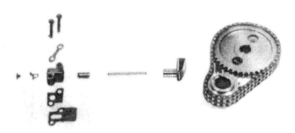

**FIGURE 25—*Timing Chain, Sprockets,
and Tensioner***

The tensioner is spring and hydraulically applied to the timing chain to maintain minimum chain looseness.

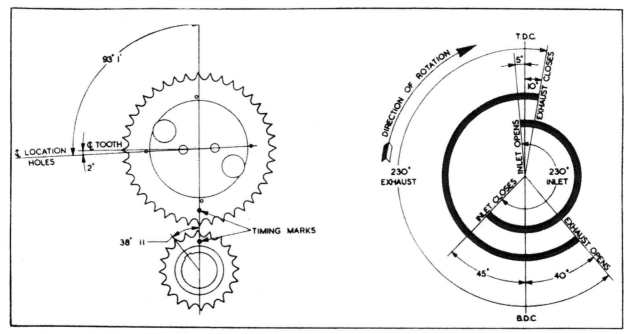

FIGURE 26—*Valve Timing Diagram and Timing Gear Arrangement*

The timing chain tensioner used for the A and B Series is illustrated in Figure 28.

Remove three cap screws from camshaft retaining and thrust plate noting the location of oil hole for lubrication of timing gears and chain assembly.

Remove oil pan, oil pump, and strainer assembly and distributor drive gear shaft.

Remove camshaft taking care not to damage camshaft bearings.

Camshaft Bearings

Camshaft bearing bores are step-bored from front to the rear, the front bearing being largest in diameter.

Camshaft bearing journal diameters are:

$$1.78875'' \qquad 1.72875'' \qquad 1.62275''$$
$$(1)\ 1.78925''\ \ (2)\ 1.72925''\ \ (3)\ 1.62325''$$

from front to rear.

The front and rear engine end plates must be removed to replace the camshaft bearings.

The original bearings can be punched out and new ones tapped into position being sure that the oil holes line up for proper lubrication. The replacement bearings must be line-reamed to afford an oil clearance of .001″-.002″.

VALVE TIMING

Proper valve timing is obtained by correct assembly of the timing gears and chain.

Before assembly of the timing chain and gears to their shafts, the gears and chain should be meshed properly on the bench. This is done by meshing the gears and chain so the timing marks or spots are indexed to their closest position (Fig. 26).

The engine crankshaft is positioned with Number 1 and 4 pistons on top dead center. The camshaft is positioned in such a manner that the Number 7 and 8 valves are in the valve overlap position. Then the timing gear and chain assembly is installed (Fig. 27).

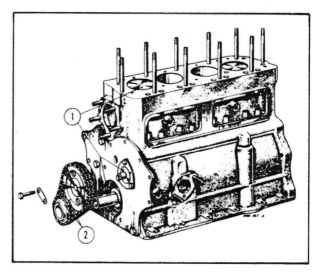

1. **Locate Piston Number One and Four T.D.C. Locate the Camshaft Gear Mounting Holes at a Diagonal With Number Seven and Eight Valves in the Valve Overlap Position**
2. **Timing Gears and Chain Assembled With Timing Marks Lined Up**

FIGURE 27—*Assembly of Timing Gears and Chain for Proper Valve Timing— A and B Series Shown*

Slide the crankshaft sprocket onto the crankshaft keeping the timing gear marks lined up, and attach the camshaft gear.

TIMING GEAR AND CHAIN LUBRICATION

The valve timing assembly is lubricated by oil flow from the front camshaft bearing (Fig. 28).

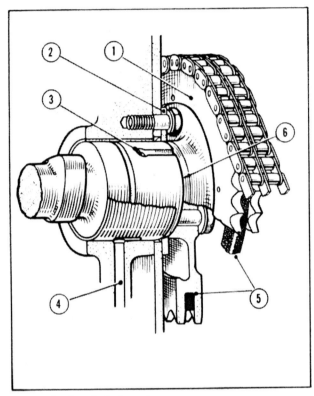

1. Camshaft Sprocket
2. Camshaft Thrust and Retaining Plate
3. Oil Feed Hole to Timing Assembly
4. Oil Feed Hole for Front Camshaft Bearing
5. Rubber Tensioner Ring for Quiet Operation
6. Check for End Play of .002″ to .008″

FIGURE 28—Timing Gear and Chain Lubrication—A and B Series Shown

ENGINE OIL PAN

The engine oil pan is readily removable from beneath the car. A drain plug is provided on the left side at the bottom of the pan.

PISTONS

A four ring, split skirt, aluminum alloy piston is used. It is cam-ground. Piston removal is accomplished from the top of the engine after cylinder head and oil pan are removed. Ridge ream, when necessary, before piston and connecting rod removal (Fig. 29).

Piston Fitting

The pistons are fitted to the bores with a clearance of .013″-.017″ at the top land and .0009″-.0015″ at the bottom of the skirt at right angles to the piston pin in the high friction area of the skirt. Piston rings are checked for ring gap clearance in the ring wear area of the cylinder bore (Fig. 30).

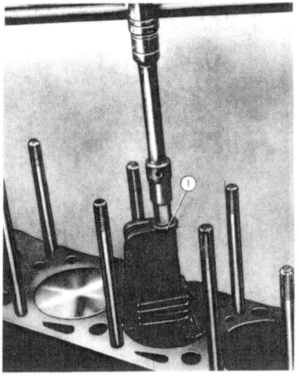

1. Ridge Reamer

FIGURE 29—Ridge Reaming Before Piston and Rod Removal

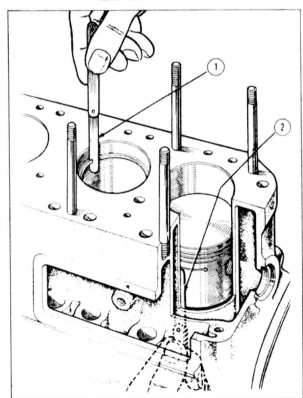

1. Ring Gap .008″ - .012″   2. Piston to Bore .0009″ - .0015″

FIGURE 30—Fitting Pistons and Rings for Proper Clearance and Gap

If the piston is fitted to just support its own weight in the usable portion of the bore, dry and inverted, it will meet the measurements given above for piston to bore clearance.

PISTON RINGS

Four rings three compression and one oil control ring are located above the piston pin. The top ring is a plain compression ring while the next two compression rings are taper face. The rings are cast iron, treated with an oxidize coating. The oil control ring is of cast iron, oxidize-coated, and installed in the bottom ring groove of the piston.

Before reassembly of piston and rod assembly to engine, the glazed surface of the cylinder wall may be removed by means of an abrasive hone, taking care not to remove any appreciable amount of metal, providing a thorough cleaning operation is performed following the glaze removal (Fig. 31).

FIGURE 32—*Cleaning Piston Ring Grooves*

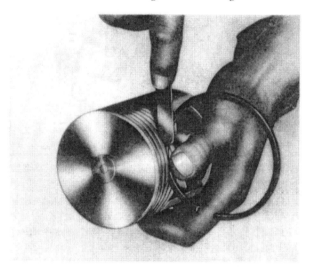

FIGURE 33—*Checking Ring Groove Clearance*

FIGURE 31—*Glaze Removal With Expanding Type Hone*

The piston ring grooves must be properly cleaned as illustrated in Figure 32.

The ring groove clearance (compression rings, .001"-.003", oil control .0025"-.003") is checked by rolling the ring around the circumference of the piston in its groove with a feeler gauge as shown in Figure 33.

Piston ring gap or joint clearance (.008"-.012", A and B Series, .008"-.013", 1500 Series) is measured in the bottom of the cylinder near the end of the ring travel area. To square the ring in the bore for check-

ing joint clearance, place the ring in the bore. Then, with an inverted piston, push the ring down near the lower end of ring travel area.

When other than standard ring sizes are used, rings should be individually fitted to their respective bores.

The rings should be installed with a ring installing tool to prevent breakage and or distortion.

When installing piston and rod assembly with the use of a ring compressor, prelubricate all parts with light engine oil to prevent initial scuffing of moving parts.

PISTON PINS

A locked-in rod type piston pin is used. A groove milled in the piston pin is used for the clamping bolt at the upper end of the connecting rod. Piston pin dimensions are: Length 2.281" — .010" + 0". The diameter is .6245" on the A and B Series; .6870" on the 1500 Series.

The pin is a push fit in the piston bosses at room temperature of 70° F. (clearance .0003" maximum).

CONNECTING RODS

The connecting rods are of the "H" section forged steel type. Replaceable bearing inserts are used on the crank pin end and a lock bolt boss is provided at the upper end for securing the piston pin. The connecting rods are removed with pistons upwardly after oil pan, oil pump assembly, and cylinder head removal. Connecting rods are stamped for cylinder location identification.

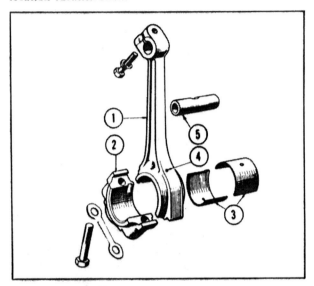

1. Connecting Rod
2. Connecting Rod Bearing Cap
3. Connecting Rod Bearing Inserts
4. Lubricating Oil Hole for Cylinder Wall Lubrication
5. Piston Pin.

FIGURE 34—*The Connecting Rod Assembly*

The bearing caps are off-set from the vertical axis toward the left or camshaft side of the engine. Each rod has an off-set from the vertical axis as shown in Figure 35.

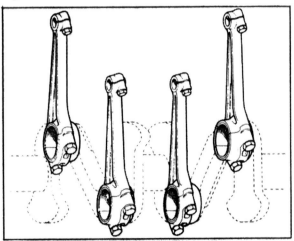

FIGURE 35—*Relative Off-Set Location of Connecting Rod Bearing End Off-Set. Note: The Off-Set Bosses of Rods One and Two and Three and Four Face Each Other as Pairs*

Whenever connecting rods are removed for service operations, they should be checked for proper alignment before replacing in engine (Figs. 36 and 37).

Tighten connecting rod bearing cap screws to 33 foot pounds torque (dry threads).

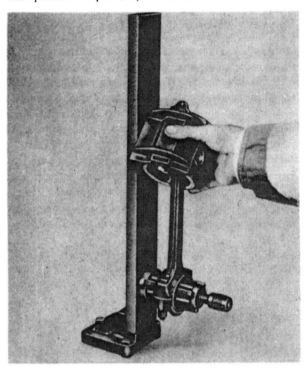

FIGURE 36—*Checking Connecting Rod Alignment for Twist*

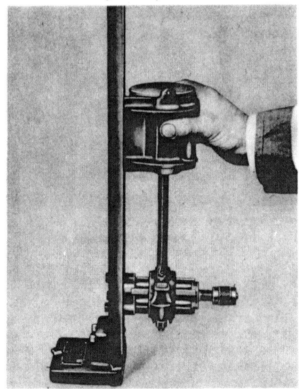

FIGURE 37—*Checking Connecting Rod Alignment for Bend*

The standard crank pin diameter is 1.8759" to 1.8764".

The crank pins can be ground .020" or .040" under size to the following limits: 1.8559" to 1.8564" or 1.8359" to 1.8364".

CONNECTING ROD BEARINGS

The bearing inserts are of the precision replaceable steel type with a tang which fits into a recess machined in the cap and rod components. See Figure 34.

Bearings are fitted to maintain an oil clearance on the crank pin of .00025" to .00150".

Connecting rod side clearance is .0085" to .0125".

To determine the amount of bearing clearance, place a piece of Plastigage crosswise in the connecting rod cap. Then tighten the cap, specified torque of 33 foot pounds, to compress the Plastigage. Remove the bearing cap and calibrate the width of the Plastigage with the scale furnished which will indicate the oil clearance.

CRANKSHAFT AND MAIN BEARINGS

A forged steel, counter balanced crankshaft, supported by three main bearings, is used.

The engine must be removed from the car to replace crankshaft bearings or remove crankshaft assembly as the front and rear engine end plates must be removed for crankshaft removal. The crankshaft and its directly related components are illustrated in Figures 38 and 39.

The crankshaft end thrust is controlled at the center main bearing location by the use of thrust washers, two in the upper bearing recess and two on the main bearing cap. Two complete recesses retain the upper thrust washers in location. A tab on the lower thrust washer indexes with a recess in the bearing cap (Fig. 38).

Crankshaft end play is .003" to .007" on the A and B Series, .002" to .003" on the 1500 Series.

The main bearing caps can be removed after engine assembly, engine end plates, and oil pump and strainer assembly are removed.

A combination tool J-5559, Main Bearing Cap and Pinion Bearing Remover, is used to pull the main bearing caps from their recessed location. The caps have a tapped hole provided for this purpose (Fig. 40).

The main bearing cap stud nuts are tightened to a torque of 70 foot pounds (dry) on the A and B Series, 77 to 80 on the 1500 Series. When replacing bearing caps, be sure to install the caps with the punch marking toward the camshaft side of the engine. Secure the nuts with cotter keys where originally used.

The standard main bearing journal diameter is 2.0005" to 2.001". The journals can be ground .020" or .040" undersize to 1.9805" to 1.981" or 1.9605" to 1.961".

The main bearing inserts are the precision replace-

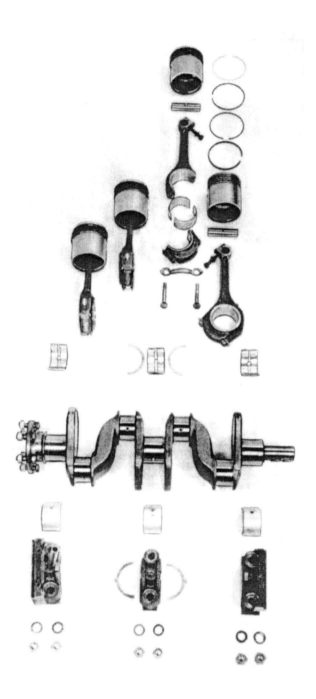

FIGURE 38—Crankshaft, Bearings, and Piston and Connecting Rod Assemblies

able type. The upper main bearing inserts can be removed by the use of a pin type tool made from a nail or cotter key as shown in Figure 41.

The main bearings are fitted to the crankshaft journals with an oil clearance of .0005" to .002".

To determine the amount of bearing clearance, place a piece of Plastigage crosswise to the bearing cap. Then tighten the cap to a specified torque, to compress the Plastigage. Remove the bearing cap and calibrate the width of the Plastigage with the scale provided with the Plastigage which will indicate the oil clearance.

ENGINE SECTION

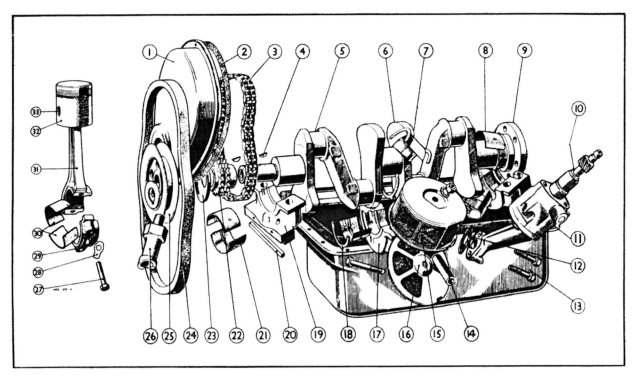

1. Timing Cover	18. Center Main Bearing Crankshaft End Thrust Washer
2. Timing Cover Gasket	19. Front Main Bearing Cap
3. Timing Chain	20. Cork Strip Front and Rear Main Bearing Oil Seal
4. Crankshaft Keys	21. Front Main Bearing Inserts
5. Crankshaft	22. Crankshaft Sprocket
6. Crankshaft End Thrust Washer	23. Oil Shedder
7. Center Main Bearing Insert	24. Fan Belt
8. Rear Main Bearing Insert	25. Fan Pulley
9. Rear Main Bearing Cap	26. Starting Nut
10. Oil Pump Drive Shaft	27. Connecting Rod Cap Screw
11. Oil Pump	28. Connecting Rod Cap Screw Lock
12. Oil Pump Strainer Gasket	29. Connecting Rod Cap
13. Oil Delivery Pipe	30. Connecting Rod Bearing Inserts
14. Spacer	31. Connecting Rod
15. Strainer Body	32. Piston
16. Strainer Cover	33. Piston Pin
17. Center Main Bearing Cap	

FIGURE 39—*Crankshaft, Oil Pan, and Pump Assembly*

1. Tool J-5559

FIGURE 40—*Removing Main Bearing Caps*

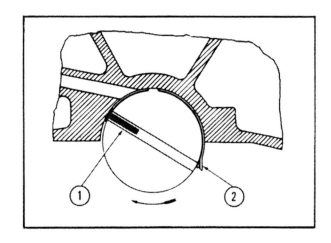

1. Removing Tool   2. Bearing Tang

FIGURE 41—*Removing Upper Main Bearing Insert*

LUBRICATION SYSTEM

Full pressure lubrication is supplied by a positive type oil pump driven off of the camshaft through an oil pump drive shaft. The oil is drawn from the oil pan through a strainer. It is forced under pressure to the main bearings, connecting rod, and camshaft bearings up to the rocker arm shaft assembly from a main oil gallery on the right hand side of the engine. On the A and B Series a small oil gallery is supplied with oil under pressure from the center camshaft bearing. This small oil gallery runs the full length of the left side of the engine block supplying oil to the valve lifters.

Oil under reduced pressure is taken from one of the camshaft bearings through passages in the cylinder head and block to the rocker arm shaft. The oil flows through holes drilled in the shaft and rocker arms to the adjusting screws and then onto the upper ends of the push rods. Excess overflow oil from the rocker arm system returns to the oil pan through the push rod holes in the cylinder head.

The front camshaft bearing supplies oil to the timing chain assembly and also the chain tensioner on the 1500 Series. The excess oil returns to the oil pan through a drilled passage in the front main bearing cap.

The rear main crank journal is provided with an oil slinger ring machined behind the journal bearing surface which directs the oil through a passage and a return pipe in the bearing cap back to the oil pan.

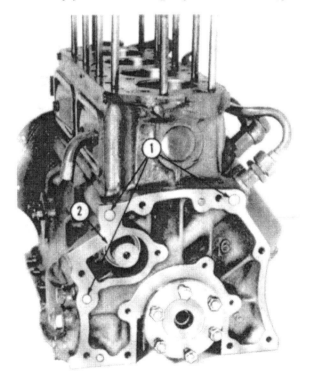

1. Brass Plugs at Rear of Oil Pressure Passages
2. Rear Camshaft Bearing

FIGURE 42—*Rear of Engine Block Assembly*

OIL PUMP

A Series

The spur gear oil pump is mounted on the left hand side of the cylinder block inside the oil pan. It is driven from a gear, cut on the camshaft, by a short drive shaft which is keyed to the oil pump drive gear at the lower end.

The oil strainer is attached directly to the oil pump body. A small connecting oil delivery pipe directs oil under pressure from the oil pump body to a connector pipe on the right bottom side of the block which connects with the main oil gallery thence through the system.

To remove the oil pump assembly, the oil pan must be removed. The connecting pipe from the pump to the block and the two nuts retaining the oil pump body to the studs in the cylinder block can be removed. The pump assembly will now slide freely from the cylinder block. The pump drive shaft will either slide out with the pump or can be pulled from the cylinder block unmeshing it from the camshaft drive gear.

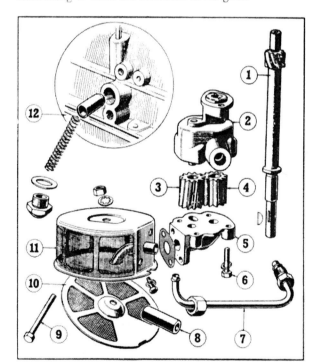

1. Drive Shaft, Oil Pump
2. Oil Pump Body
3. Oil Pump Driven Gear
4. Oil Pump Drive Gear
5. Oil Pump Bottom Cover
6. Oil Pump Body Screw
7. Oil Delivery Pipe
8. Oil Strainer Spacer
9. Oil Strainer Bottom Cover Attaching Screw
10. Oil Strainer Bottom Cover
11. Oil Strainer Body
12. Oil Release Valve Assembly

FIGURE 43—*Exploded View of Oil Pump and Oil Release Valve Assembly—A Series*

B and 1500 Series

The rotor oil pump is mounted on the left hand side of the cylinder block inside the oil pan. It is driven from a gear, cut on the camshaft, by a short drive shaft which is keyed to the oil pump drive gear at the lower end.

The oil strainer is attached directly to the oil pump body. Oil under pressure from the oil pump enters the main oil gallery thence through the system.

To remove the oil pump assembly, the oil pan must be removed. The two nuts retaining the oil pump body to the studs in the cylinder block can then be removed. The pump assembly will now slide freely from the cylinder block. The pump drive shaft will either slide out with the pump or can be pulled from the cylinder block unmeshing it from the camshaft drive gear.

OIL RELEASE VALVE

The oil pressure release valve consists of a plunger piston, calibrated spring, and retaining nut and washer. It is located in a passage between the oil pump and main oil gallery. (Figs. 43 and 44).

The oil pressure for normal operation is 40-45 pounds and proportionately lower at idle. Check oil pressure for 40-45 P. S. I. at 30 M. P. H.

FULL FLOW OIL FILTER

A full flow oil filter became effective at car serial number E-43116. All oil from the pump is filtered prior to being delivered to the engine parts.

It is recommended that the oil filter assembly be changed at 3000 mile intervals.

The oil filter incorporates a relief valve to prevent lack of engine lubrication in the event the filter material becomes clogged with sludge or dirt.

The relief valve is of the ball and seat type "staked" in place in the upper section of the filter assembly.

FLYWHEEL

The flywheel is attached to the crankshaft by four studs and nuts. The diameter of the flywheel is 11-5/16". A 117 tooth starter ring gear is shrunk-fitted to the flywheel. The ring gear diameter over the teeth is 11.786".

A torque of 32 foot pounds is used on the flywheel stud nuts.

PILOT BEARING

An oillite bushing is pressed into the rear journal (stock of the crankshaft) for support of the transmission clutch shaft. A very light application of engine oil is applied to the bushing only upon reassembling transmission to engine assembly.

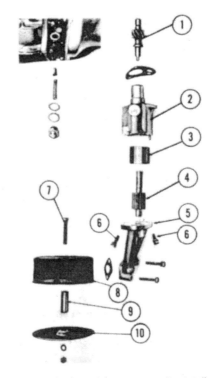

1. Drive Shaft, Oil Pump
2. Oil Pump Body
3. Oil Pump Driven Rotor
4. Oil Pump Drive Rotor
5. Oil Pump Bottom Cover
6. Oil Pump Body Screw
7. Oil Strainer Bottom Cover Attaching Screw
8. Oil Strainer Body
9. Oil Strainer Spacer
10. Oil Strainer Bottom Cover

FIGURE 44—*Exploded View of Oil Pump and Oil Release Valve Assembly—B and 1500 Series*

FIGURE 45—*Oil Filter Assembly "1500" Series*

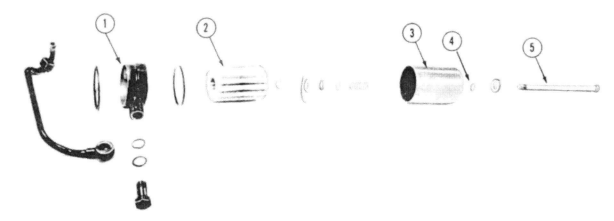

1. Filter Adapter
2. Filter Element
3. Filter Housing

4. Through Bolt Seal
5. Bolt

FIGURE 46—*Oil Filter Components—"1500" Series*

CYLINDER BLOCK ASSEMBLY

The cylinder block is cast iron of the monobloc type. The maximum rebore oversize is 1/16″. It is provided with three main bearing webs for support of the crank-shaft and camshaft and to absorb stresses from these rotating assemblies.

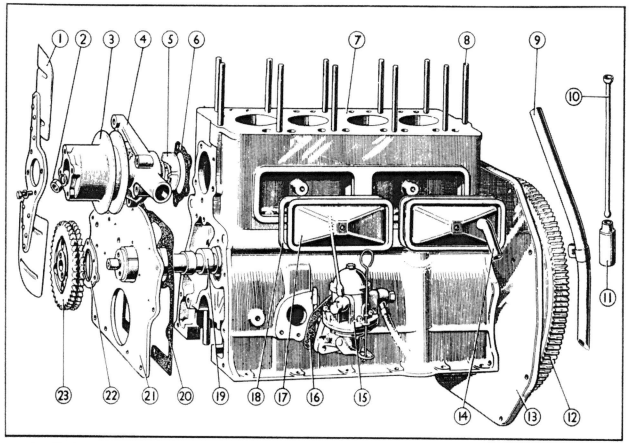

1. Fan Blade	9. Crankcase Breather Pipe	17. Engine Side Cover
2. Retaining Nut	10. Push Rod	18. Engine Side Cover Gasket
3. Fan Pulley	11. Tappet	19. Camshaft
4. Water Pump	12. Flywheel	20. Front Engine End Plate Gasket
5. Water Pump Impeller Assembly	13. Rear Engine End Plate	21. Engine Front End Plate
6. Water Pump Gasket	14. Breather Pipe Elbow	22. Camshaft Retaining Plate
7. Cylinder Block	15. Fuel Pump	23. Camshaft Sprocket
8. Cylinder Head Stud	16. Fuel Pump Gasket	

FIGURE 47—*Cylinder Block Assembly (Exploded View)—A and B Series*

ENGINE SPECIFICATIONS

Series	A and B	1500
Type	Valve-In Head — In Line	Valve-In Head — In Line
No. of Cylinders	4	4
Bore	$2^{37}/_{64}''$	$2^{7}/_{8}''$
Stroke	$3^{1}/_{2}''$	$3^{1}/_{2}''$
Compression Ratio	7.2:1	7.2:1 *8.3:1
Piston Displacement Cubic Inch	73.17	90.89
Compression Pressure at Cranking Speed (300-350 R.P.M.) .	130 + P.S.I.	130 + P.S.I.
Horsepower S.A.E. Brake (Maximum)	42 @ 4500 R.P.M.	52 @ 4500 R.P.M. *55 @ 4600 R.P.M.
Maximum Engine Torque.....	62 Foot Pounds @ 2400 R.P.M.	77 Foot Pounds @ 2500 R.P.M. *82 Foot Pounds @ 2400 R.P.M.
Engine Lubrication	Pressure	Pressure

*Applies to Engines having Engine Number Prefix 15-CNH.

VALVE SPECIFICATIONS

Series	A	B	1500
Stem Diameter			
Intake	.3089″-.3094″	.34175″-.34225″	.34175″-.34225″
Exhaust	.3089″-.3094″	.34175″-.34225″	.34175″-.34225″
Stem to Guide Clearance			
Intake	.001″-.003″	.0015″-.0025″	.0015″-.0025″
Exhaust	.001″-.003″	.0015″-.0025″	.0015″-.0025″
Head Diameter			
Intake	$1^{3}/_{8}''$	$1^{3}/_{8}''$	$1^{3}/_{8}''$
Exhaust	$1^{3}/_{16}''$	$1^{3}/_{16}''$	$1^{3}/_{16}''$
Seat Angle			
Intake	45°	45°	45°
Exhaust	45°	45°	45°
Valve Face Angle			
Intake	45°	45°	45°
Exhaust	45°	45°	45°
Valve Spring Free Height.....	$1^{13}/_{16}''$	$2^{1}/_{32}''$	$2^{1}/_{32}''$
Valve Spring Pressure			
Valve Open	103#-107# @ $1^{5}/_{32}''$	130# + or — 2 @ 1.206″	130# + or — 2 @ 1.206″
Valve Closed	53#-57# @ $1^{15}/_{32}''$	77.5# + or — 2 @ $1^{17}/_{32}''$	77.5# + or — 2 @ $1^{17}/_{32}''$
Spring Retainer Lock........	Split Two Piece With Hair Pin Retainer	Split Two Piece With Hair Pin Retainer	Split Two Piece With Hair Pin Retainer

ENGINE SECTION

Tappet Clearance or Valve Lash	0.15″ Both Intake and Exhaust. Set at Room Temperature.	0.15″ Both Intake and Exhaust. Set at Room Temperature.	0.15″ Both Intake and Exhaust. Set at Room Temperature.
Valve Lift	.312″	.325″	.325″

PISTON RINGS

Series	A and B	1500
No. of Rings Per Piston......	4	4
End Gap	.008″-.012″	.008″-.013″
Compression Ring Width.....	.077″-.078″	.0615″-.0625″
Oil Ring Width............	.1552″-.1562″	.1552″-.1562″
Clearance in Ring Groove Compression	.001″-.003″	.001″-.003″
Oil Control	.0025″-.003″	.0025″-.003″

OIL SYSTEM

Series	A	B and 1500
Oil Pump Type.............	Spur Gear	Rotor
Normal Oil Pressure.........	40-45 P.S.I. @ 30 M.P.H.	40-45 P.S.I. @ 30 M.P.H.
Engine Oil Refill Capacity....	4 Quarts	4 Quarts

CRANKSHAFT AND BEARINGS

Series	A and B	1500
Bearing Type	Replaceable	Replaceable
No. of Main Bearings........	3	3
Main Bearing Oil Clearance..	.0005″-.002″	.0005″-.002″
Main Bearing Journal Diameter	2.0005″-2.001″	2.0005″-2.001″
Crank Pin Diameter.........	1.8759″-1.8764″	1.8759″-1.8764″
Shaft End Play.............	.003″-.007″	.002″-.003″
End Thrust Taken By........	Center Bearing	Center Bearing
Bearing Cap Torque........	70 Ft. Lbs. (Dry)	77-80 Ft. Lbs. (Dry)

CONNECTING ROD AND BEARING

Bearing Type	Replaceable
Bearing Clearance	.00025″-.0015″
Crank Pin Diameter.........	1.8759″-1.8764″
Bearing End Play...........	.0085″-.0125″
Bearing Cap Adjustment......	33 Ft. Lbs. (Dry)

PISTON PIN

Series	A	B and 1500
Type	Locked-In Rod	Locked-In Rod
Length	2.281″	2.281″
Diameter	.6245″	.6869″-.6871″
Clearance in Piston.........	.0003″ Maximum (Palm Press Fit at Room Temperature 70°)	.0003″ Maximum (Palm Press Fit at Room Temperature 70°)

TUNE-UP DATA

Compression Pressure @ Cranking Speed............	130 + P.S.I. @ 300-350 R.P.M.
Cylinder Head Nut Torque......................	40 Ft. Lbs. (Dry)
Ignition Timing	
A Series	7° B.T.D.C. Mark on Crankshaft Pulley
B Series	11° (1½″) B.T.D.C. Mark on Crankshaft Pulley
1500 Series	7° B.T.D.C. Mark on Crankshaft Pulley
Firing Order	1, 3, 4, 2
Distributor Point Gap	.014″-.016″
Spark Plug Gap	.023″-.025″
Torque	30 Ft. Lbs. (Dry)
Type	Champion N-8 (¾″ Thread Reach)
Fuel Pump Pressure......................	1½-2½ P.S.I.
Carburetor Idle Mixture..................	From 0-1 Turn Out
Idle Speed	625 R.P.M.
Charging Circuit	
Circuit Breaker Closing Voltage.............	12.7-13.3 Volts @ 1050-1200
Operating Voltage @ 1000	Generator R.P.M.
Generator R.P.M. Minimum.................	15.8 Volts 68° F. Air Temperature
Operating Amperage	Controlled by Resistor and Tap-Off on Series Winding of Regulator Relay

TECHNICAL SERVICE LETTER REFERENCE

Date	Letter No.	Subject	Changes information on Page No.

Technical Service Manual

Cooling

COOLING SYSTEM

WATER PUMP

A centrifugal type water pump is constructed integrally with the fan and pulley assembly. A carbon spring loaded seal coupled with a rubber seal prevents leakage of coolant along the water pump shaft.

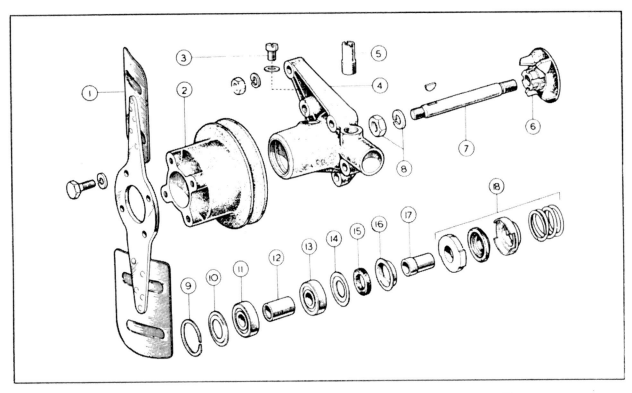

1. Fan Blade
2. Pulley
3. Oil Plug and Washer
4. Pump Body
5. By-pass Pipe
6. Impeller
7. Shaft and Key
8. Shaft Nut and Washer
9. Snap Ring
10. Bearing Shield
11. Front Bearing
12. Spacer
13. Rear Bearing
14. Rear Bearing Shield
15. Felt Washer
16. Felt Washer Retainer
17. Spacer
18. Seal Gland Assembly

FIGURE 1—*Water Pump Assembly—A Series*

Water Pump Disassembly and Repair

Remove the water pump from the car.

Remove the nut and lock washer retaining the pulley hub and fan to the water pump shaft.

A universal puller can now be used to pull the pulley from the shaft.

Tap out the impeller shaft and seal assembly.

Remove the front bearing retaining snap ring and bearing shield.

Use Tool J-5558-3, Water Pump Bearing Remover and Installer and tap out the front bearing and spacer (Fig. 4).

Assemble J-5558-1 and 2 and drive out the rear bearing. This tool is required to maintain the bearing in alignment, in the housing, when removing or replacing the bearings.

Remove the bearing shield, felt washer, and retainer.

Inspect and replace all defective parts.

Install retainer, felt washer, and bearing shields.

Install rear bearing, using Tool J-5558-1, 2, and 3.

Install spacer, front bearing, bearing shield, and snap ring.

Assemble the impeller, seal assembly, and spacer.

Install impeller shaft assembly into the pump body.

Install fan pulley and fan.

Fill oil reservoir of pump with engine oil and install on engine using a new water pump gasket.

RADIATOR

The radiator is of the vertical flow type using tube and fin construction. An expansion tank is soldered to the tops of the tubes.

COOLING SYSTEM

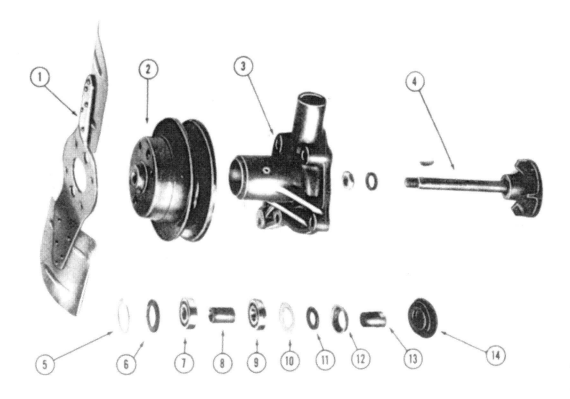

1. Fan Blade	6. Grease Retainer	11. Felt Washer
2. Pulley	7. Front Bearing	12. Felt Washer Retainer
3. Pump Body	8. Bearing Spacer	13. Spacer
4. Shaft and Impeller	9. Rear Bearing	14. Seal Assembly
5. Snap Ring	10. Rear Bearing Shield	

FIGURE 2—*Water Pump Assembly—B Series*

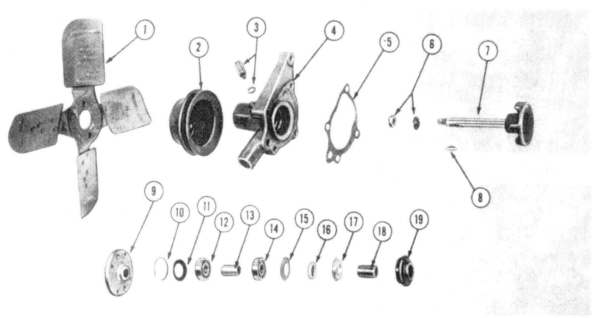

1. Fan Blades	7. Shaft and Impeller	13. Bearing Spacer
2. Pulley	8. Key	14. Rear Bearing
3. Oil Plug and Washer	9. Hub	15. Rear Bearing Shield
4. Pump Body	10. Snap Ring	16. Felt Washer
5. Pump Gasket	11. Grease Retainer	17. Felt Washer Retainer
6. Shaft Nut and Washer	12. Front Bearing	18. Spacer
		19. Seal Assembly

FIGURE 3—*Water Pump Assembly—1500 Series*

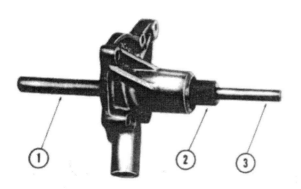

1. Tool J-5558-3   3. Tool J-5558-2
2. Tool J-5558-1

FIGURE 4 — *Water Pump Bearing Remover and Installer Tool J-5558*

To avoid loss of coolant, fill radiator only when engine is cold. The system is normally pressurized to a value of 3.5 to 4.5 P.S.I. The heater valve should be wide open or full hot position when filling the radiator with engine running to bleed all air from the system.

A drain cock (Fig. 5) is located at the right side bottom of the radiator core and a block drain is located at the right side of the cylinder block near the oil stick on the "A" Series (Fig. 6) and at the right rear of the cylinder block on all later Series (Fig. 7).

The cooling system capacity is 8 qts. with heater.

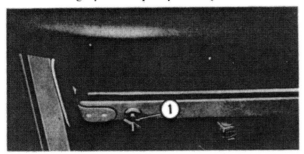

FIGURE 5 — *Radiator Core Drain Cock*

FIGURE 6—*Cylinder Block Drain—A Series*

FIGURE 7—*Cylinder Block Drain—B and 1500 Series*

RADIATOR FILLER CAP

In order to pressurize the cooling system to a value of 3.5 to 4.5 P.S.I., a pressure type filler cap is used. There are several advantages to a pressurized cooling system. The boiling point of the coolant is raised approximately 3° per each pound of pressurizing and there is almost no loss of coolant through evaporation in a leak-proof system with the filler cap in place.

The filler cap incorporates two calibrated valves, one to maintain pressure within the system while coolant is heated and expanded and the other to bleed atmospheric pressure into the expansion tank as the coolant cools and contracts (Fig. 8).

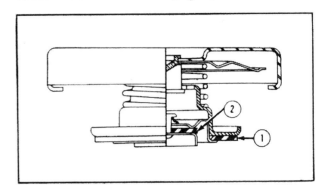

1. Pressure Valve Seal (Relieves at 3.5 to 4.5 P.S.I. — Vents to Overflow Pipe Chamber)
2. Vacuum Relief Valve (Air Vent)

FIGURE 8—*Pressure Type Radiator Filler Cap*

THERMOSTAT

A thermostat is located in the thermostat housing of

the cylinder head outlet. Its operation is of utmost importance to obtain economy, proper engine operating tolerances and efficient heater operation.

A 158° F. to 167° F. thermostat is supplied as standard. For service, to improve heater operation in cold weather, a 180° F. thermostat is available. This should only be used with a permanent type anti-freeze.

Never operate the engine without a properly operating thermostat installed. Remember, it is possible to do engine damage by operating over-cooled as well as over-heated.

FIGURE 10—*Fan Belt Adjustment*

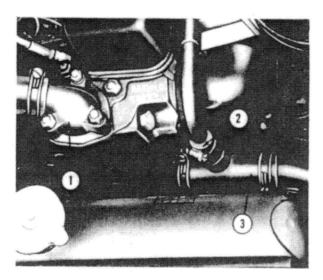

1. **Thermostat Housing, Cylinder Head Water Outlet**
2. **Heater Return Line**
3. **Water Inlet to Water Pump**

FIGURE 9—*Thermostat Location*

FAN ASSEMBLY

The 13 inch two bladed fan used on the A and B Series and the 13 inch four bladed fan used on the 1500 Series is driven at a ratio of 1.2 to 1 crankshaft revolutions. The fan pulley hub is a light press fit and keyed in position on the water pump shaft. A universal gear puller can be used to remove it after removing the retaining nut and lockwasher.

FAN BELT

A single "V" type fan belt is used to drive the generator, fan and water pump assembly from the crankshaft pulley.

The angle of the belt "V" is 32°; its outside length is 34⅞", and it is ⅝" wide.

The belt should not be over-tightened or loose enough to slip. A properly adjusted belt can be deflected 1" each way at right angles to belt path between generator and crankshaft pulley.

SEASONAL PREPARATION OF COOLING SYSTEM

The cooling system seasonal tune-up is as important as is done on the engine, ignition, and carburetor. The spring and fall tune-up should include an inspection of the cooling system. The operations performed are necessary and beneficial to performance, efficiency, and economy.

Perform a visual inspection of the cooling system for leaks and general condition of the radiator, hoses, hose clamps, fan belt, and water pump.

Radiator — Clean the radiator core of all obstructions, such as leaves and bugs at the frontal area. Any such obstructions will reduce the air flow through the radiator core and reduce its cooling efficiency. It should also be inspected for leaks. Minor leaks can be eliminated by using American Motors Sealer-Lubricant following directions as outlined on the container.

Thermostat — The thermostat's function is to restrict the coolant flow during engine warm-up and thereby shorten the warm-up period. Since the engine operates most efficiently when hot (normal operating temperature), it is only practical to bring it up to that temperature as quickly as possible. The thermostat also helps to maintain normal operating temperature by allowing the coolant to circulate and cool when engine temperature begins to rise above normal. It also restricts coolant flow when engine temperature drops below normal.

A 158° F. to 167° F. thermostat is supplied as standard. For service, to improve heater operation in cold weather, a 180° F. thermostat is available. This should only be used with a permanent type anti-freeze.

The thermostat should be checked at least twice a

year at time of cooling system draining and flushing. To test a thermostat for proper operation, suspend it in a pan of water together with a thermometer. Heat the water and note the temperature at which the thermostat begins to open. This should be within 10° F. of the thermostat rating or the thermostat should be replaced.

Water Pump — Inspect the water pump for leaks at the gasket area. The water pump oil reservoir should be filled with engine oil every 1,000 miles.

Radiator and Heater Hoses — All hoses should be examined for cracks and leaks. Hoses will harden and crack allowing coolant to leak out of the system or air to leak in. Often the outer surfaces may appear to be satisfactory yet the inside may be badly deteriorated. When in doubt about their condition, remove, inspect, and replace them. Before installing new radiator or heater hoses, thoroughly clean the metal tube connections. When servicing the cooling system, always check all hose clamps for tightness.

Radiator Cap — The radiator pressure cap provides 4 pound pressurizing of the cooling system which raises the normal atmospheric boiling temperature approximately 3° F. for every pound of pressure built up in the system. For this device to function properly, the cooling system must be air tight and free from coolant leaks. Inspect the pressure cap sealing surfaces and radiator filler neck for nicks or breaks and make certain the locking mechanism on the cap and radiator is not bent or worn.

CAUTION: *When removing the radiator cap while the engine is hot, first loosen cap to the first notch to reduce pressure before removing the cap.*

Fan Belt Adjustment — For the water pump to operate satisfactorily, proper fan belt tension must be maintained (Fig. 10). Too much tension will cause excessive wear on the fan and generator bearings. Too little tension will allow the belt to slip and reduce the efficiency of the water pump and generator.

Flushing — The cooling system is drained at the lower right hand side of the radiator and at the block drain on the right side of cylinder block. Flush the system thoroughly. If necessary, use a cleaning solution such as American Motors Radiator Kleen, following the instructions outlined on the container. For best results, remove the thermostat prior to flushing. With the engine running at idle speed, drain cocks open, fill the radiator with clean water until signs of discoloration disappear in the water draining at the bottom of the radiator.

With the cooling system drained, perform the necessary maintenance determined by the visual inspection.

For winter operation in colder regions, replace the thermostat with one suitable to the type of anti-freeze to be used.

Tighten radiator drain cock and fill cooling system with the required amount of anti-freeze to give the necessary protection. Top off the radiator with water to about 2" below the radiator filler neck.

Start and run the engine until it reaches normal operation temperature. Keep the radiator cap off and the Weather Eye valve open to rid the system of any pockets of trapped air. After approximately 10 minutes of running, top off with water and replace the radiator cap.

The cylinder head stud nuts should now be properly tightened to the torque specifications as outlined in the Engine Section.

CAUTION: *Never add large amounts of cold water or anti-freeze to a hot engine. Serious damage can result. Small amounts of water may be added to top off the radiator while the engine is running.*

TECHNICAL SERVICE LETTER REFERENCE

Date	Letter No.	Subject	Changes information on Page No.

Technical Service Manual

ELECTRICAL SECTION

Electrical

ELECTRICAL SECTION

BATTERIES

A Lucas 12 volt battery is installed under the rear seat (Fig. 1). The positive terminal is grounded.

FIGURE 1—*Battery Box Cover*

Battery Specifications

	Series	A and B	1500
Make	....	Lucas 12-V	Lucas 12-V
Model	....	GTW-9-A	BT-9-A
Ampere Hour Capacity:			
20 Hour Rating	......	58	57
No. of Plates Per Cell	....	9	9

Checking Battery Condition

Check electrolyte level every thousand miles or once a week.

Under each vent plug is a plastic tube with perforated flange. Bring level of electrolyte up to top of flange with distilled water. Then lift tube slightly and replace vent plug.

The battery specific gravity should be checked at least once every month to determine the state of charge and general cell condition. The readings should be uniform between cells. A battery capacity test will confirm the cell condition as to good or bad.

A cell breakdown tester consisting of a heavy shunt resistor with a sensitive voltmeter 2-3 volts can be used across the cells. The resistor should be capable of drawing several hundred amperes. Under the tester load, the cell should indicate a voltage of 1.2 to 1.5 volts for at least six seconds. If under load the voltage indication of a cell drops off rapidly, a faulty plate group is indicated. The battery should then be replaced or repaired.

Battery Charging

Charge battery at 5 ampere rate, until specific gravity reading stabilizes at 1.280 to 1.300 for all cells. The specific gravity varies with temperature. All readings are corrected to the standard 60° F. temperature. This is done by the following method:

For every 5° F. below 60° F., deduct .002 from the observed specific gravity reading to obtain the true reading for 60° F.
For every 5° F. above 60° F. add .002 to the observed specific gravity reading to obtain the true reading for 60° F.

Battery Terminal Location

Due to a difference between the British and American cell connection arrangement, the battery terminal locations differ. To accommodate this terminal location difference, the negative battery cable is located so it enters the central part of the front end of the battery box. (Fig. 2).

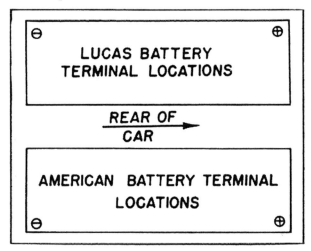

FIGURE 2—*Battery Terminal Location*

GENERATOR

A Lucas 12 volt model C-39-PV-2 generator is used. It is a two pole, two brush, shunt wound type, designed to work with a compensated voltage and current control unit.

Lubrication

A sealed ball bearing is installed in the generator drive end frame.

In the commutator end frame an oil impregnated bushing is used. Lubricate every 6,000 miles. Unscrew the lubrication cap, lift out the felt pad and spring, and half-fill the cap with engine oil. Replace the felt pad and spring and reinstall the cap.

ELECTRICAL SECTION

1. Starting Motor Switch
2. Distributor
3. Starting Motor
4. Generator

FIGURE 3—*Generator Location*

Inspection

At approximately 12,000 miles, remove the brush cover, inspect the brushes, brush holders and commutator.

The brushes should slide free in their holders. Brushes which have worn down enough to expose the connecting pig tail on the contact area moulded into the brush must be replaced. The commutator should show a clean shining condition. If a gummy blackened commutator is noted, clean with a solvent

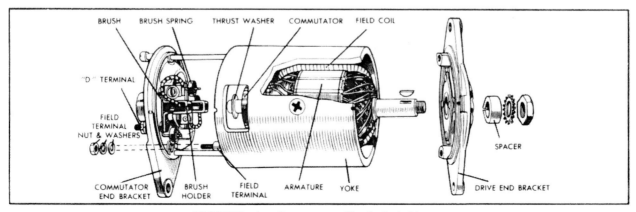

FIGURE 4—*Generator Exploded View*

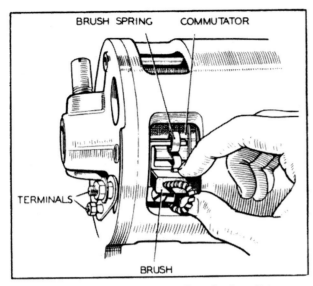

FIGURE 5—*Inspecting Brush Condition*

soaked rag held against it while turning the armature. The brushes should be removed while this cleaning operation is performed.

The brush spring tension should be checked for a tension of not less than 15 ounces. The normal tension when new is 22 to 25 ounces (Fig. 6).

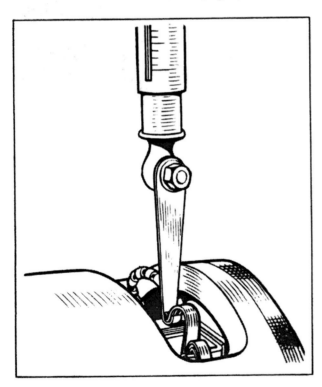

FIGURE 6—*Checking Generator Brush Spring Tension*

If commutator is badly worn, dress lightly in a lathe and finish by polishing with #00 sandpaper. Never use emery cloth. Undercut the mica insulator between the commutator segments with a hacksaw blade ground down to the thickness of the insulator.

Fan Belt Adjustment

The fan belt is adjusted by rotating the generator assembly clockwise with the mounting bolts loose. The belt is adjusted so that upon application of light finger pressure applied at a point midway between the generator and crankshaft pulleys, it will deflect approximately one inch.

Over-tightening the fan belt will cause undue strain on the generator bearings.

FIGURE 7—*Fan Belt Adjustment*

Generator Specifications

Model	C-39-PV-2
Type	Two Pole, Two Brush, Shunt Wound
Rotation	C.W. Drive End
Brush Spring Tension	22-25 Ozs. Not Less Than 15 Ozs.
Cut-In Speed	1050-1200 R.P.M. at 13 Volts
Field Resistance	6.2 Ohms
Max. Controlled Charging Rate (Controlled by Current Regulator Winding)	19 Amperes — 13.5 Volts at 2000-2150 Generator R.P.M.

Generator Testing on the Car

Check the fan belt adjustment. Inspect the wiring of the charging circuit for proper connection of the units. The generator "D" and "F" terminals must be connected to the regulator "D" and "F" terminal respectively.

The "E" terminal must be satisfactorily grounded. Switch off all electrical load in the system.

Disconnect the wires from terminals "D" and "F" on the generator and connect the two terminals together with a short jumper wire.

Start the engine and let idle at normal idle speed. Attach the (—) negative lead of a sensitive voltmeter 0-20 volt range to either of the generator terminals and the (+) positive lead of the voltmeter to the generator frame for ground.

Accelerate the engine to about 1000 R.P.M. A steady rapid rise in voltage should be indicated. Do not allow the voltage to build up above 20 volts. Do not race the engine to try to indicate a higher voltage. A higher engine speed than 1000 R.P.M. should not be required for proper check. If no voltage reading occurs, the generator brushes are usually at fault. If a low reading exists, $\frac{1}{2}$-1 volt, the generator field winding is at fault. If there is a reading of 4-5 volts, the armature may be at fault.

Check the brush assembly.

Clean the commutator and re-test.

If the generator was in good condition and the voltage indicated a good steady rise, remove the jumper wire from the generator terminals.

To check for a short internally between the "D" and "F" terminals on the generator, remove the generator lead wires and attach (—) negative lead from the voltmeter to the "D" terminal on the generator and the (+) positive voltmeter lead to the generator frame for ground. Increase engine speed to approximately 1500 R.P.M. A voltage reading of 1.5 to 3 volts as engine speed is increased is normal. Zero reading indicates open or poor circuit through brush assemblies or armature.

A rising voltage with increased engine speed indicates internal short between "D" and "F" terminals of generator.

The above checks determine the generator condition as an independent unit in the charging circuit. If trouble is still indicated in the charging circuit, the wiring, battery, or current and voltage control unit must be tested.

VOLTAGE AND CURRENT CONTROL UNIT (VOLTAGE REGULATOR)

The voltage regulator contains both the voltage and current control unit, and the cut-out unit. Although combined structurally, the regulator and cut-out are electrically separate.

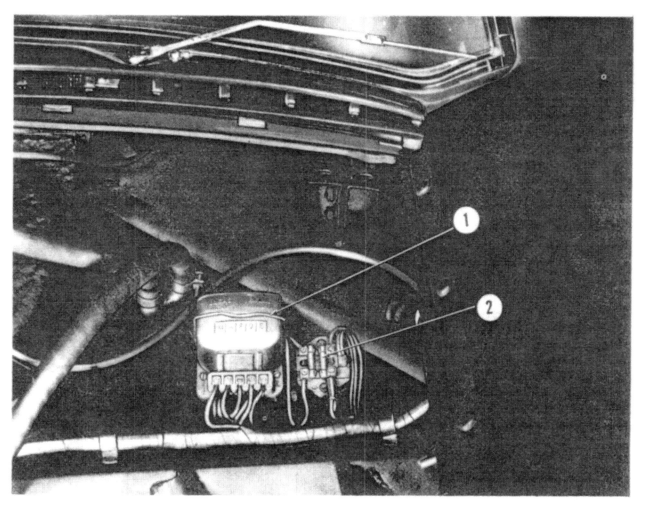

1. Regulator   2. Fuse Block

FIGURE 8—*Regulator Location*

The Regulator Action

The regulator is adjusted to maintain a certain voltage at all speeds above the regulating point, the generator field strength being controlled by the automatic insertion of a resistance in the generator field circuit. At a predetermined voltage, the magnetic field due to the shunt or voltage winding becomes sufficiently strong to attract the armature. This causes the contacts to open, inserting the resistance in the generator field circuit. The resulting reduction in field current reduces the generator voltage permitting the regulator armature to return to its original position by spring tension, closing the contact points and again building up the generator output voltage. The cycle is repeated and the regulator armature is set into a vibration. As the generator voltage rises, the amplitude of the vibrations increases, while the periods of interruption increase in length. This results in an even uniform controlled operating voltage once generator operating speed is reached.

The series or current winding provides a compensating control for the regulator, because voltage control only would be injurious to the generator, overloading it when the battery internal resistance is low, as in a discharged condition. This would especially be so if lights and other electrical loads were applied. The series winding assists the shunt or voltage winding so that the regulator comes into operation during a high current delivery with a lower voltage condition to limit the current output accordingly.

A split series winding is used; a center junction carrying the battery charging current while the whole winding carries the lighting and ignition loads.

A bi-metal spring located behind the tensioning spring of the regulator armature serves to give the regulator a temperature compensation feature.

Cut-Out Relay Action

The cut-out relay is made up of a relay core armature, contacts, and two windings, a series current winding of heavy wire and a voltage shunt winding of lighter wire. As the generator output builds up through the shunt or voltage winding, a magnetic field increases in strength, closing the cut-out points permitting a charging current to flow to the battery. The series coil now aids the shunt coil to maintain a strong magnetic field to hold the cut-out points closed.

As the generator speed decreases to a point where its output voltage is less than the battery output voltage, the relay points open, breaking the charging circuit.

Testing Voltage Regulator on the Car

If the battery and generator are normal, test the voltage regulator as follows:

First check the wiring connecting the regulator in the charging circuit. Disconnect the wire from the

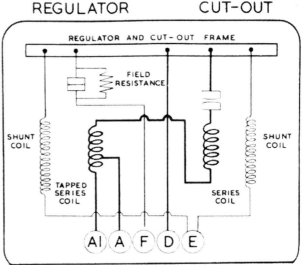

FIGURE 9—*Voltage Regulator Wiring Diagram*

"A" terminal of the regulator. Attach the negative (—) lead of the voltmeter to the wire and the positive (+) lead to a good ground. The voltmeter should read battery voltage. If a low reading or no reading exists, check the connections and wiring to the starting motor switch and battery.

Remove the wire from the regulator terminal marked "A-1" and connect it to the wire removed from the "A" terminal. Connect the voltmeter across the generator from the "D" terminal to ground.

Start the engine and increase the speed until the voltmeter reading is steady. The reading should be 15.8 volts at approximately 765 Engine R.P.M. with the RB-106-1 regulator; 15.6 to 16.2 volts at 1145 Engine R.P.M. with the RB-106-2 regulator. If a reading out of this range occurs, adjustment must be made. Remove the cover and with a small wrench, unlock regulator adjustment screw lock nut (Figs. 10 and 12) while holding adjustment screw. Turn adjustment screw clockwise to increase voltage setting or counterclockwise to reduce voltage. Make small changes in adjustment, checking after each adjustment, to obtain correct setting.

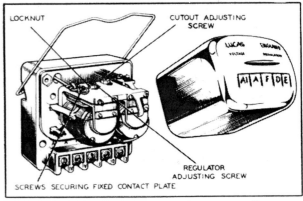

FIGURE 10—*Regulator Adjustment Screw Location—Model RB-106-1*

In the event satisfactory electrical setting cannot be obtained on the car, the regulator unit will have to be removed for replacement or further calibration. Before making any mechanical adjustments, the contact should be removed and dressed with a fine carborundum stone.

Model RB-106-1 Regulator

To adjust the regulator armature air gap, loosen the armature attaching screws (Fig. 11) and press the armature downward and backward against an .018" feeler gauge held between it and the regulator frame. Tighten the two attaching screws.

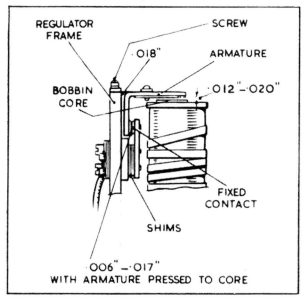

FIGURE 11—*Checking Regulator Armature Air Gap and Point Spacing—Model RB-106-1*

Check the gap at the space between the armature and the relay core. This should be .012" to .020". If the gap is not within these limits, correct by adding or removing shims from behind the fixed contact.

The point spacing should be between .006" to .017" with armature held down on relay core.

Model RB-106-2 Regulator

To adjust the regulator armature air gap, loosen the fixed contact lock nut and loosen the adjustment screw until the contact is clear of the armature moving contact.

Loosen the voltage adjusting screw lock nut on the rear of the regulator frame. Loosen the adjustment screw until it is clear of the tension spring (Fig. 12).

Loosen the two armature fastening screws and insert a .015" feeler gauge between the armature and core shim. Be careful not to damage the edge of the shim.

Press the armature squarely down against the gauge and tighten the two armature fastening screws.

With the gauge still in position, tighten the adjustable contact until it just touches the armature contact. Tighten the lock nut and remove the feeler gauge.

Recheck and adjust voltage regulator setting as outlined in preceding paragraphs. Tighten adjusting lock nut (Fig. 12).

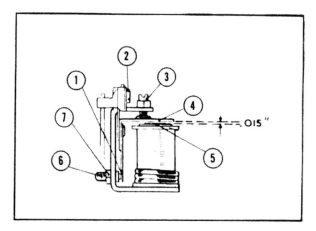

1. Armature Tension Spring
2. Armature Fastening Screws
3. Fixed Contact Adjustment Screw
4. Armature
5. Core Face and Shim
6. Voltage Adjusting Screw
7. Lock Nut

FIGURE 12—*Checking Regulator Armature Air Gap and Point Spacing—Model RB-106-2*

Cut-Out Relay Adjustment

The cut-out closing voltage is checked on the car in the following manner:

Remove the regulator cover assembly so that the opening and closing of the cut-out points can be seen and heard.

Attach the (—) negative voltmeter lead to the "D" terminal of the generator or regulator and the (+) positive terminal to a good ground.

Start the engine and slowly increase the speed noting the voltmeter and watching the cut-out points. The voltmeter will rise and flicker at the time the cut-out points close. Observe the voltage at the time the points close. The voltage should be 12.7 to 13.3 volts at 1050 to 1200 generator R.P.M. (approximately 865 Engine R.P.M.).

If the closing voltage is not within the range given, adjust as follows:

Loosen the lock nut (Figs. 10 and 14) while holding the adjustment screw. Then turn the adjustment screw clockwise to increase the closing voltage and counter-clockwise to reduce it. Make small changes and recheck. When adjustment is satisfactory, be sure to tighten lock nut.

If the cut-out relay does not respond to on-the-car adjustment, the regulator must be removed for further checking or replacement.

Model RB-106-1 Cut-Out Relay

Adjust the armature air gap by loosening the armature

attaching screws and fixed contact screw, and inserting a .011" to .015" gauge between the core face and the brass shim on the armature and an .008" feeler gauge between the armature bar and the regulator frame (Fig. 13). Press the armature down and back against the two gauges and tighten the armature attaching screws.

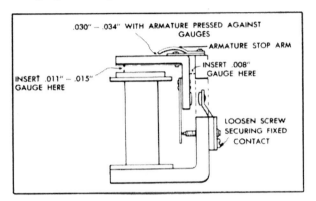

FIGURE 13—*Adjusting the Cut-Out Relay Armature Air Gaps—Model RB-106-1*

With the gauges still in position, set the armature stop arm to a clearance of .030" to .034" by carefully bending it (Fig. 13).

Remove the gauges and tighten the point attaching screw.

Insert a .025" gauge between the relay core face and the armature. Press the armature down onto the gauge. The gap between the contact points should now be .002" to .006". Adjust the point gap, if necessary, by adding or removing shims beneath the fixed contact plate.

Model RB-106-2 Cut-Out Relay

To adjust the armature air gap, loosen the adjusting screw lock nut at rear of cut-out relay frame and loosen the screw until it is clear of the armature tension spring (Fig. 14).

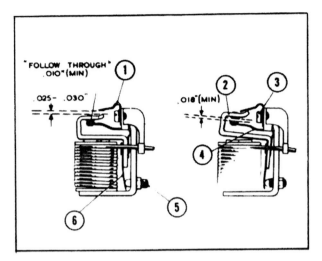

1. Stop Arm
2. Armature Tongue and Moving Contact
3. Armature Fastening Screws
4. Fixed Contact Blade
5. Cut-Out Adjusting Screw
6. Armature Tension Spring

FIGURE 14—*Adjusting the Cut-Out Relay Armature Air Gaps—Model RB-106-2*

Loosen the two armature fastening screws and press the armature squarely against the copper sprayed face of the relay core. Then retighten the fastening screws.

With a pair of round-nose pliers, adjust the gap between the armature stop arm and the armature tongue by bending the stop arm. The gap must be .025" to .030" when the armature is pressed squarely down on the core face.

The insulated contact arm must be bent in a similar manner so that when the armature is pressed against the core face a clearance of .010" is provided between the stop arm and armature tongue.

The contact gap when the armature is in the free position must be .018" minimum.

Recheck and adjust cut-out relay as outlined in preceding paragraphs. Tighten adjusting lock nut.

Regulator Specifications

Series	A and B	1500
Model	Lucas RB-106-1	RB-106-2
Regulator Relay		
Operating Voltage @ 68° F. and Generator R.P.M.	15.8 @ 1000	15.6-16.2 @ 1500
Air Gap	.012"-.020"	.015"
Point Gap	.006"-.017"	. . . . .
Cut-Out Relay		
Closing Voltage	12.7-13.3 Volts @ 1050-1200 Generator R.P.M.	12.7-13.3 Volts @ 1050-1200 Generator R.P.M.
Cut-Out Voltage and Reverse Current	9-10 Volts — 3-5 Amps.	8.5-11 Volts — 3.5-5 Amps.
Air Gap	.011"-.015"	.025"-.030"
Point Gap	.002"-.006"	.000"-.010"

STARTING MOTOR

A Lucas 12 volt M-35-G-1 starting motor is used. It is a series wound four brush, four pole type (Figs. 15 and 16).

Inspection

At time of inspection, the motor should be removed to inspect the brushes, commutator and general condition.

The brushes should be free in their holders and not worn enough to expose the pig tail brush lead on the contact surface.

Two of the brushes are attached by their pig tails to eyelets in their brush holders. (Fig. 17). These are ground brushes.

The other two brushes are attached to the end of the field windings by a common connection. These are the insulated brushes. When replacing brushes, unsolder old brushes and solder new brushes into place either at eyelets for ground brushes or at the field coil connection for the insulated brushes.

Brush tension should be 15 to 25 ounces.

Clean the commutator with a soft cloth moistened with solvent. If the commutator is rough or scored, dress lightly in a lathe and polish with fine sandpaper #00. Never undercut the insulators between the segments.

Test the field coils for continuity with a series connected 12 volt light and battery. If the light lights when the field circuit is connected in this series circuit, it is an indication that the field coils are intact.

A check for proper amperage draw is made with the

1. Starting Motor Switch
2. Starting Motor Cable
3. Starting Motor

FIGURE 15—*Starting Motor Location*

complete assembly after reassembly to determine if the field circuit is in order.

A check can be made of the field circuit for short to ground by the use of a 110 volt test lamp. Place

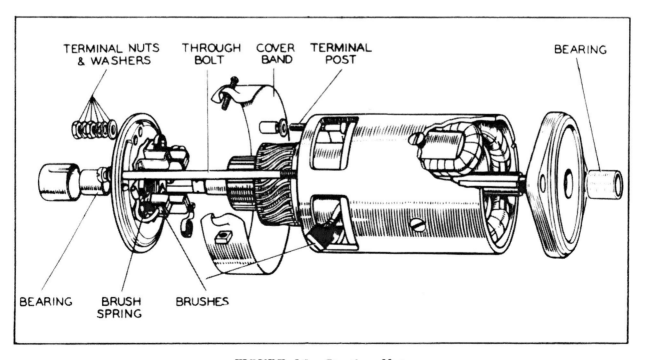

FIGURE 16—*Starting Motor*

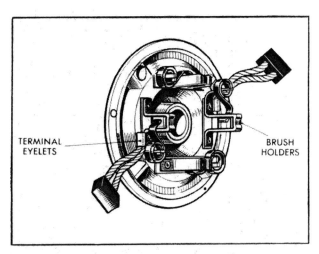

FIGURE 17—*Ground Brushes Attached to Commutator End Frame*

one test prod on the field brush connection with the brushes hanging free from any contact with the starting motor frame. Touch the other test prod to the starting motor frame. If the light lights, a short to ground exists in one of the field coils or field leads.

If a faulty field coil is indicated, the field coils must be replaced.

Test Data

Lock Torque	9.3 Ft. Lbs. With 370-390 Amperes at 7.3-7.7 Volts
Torque at 1000 R.P.M.	4.9 Ft. Lbs. With 250-270 Amperes at 8.9-9.3 Volts
No Load Test	45 Amperes at 5800 R.P.M.

STARTING MOTOR DRIVE

Removal of the Starting Motor Drive

The drive is retained on the armature shaft by means of the drive retaining nut.

Remove the cotter key from the nut and remove the nut.

Rotate and slide the main drive spring, thrust washer, and pinion barrel assembly from the armature shaft.

Inspection and Cleaning

After the drive is removed from the armature shaft, it can be further disassembled by removing the snap ring and wave washer from the barrel assembly. This will permit removal of the control nut, anti-drift spring, and spring limiting washer (Figs. 18 and 19).

Clean all parts in solvent and inspect.

Replace all damaged or badly worn parts. It is essential to replace the spiral sleeve and control nut as a pair. Coat all parts with a very thin film of light engine oil and reassemble.

STARTING MOTOR SWITCH

A Lucas switch, Model ST-19/1, cable controlled from the dash mounted knob is used.

Care must be used in mounting of switch to insure a slack cable, when switch is not in use, to prevent inadvertent closing of the switch contacts.

When testing reveals a faulty switch, the switch assembly must be replaced as a unit.

The switch is located behind and to the right of the engine on the fire wall (Fig. 3), and can be operated from engine side by pressing switch shaft extension.

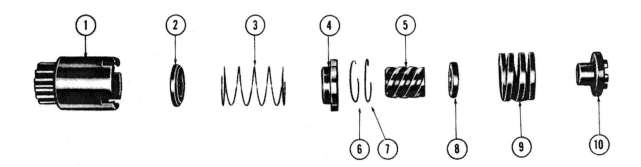

1. Pinion and Barrel Assembly
2. Spring Limiting Washer
3. Pinion Anti-Drift Return Spring
4. Control Nut
5. Spiral Sleeve

6. Wave Spring Washer
7. Retaining Snap Ring
8. Thrust Washer
9. Main Drive Spring
10. Drive Retaining Nut

FIGURE 18—*Exploded View of Starting Motor Drive*

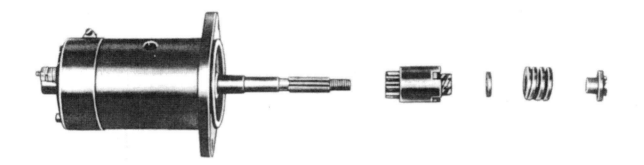

FIGURE 19—*Starting Motor Drive Removed from Armature Shaft*

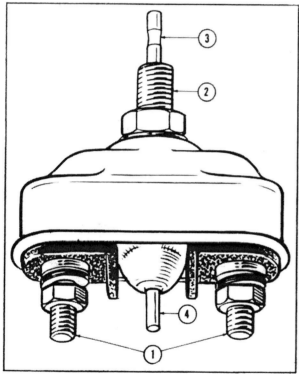

1. Terminals
2. Bracket Mounting Threaded Shaft
3. Cable Adapter Shaft
4. Switch Shaft Extension

FIGURE 20—*Starting Motor Switch*

IGNITION COIL

A Lucas 12 volt ignition coil (Model Q-12, A and B Series, or LA-12, 1500 Series) is mounted on top of the generator.

No service is required other than to keep the coil clean. The terminals especially must be kept clean and tight.

DISTRIBUTOR

A Lucas Model DM-2 distributor equipped with centrifugal and vacuum advance mechanism is used. A micrometer advance adjustment is provided for changes in fuel or engine carbon build up.

1. Ignition Coil

FIGURE 21—*Ignition Coil Location*

Radio interference is reduced by a carbon rotor contact built into the distributor cap.

The condenser is of the completely sealed metalized paper type.

Lubrication

At every 1000 mile period, place a few drops of light machine oil through the opening at the edge of the contact breaker cam to lubricate the automatic spark advance mechanism.

Apply a light film of high melting point grease to the cam and pivot.

Remove the rotor and apply a few drops of light machine oil to the shaft to lubricate the cam bearing.

Distributor Disassembly and Servicing

Remove the nut holding the primary lead pig tail, condenser lead, and movable contact spring to the anchor stud. Do not lose the two insulating washers assembled on the spring anchor stud.

Lift off the movable arm and spring.

Remove the two screws retaining the stationary point plate to the vacuum advance plate.

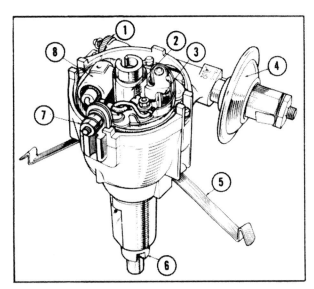

1. Micrometer Spark Advance Adjustment
2. Breaker Cam
3. Contact Points
4. Vacuum Advance Mechanism
5. Distributor Cap Retaining Clip
6. Distributor Drive Coupling
7. Primary Terminal
8. Condenser

FIGURE 22—Distributor Assembly Removed from Engine for Servicing

Remove the screw retaining the condenser and remove condenser.

Remove the two screws at the edge of the base plate supporting the breaker vacuum advance plate.

Remove the pin clip holding the vacuum link to the rotating breaker plate.

Remove the ground pig tail.

Lift the contact breaker plate and support plate out of the distributor body.

NOTE: *The primary terminal is attached with its insulating block to the lower sup-port plate.*

The breaker plate can now be separated from the support plate by removing the snap ring and star shaped finger spring (Fig. 23).

Remove the screw from the top of the shaft inside of breaker cam. Remove the cam and cam foot.

Note the location of the offset drive tang to the rotor shaft and mark to aid in reassembly, then remove the pin securing the drive tang.

Remove the shaft spacer, and shaft.

Remove the vacuum unit adjusting nut snap ring, nut, and vacuum unit assembly.

Distributor Reassembly

Place the spacer over the distributor shaft. Coat the shaft assembly with clean engine oil and install it into its bearing in the distributor body.

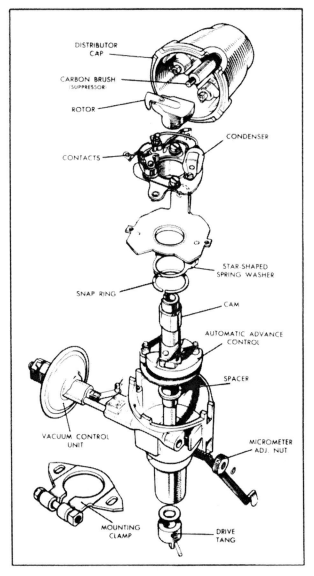

FIGURE 23—Exploded View of Distributor Assembly

Reassemble the vacuum unit into its housing on the distributor body and replace the springs, milled adjusting nut, and snap ring.

Assemble the automatic advance control. Check the springs for stretch or damage. Check to see that a washer is in position below each toggle. Place the cam and cam foot over the distributor shaft engaging the projecting pins on the cam foot with the toggles. Install the cam screw on top of the shaft.

Install the rotating breaker plate onto the main support plate. Retain the assembly with the spring washer and snap ring. Install the plate assembly into the distributor body engaging the vacuum link pin. Install the two support plate retaining screws, ground pig tail lead, and clip to vacuum link pin.

Install the condenser locating the plate ground pig tail wire below the condenser attaching screw.

Install the stationary contact point securing it with its two attaching screws. One plain and one lockwasher is used beneath each of these screws.

Install the movable point and spring after placing the two lower insulating washers in place, one on the point pivot and the other on the terminal stud to which the spring is anchored.

Slide insulator shoulder washer through condenser lead and primary lead terminal and into spring eye. This shoulder washer isolates the primary from ground other than through the contact points.

Install terminal nut and washer.

Set point gap to .014″ to .016″. Both attaching screws must be loosened.

Install drive tang according to marks and secure with pin. Install rotor.

Distributor Timing

The distributor assembly can only be installed in one position as the drive tang is offset. Before tightening

Timing, Breaker Points Open

A Series

1500 Series With Engine Number Prefix 15-CNH

B Series and 1500 Series With Engine Number Prefix IH

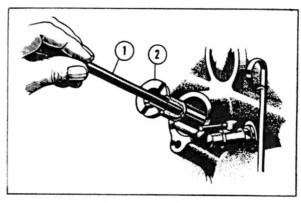

1. Screw Tipped Rod
(5/16″-24 THD-NF)
2. Drive Shaft and Gear

FIGURE 24—*Removing or Installing Distributor Drive Shaft*

the clamp, rotate distributor body so that points just open with number one piston in firing position to the required specifications as listed below:

7° B.T.D.C. (5/16″ B.T.D.C. Mark on Pulley)
5° B.T.D.C. (7/32″ B.T.D.C. Mark on Pulley)

11° B.T.D.C. (1/2″ B.T.D.C. Mark on Pulley)

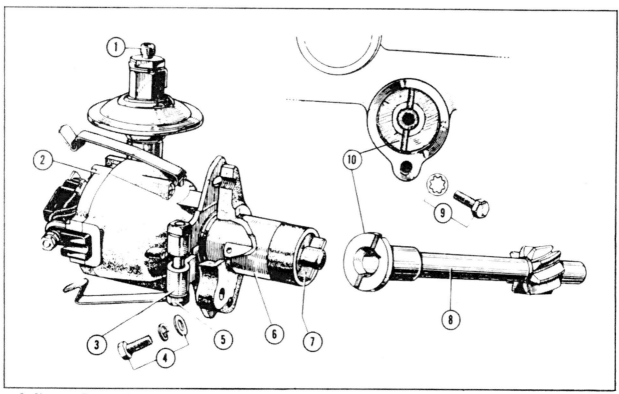

1. Vacuum Control Tube Connection
2. Distributor Body
3. Mounting Clamp
4. Mounting Clamp Attaching Screws (2)
5. Mounting Clamp Bolt
6. Distributor Drive Bushing
7. Distributor Drive Tang
8. Distributor Drive Shaft
9. Distributor Drive Bushing Attaching Screw
10. Offset Slot in Drive Shaft

FIGURE 25—*Components of the Distributor Drive*

The mark on the crankshaft pulley is located at T.D.C. Therefore, in order to obtain the required degrees advance, it is necessary for the points to open before T.D.C. as measured on the outside diameter of the crankshaft pulley.

Should it become necessary to remove the distributor drive bushing and main drive shaft, remove the mounting bracket and bushing. Then insert a threaded rod (5/16"-24 N.F.) into the end of the distributor main drive shaft and remove the shaft with a turning movement as it is withdrawn (Fig. 24). The use of the threaded rod will prevent the shaft dropping into the engine oil pan at time of removal and installation.

At time of installation, locate the number one piston in firing position at T.D.C. Install the shaft, using the threaded rod, in such a manner that the offset slot is located in a diagonal (12:30-6:30) position, the larger side of the offset being to the rear of the engine (Fig. 25).

Inspect the distributor cap for cleanliness and a free sliding contact brush. The ignition wires are retained in the distributor cap by pointed set screws (Fig. 26).

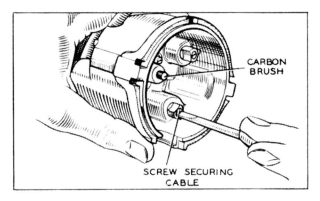

FIGURE 26—*Replacing Spark Plug Lead Cable (High Tension)*

Distributor Specifications

Make	Lucas
Type	DM-2
Cam or Dwell Angle	60° (+ or —3°)
Open Period	30° (+ or —3°)
Contact Point Gap	.014"-.016"
Contact Point Spring Tension Measured at Contacts	20-24 Ozs.
Condenser Capacity	.2 Microfarads

Automatic Advance
Centrifugal
Distributor Degrees & R.P.M.

A Series	0°- 1° @ 500
	14°-16° @ 1900
B Series	0°- 1° @ 380
	8°-10° @ 1500
1500 Series With Engine Number Prefix IH	0°- 1° @ 600
	7° @ 1700
1500 Series With Engine Number Prefix 15-CNH (Car Serial #E-43116)	0°- 1° @ 300
	½°- 2½° @ 450
	6°- 8° @ 1130
	9°-11° @ 1500
	11°-13° @ 2400

Vacuum Advance

A Series	1°- 3° @ 6.5" Hg.
	9°-11° @ 17" Hg.
B Series	1°- 3° @ 6.04" Hg.
	10°-12° @ 20.8" Hg.
1500 Series With Engine Number Prefix IH	0°- 1° @ 6" Hg.
	12° @ 16" Hg.
1500 Series With Engine Number Prefix 15-CNH (Car Serial #E-43116)	0°- 1° @ 5" Hg.
	17° @ 10" Hg.

SPARK PLUGS

A long reach thread spark plug, Champion N-8 is used as standard equipment. It is a 14 m.m. thread and has 13/16" hex for socket wrench installation. The plug is always installed with new gasket to a torque of 30 foot pounds with clean dry thread.

Clean plugs with sand blaster every 3,000 to 5,000 miles of service. Replace at approximately 10,000 miles service.

Plug gap is .023" to .025".

1. Instrument Cluster Lights
2. Knurled Nut
3. Fuel Gauge Dash Unit
4. "L" Shaped Retaining Bracket
5. Cluster Housing
6. Speedometer Head Assembly
7. Lens and Bezel Assembly

FIGURE 27—*Instrument Cluster
Exploded View*

INSTRUMENT CLUSTER

The instrument cluster is located in the dash panel above the steering jacket tube. It contains the speedometer, odometer, fuel gauge, and high beam, oil pressure and no-charge indicator lights.

Instrument Cluster Removal

To remove the cluster assembly, disconnect the speedometer cable at the rear of the speedometer head and remove the two knurled nuts and "L" shaped brackets from the instrument cluster housing. This will allow the complete unit to be pulled forward through the dash panel. The wires and light sockets can then be removed and tagged for identification on reassembly.

INSTRUMENT LIGHT

To illuminate the instrument cluster for night driving, two light bulbs are fitted into the back of the cluster housing and are controlled by the light switch in either "park" or "headlight" position. The bulbs are easily replaced from the rear of the panel by pulling the bulb sockets from the housing and changing the bulbs. A Lucas #987 bulb is used in the two instrument bulb locations (Fig. 27).

HIGH BEAM INDICATOR

A Lucas #987 bulb is installed behind the red jewel at the top of the instrument cluster for indication of country driving light operation. The bulb is controlled by the dimmer switch, and is connected to the country driving light circuit at a four way connector (see Wiring Diagram) at the left inner wheelhouse panel. The bulb can be easily changed from the rear of the panel.

NO-CHARGE INDICATOR LIGHT

The no-charge indicator light is located at the lower right of the instrument cluster. It serves to indicate general condition of the charging circuit and warns operator when ignition switch is left on with engine inoperative. It is a series connected light in an insulated socket. It is connected across the charging circuit from the voltage regulator "D" terminal to the ignition side of the ignition circuit. When the voltage regulator cut-out points are open, electrical energy from the battery, with the ignition switch on, flows through the no-charge light illuminating the red jewel and back to the battery by way of the generator ground brush or voltage regulator ground connection. Due to the reversal of current flow as the generator begins to charge, and the decrease of resistance through the closed cut-out points, the no-charge light goes out. If the no-charge light is on during engine operation, at approximately 30 M.P.H., it is an indication that the battery is not receiving a charging current.

A Lucas #987 bulb is used and is easily changed from the back of panel.

FUEL QUANTITY GAUGE

The fuel gauge is of the balanced coil magnetic type.

The sending unit is a variable resistor operated through movement of the float.

No field service is performed on the dash or tank units. If trouble exists. the faulty unit is replaced with a new one.

Test for circuit continuity. and if improper operation still exists. substitute a good tank unit of the identical type in the circuit and hand operate to give the dash unit readings of empty. half full and full. If the dash unit then reads correctly. the tank unit is at fault. If the dash unit reads incorrectly. it is at fault.

The dash unit is retained by two screws to the cluster housing and is readily accessible from the back of the panel.

The tank unit replacement requires removing the gas tank.

The fuel gauge circuit is protected by a 30 ampere fuse in the fuse block.

LOW OIL PRESSURE LIGHT

A warning light located in the lower left of the instrument cluster lights when the oil pressure is seven P.S.I. or less. The energy for the light is obtained from an ignition circuit energized thirty ampere fuse on the fuse block. The energy is routed to the battery labeled terminal of the gas gauge dash unit and then to one side of the series connected insulated light socket assembly. The other side or lead from the light socket assembly connects to the terminal of the pressure switch mounted on the engine. A set of contacts in the pressure switch is opened by oil pressure at approximately seven P.S.I. making the light go out. Below seven P.S.I.. the contacts close completing the warning light circuit to ground and the light goes on.

The light bulb. a Lucas #987. is readily accessible from the back of the panel.

The pressure switch is located on the right side of the engine just behind the distributor.

IGNITION AND LIGHT SWITCH ASSEMBLY

A combination switch assembly is used for ignition and lighting. The knob serves to operate the light switch section. while the ignition lock cylinder is contained in the center of the unit. A wire spring clamp and clamp bolt retain the switch to the dash panel.

1. **Choke Control**	8. **No-Charge Indicator**
2. **Heater Control**	9. **Fuel Gauge**
3. **Windshield Wiper Control**	10. **Starter Switch**
4. **Directional Signal Pilot Flasher**	11. **Ignition and Light Switch**
5. **High Beam Indicator**	12. **Dimmer Switch**
6. **Speedometer**	13. **Low Oil Pressure Warning Light**
7. **Odometer**	

FIGURE 28—*Instrument Cluster*

To remove the light and ignition switch assembly, disconnect the battery lead at the starter switch.

Remove the spring clamp screw and clamp. The switch can then be pulled forward through the dash.

A hole has been provided in the metal shell of the switch assembly to permit the removal of the lock cylinder in the event a change in keys is desired (Fig. 29).

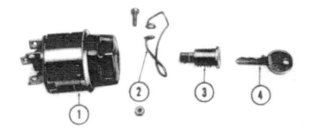

1. Switch Body
2. Retaining Clamp
3. Lock Cylinder
4. Ignition Key

FIGURE 31—*Main Removable Components of Ignition Light Switch Assembly*

1. Access Hole to Remove Lock Cylinder
2. Light Switch Control Knob
3. Ignition Switch Key

FIGURE 29—*Light and Ignition Switch Assembly*

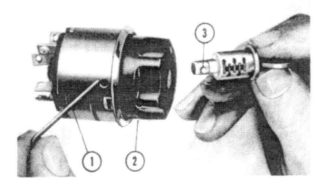

1. Small Allen Wrench
2. Rotate Black Knob Until Cylinder Retaining Pin, Item 3, Lines Up With Access Hole. Insert Ignition Key and Depress Plunger with Allen Wrench Permitting Cylinder to be Withdrawn with Key.
3. Lock Cylinder Retaining Pin

FIGURE 30—*Removing Lock Cylinder from Ignition Switch Assembly*

FUSE BLOCK

A fuse block assembly located on the forward side of the dash affords protection for main electrical circuits (Fig. 8).

The fuse unit is a Lucas Model SF-6 consisting of an open insulated moulding, mounting two active and two spare fuses.

The fuse connected across section "A-1" to "A-2"

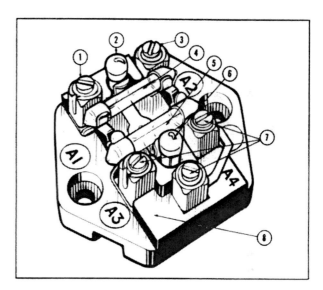

1. Wire Terminal
2. Spare Fuse
3. Wire Terminal
4. Main Lighting Fuse
5. Ignition Energized Fuse
6. Spare Fuse
7. Wire Terminals
8. Fuse Unit Body

FIGURE 32—*Fuse Unit*

protects the lighting circuits consisting of the headlamps, license plate lamp, parking and tail lamps, courtesy light, panel lights, and high beam indicator light.

The circuits protected by the fuse connected across the "A-3" to "A-4" section and controlled by the ignition switch are the heater motor, windshield wiper, fuel gauge, low oil pressure warning light, directional signal, and stop light. The horns, ignition coil, no-charge light and cigar lighter are not fuse protected.

A thirty ampere fuse $1\frac{1}{4}''$ long, $\frac{1}{4}''$ diameter is used in each of the sections of the fuse block.

HEADLAMPS

The headlamps are of the sealed beam type. Beam

direction is adjusted by the method outlined below:

For access to the adjustment screws on each sealed beam, remove the headlamp door.

1. **Vertical Adjustment**
2. **Horizontal Adjustment**
3. **Front Parking and Directional Signal Lamp**

FIGURE 33—*Headlamp Adjustment*

Locate the car on a level floor twenty-five feet ahead from a vertical wall. Draw a horizontal line on the wall three inches below the headlamp center level, and a vertical line directly ahead of each lamp. Another vertical line, midway between the headlamps, may be located by sighting through the center of the rear window and over the center of the hood.

> CAUTION: *If your state requires a loading allowance, draw the horizontal line below the level line by the amount required in your particular state.*

Cover one lamp and adjust the other lamp by centering the high intensity beam.

Repeat the operation for the second lamp. No further adjustment is needed for the lower beam.

Headlamp bulbs are #4430.

HEADLAMP DIMMER SWITCH

A dimmer switch is located above and to the left of the clutch pedal (Fig. 28). It is readily accessible from inside of the car after folding back floor mat.

Three wire terminals are provided. One wire connects to the headlight terminal on the light switch.

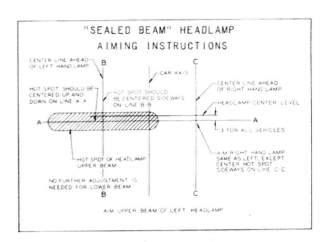

FIGURE 34—*Headlamp Adjusting Chart*

One wire connects to the high beam element of each headlamp sealed beam unit and the high beam indicator light. One wire connects to the low beam element of each headlamp sealed beam unit.

PARKING, TAIL, STOP AND DIRECTIONAL LIGHTING

The left and right front parking and directional signal lights are each contained in a single lamp unit and use a double element bulb #1016. The heavy element 21 cp is for the directional signal and the light element 6 cp for the parking light. A rubber gasket serves to retain both the lens and lens bezel, and also serves to seal the socket assembly in the fender.

To change the bulb, a small screwdriver is carefully used to pry out the lens bezel and lens (Figs. 35 and 36).

The socket assembly is retained to the fender by three screws.

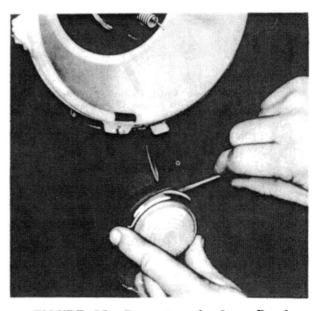

FIGURE 35—*Removing the Lens Bezel*

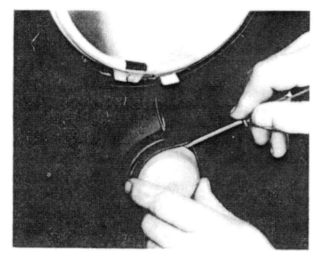

FIGURE 36—*Removing Lens*

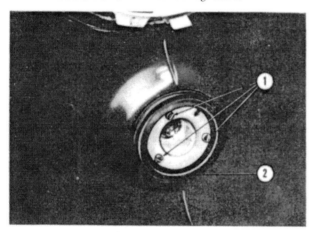

1. Attaching Screws
2. Seal and Lens Retaining Gasket

FIGURE 37—*Directional Signal and Parking Lamp Socket Assembly*

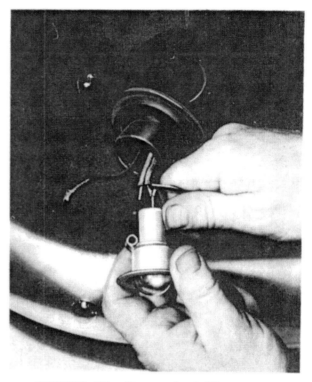

FIGURE 38—*Removal of Wires from Socket Assembly*

The tail, stop and rear directional lights are contained in single assemblies containing two sections. The upper section contains the stop and tail light bulb. The lower section contains the directional signal bulb (Fig. 39).

A #1016 bulb is used in the tail and stop light socket.

A #1141 bulb is used in the rear directional light socket.

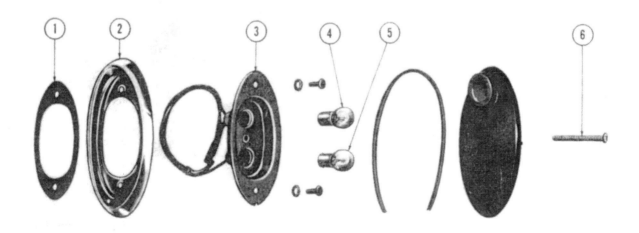

1. Housing to Fender Seal Gasket
2. Housing Trim Plate Body
3. Socket Housing Assembly
4. Tail and Stop Light Bulb
5. Directional Signal Bulb
6. Lens Retaining Screw

FIGURE 39—*Components of Rear Tail, Stop, and Directional Signal Light Assembly*

BRAKE LIGHT SWITCH

A hydraulic operated brake light switch is used in the service brake pressure line to the front wheel brakes, and is located on the inside of the left front wheelhouse panel.

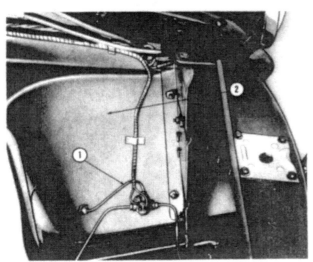

1. Brake Light Switch
2. Left Inner Wheelhouse Panel

FIGURE 40—*Hydraulic Brake Light Switch Location*

LICENSE LAMP

A license plate lamp is energized by the park and headlight position of the light switch. In the "park" position, the courtesy light is also in the circuit.

A #57 bulb is used for the license lamp. To change the bulb, the shield only has to be removed. It is held by two small screws (Fig. 41).

DIRECTIONAL SIGNAL

The signal is controlled through the directional signal switch assembly located in the hub section of the steering wheel. The switch lever is moved manually to indicate the desired turn and cancelled automatically during the recovery from the turn through cam action.

Electrical energy from the ignition energized thirty ampere fuse flows to the flasher then up to the signal switch, which will be closed to right or left position, and to the indicator pilot light and signal lights on the side of the car selected.

The flasher is located behind the dash panel on the ceiling of the cowl.

The pilot indicator light is connected in series with the circuit not in operation to obtain a ground, and energized by the circuit that is in operation. The socket assembly is insulated from the ground. Due to the series resistance of the indicator bulb (approximately 7 ohms) insufficient energy is available to light the bulbs through which the indicator bulb gets its ground.

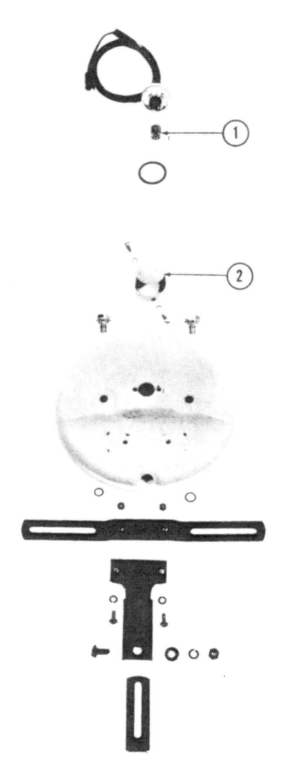

1. License Lamp Bulb
2. Bulb Shield

FIGURE 41—*License Lamp Assembly*

The bulb socket assembly is held in the bulb housing by spring clip tension, and is removed from the back of the dash panel.

A #970 bulb is used.

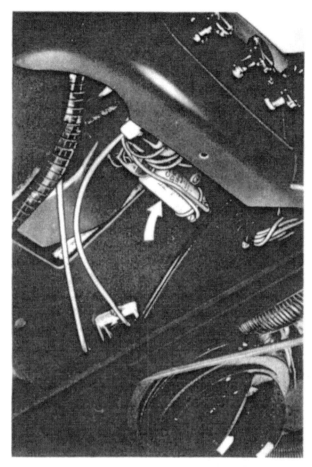

FIGURE 42—*Directional Signal Flasher Location*

1. Red Plastic Bulb Housing
2. Dash Retaining Nut

FIGURE 43—*Directional Signal Pilot Light Indicator*

Directional Signal Switch

To remove the switch, disconnect the directional and horn leads at the lower end of the switch harness near the end of the steering worm tube. Remove the three screws from the side of the steering wheel hub and pull the assembly from the steering wheel (Fig. 44).

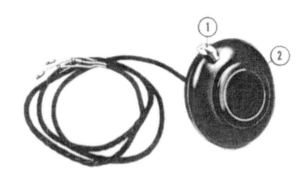

1. Directional Switch Lever
2. Horn Button

FIGURE 44—*Directional Signal and Horn Button Assembly Removed from Steering Wheel*

Remove the three screws and remove retaining ring, horn button, horn button return springs, and contact plate (Figs. 45 and 46).

FIGURE 45—*Removing Horn Button Assembly*

With a screwdriver shift brass lock plate to the right to expose the three cam plate to switch assembly retaining screws (Fig. 47).

Remove the three screws which retain the switch assembly to the cam plate (Figs. 48 and 49).

Remove the nuts and long screws that retain the horn finger contact plates and signal terminal block to signal switch unit (Fig. 50).

ELECTRICAL SECTION

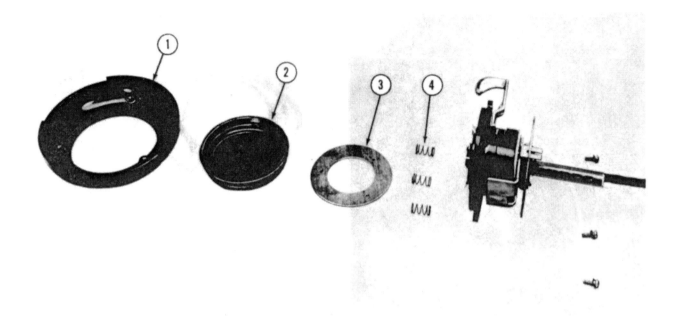

1. Horn Button Retainer
2. Horn Button

3. Horn Button Contact Plate
4. Horn Button Return Springs

FIGURE 46—*Horn Button Assembly Removed from Control Unit*

FIGURE 47—*Moving Brass Lock Plate to Uncover the Three Screws Retaining Directional Switch to Cam Plate*

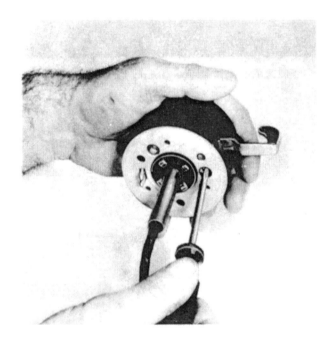

FIGURE 48—*Removing the Three Screws Retaining Cam Plate to Signal Switch Assembly*

The horn finger plates can be further disassembled as shown in Figure 51.

The switch (directional signal) block unit can be removed from the horn button retaining plate by the removal of the retaining screw (Item 4, Fig. 52).

The signal switch block unit can be disassembled into the components shown in Figure 53.

Before installing the directional signal switch and horn blowing assembly, be sure the conduit tube is flush with the top of the steering worm tube, and the nut and sleeve tight at the bottom of the steering gear box.

ELECTRICAL SECTION

HORNS

A pair of Lucas Model WT-614 electric horns are used. One has a higher note than the other. The high note horn is recognized by its smaller air column casting and by the yellow band fitted to one of its internal connections. All the connections in the low note horn are identified by a red band. The horns are marked "H" and "L" inside the flare of the trumpet for high and low note horns respectively. The high and low note horns differ in frequency by an interval of a major third.

FIGURE 49—Cam Plate Separated from Signal Switch Assembly

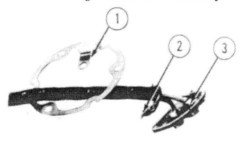
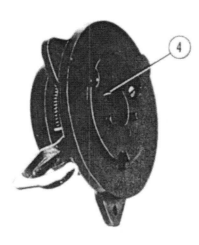
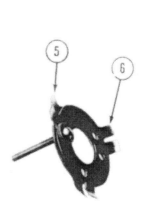

1. Horn Ground Plate
2. Horn Energy Feed Wire
3. Signal Energy Feed Wire

4. Signal Switch Unit
5. Horn Feed Finger Plate
6. Horn Ground Finger Plate

FIGURE 50—Horn Contact Finger Plate, Ground Contact Plate, and Signal Switch Unit

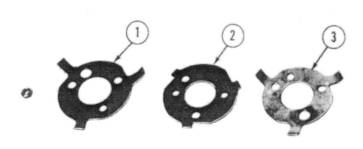
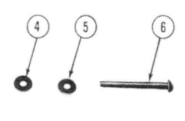

1. Horn Energy Feed Finger Plate
2. Finger Plate Insulator
3. Horn Ground Contact Finger Plate

4. Terminal Screw Insulator Washer
5. Terminal Screw Washer
6. Terminal Screw

FIGURE 51—Horn Contact Finger Plate Assembly Sequence

ELECTRICAL SECTION

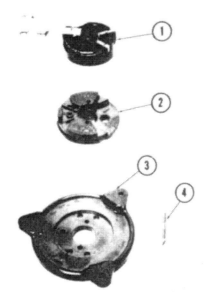

1. **Switch Block**   3. **Retaining Plate**
2. **Switch Block Base**   4. **Retaining Screw**

FIGURE 52—*Signal Switch Block Unit Removed from Retainer Plate*

Service Operations

Horns may require adjustment to compensate for the wear of the moving parts. The adjustment will not alter the pitch of the note, but if not adjusted, the horn may lose power and become rough in tone. Horns should not be used, when out of adjustment, as a high current draw may cause damage.

To check the current draw of one or both horns, attach a 0-30 ampere range ammeter in the circuit in series to the single or to both horns at a convenient point. The reading for a single operating horn should be 6.5 amperes, for both operating horns 13 amperes. The car should be stationary and the battery voltage at 12 volts during this check.

It is advisable to remove the horns for cleaning and adjustment when required. A 12-volt battery, 0-30 ammeter, and connecting wire of the size used in the car will provide the needed equipment to bench test and calibrate the horns.

To adjust a horn, remove the cover securing screws and cover. Loosen the lock nut on the fixed contact

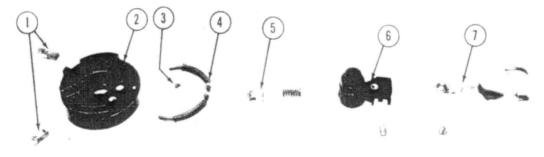

1. **Switch Toggles**
2. **Switch Terminal Block**
3. **Switch Moving Contact Plate**
4. **Signal Lever Return Spring Unit**

5. **Lever Trip Roller**
6. **Lever Trip Roller Housing**
7. **Signal Switch Lever**

FIGURE 53—*Components of Signal Switch Block Unit*

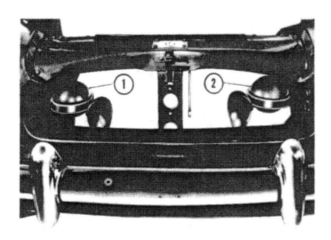

1. **High Note Horn (Right Side)**
2. **Low Note Horn (Left Side)**

FIGURE 54—*Horn Location, Radiator and Grille Removed*

and rotate the adjusting nut in a clockwise direction until the contacts are just separated, as indicated by the horn failing to sound. Turn the adjusting nut half a turn in the opposite direction and hold it while tightening the lock nut. Check the current consumption of the horn, which must not exceed 6.5 amperes.

If the current is incorrect, make further fine adjustments to the contact breaker turning the adjusting screw in a clockwise direction to decrease the current and vice-versa. When normal adjustment is not possible, it is a fault of some internal part listed below:

Contacts Badly Worn	Replacement Needed
Incorrect Contact Spring Pressure	Pressure to Just Separate the Contacts at End of Spring Should Be 3.5 to 4.5 Pounds. Replacement Needed
Steel Push Rod Binding	Clean and Free-up

ELECTRICAL SECTION

Push Rod Too Slack;
   Rattles when Horn
     Is Used   Replace Push Rod or Horn Unit
Armature Fouling
   Base Plate   Clearance of .020" Should Exist
               Between Armature and Base
               Plate. Loosen Base Plate,
               Centralize Armature in Open-
               ing and Retighten Base Plate.

The horn circuit is not fused, so it is advisable to disconnect the battery lead at the starter switch, before working on horns for removal.

Before reinstalling horns, a 500 volt test should be made to check the horn insulation for breakdown. Test prods should be placed on the horn mounting base and horn feed terminal.

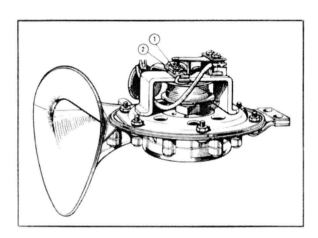

1. Adjusting Nut
2. Lock Nut

FIGURE 55—*Horn Adjustment*

SPEEDOMETER

A Smith magnetic type speedometer, cable driven from the rear of the transmission, is used.

To remove the speedometer head for service, the instrument cluster must be removed from the dash. It is retained to the dash by two "L" shaped brackets and knurled nuts.

Disconnect speedometer cable at back of head.

Remove the knurled nuts, washers, and "L" brackets; then pull cluster forward through dash. Disconnect and mark all wiring and light bulb sockets to aid in reassembly.

Remove two screws retaining speedometer head to cluster housing; uncrimp lens bezel from cluster housing and remove lens and bezel.

Remove speedometer head.

Always inspect the speedometer cable housing, whenever working on the speedometer, for kinks or sharp bends in the housing. Make sure that the cable is of the correct length for the series required.

Speedometer Cable

At approximately 5,000 miles, the inner speedometer cable core should be removed, cleaned thoroughly, dipped in #30 engine oil, and reinstalled.

To insure the use of speedometer cable cores which will give quiet and satisfactory service, locate the cable core on a flat surface in the form of an inverted "U" and then cross the open ends. Hold one end in the left hand, the other in the right hand.

Twist one end, applying light finger pressure to the other end. If the core is satisfactory, the turning action will be smooth.

On a damaged core, although not noticeable by visual inspection, the turning action will be jerky and, in a severe case, the core will leap or jump.

The speedometer cable requires no lubrication but as a sound deadener, it is beneficial to coat the cable with a light coating of #30 engine oil.

The A Series speedometer cable and driven gear components are illustrated in Figure 56.

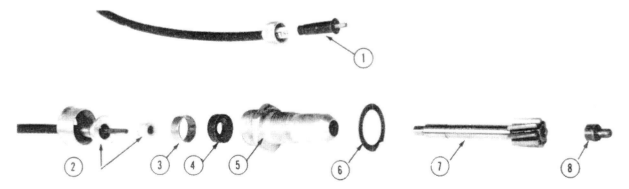

1. **Upper End of Speedometer Cable Assembly**
2. **Transmission End of Speedometer Cable**
   Which Contains Felt Seal
3. **Speedometer Driven Gear Oil Seal Retaining Ring**
4. **Speedometer Driven Gear Oil Seal**
5. **Speedometer Driven Gear Bushing**
6. **Speedometer Driven Gear Bushing Gasket**
7. **Speedometer Driven Gear, 8 Teeth**
8. **Speedometer Driven Gear Thrust Button**

FIGURE 56—*Speedometer Cable and Driven Gear Components—A Series*

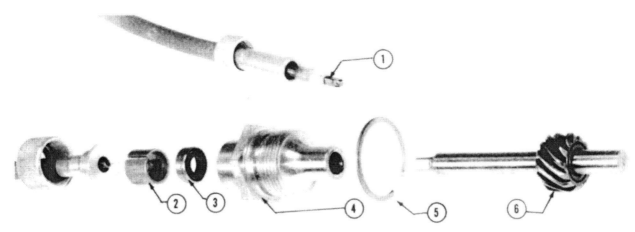

1. Speedometer End of Cable Assembly, Oil Control
   Groove Provided in Plastic Stop
2. Speedometer Driven Gear Bushing Oil Seal
   Retaining Ring

3. Speedometer Driven Gear Bushing Oil Seal
4. Speedometer Driven Gear Bushing
5. Speedometer Driven Gear Bushing Gasket
6. Speedometer Driven Gear, 13 Teeth

FIGURE 57—Speedometer Cable and Driven Gear Components—B Series
and 1500 Series to Car Serial Number E-28705 Inclusive

Figure 57 illustrates the driven gear components effective with the B Series to car Serial E-28705 on the 1500 Series. At Serial Number E-28217 an oil control groove was incorporated in the plastic guide at the speedometer end of the cable core.

At car Serial Number E-28706, a new transmission extension housing required additional changes in the speedometer driven gear and bushing. The driven gear is of nylon construction, for quietness, with a spiral oil control groove provided on the shaft as illustrated in Figure 58.

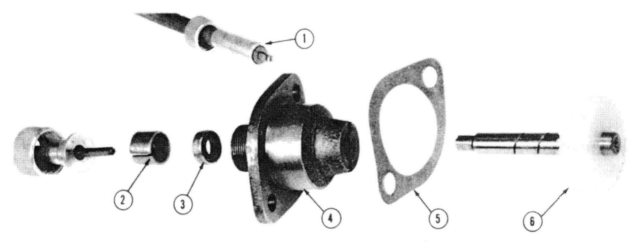

1. Speedometer End of Cable Assembly
2. Speedometer Driven Gear Bushing Oil Seal
   Retaining Ring
3. Speedometer Driven Gear Bushing Oil Seal

4. Speedometer Driven Gear Bushing Adapter
5. Speedometer Driven Gear Bushing Adapter Gasket
6. Speedometer Driven Gear, 28 Teeth

FIGURE 58—Speedometer Cable and Driven Gear Components—
1500 Series at Car Serial Number E-28706

BATTERY SPECIFICATIONS

Series	A and B	1500
Make	Lucas 12-Volt	Lucas 12-Volt
Model	GTW-9-A	BT-9-A
Ampere Hour Capacity; 20 Hour Rating	58	57
No. of Plates Per Cell	9	9

ELECTRICAL SECTION

GENERATOR SPECIFICATIONS

Make	Lucas
Model	C-39-PV-2
Type	Two Pole, Two Brush, Shunt Wound
Rotation	C.W. Drive End
Brush Spring Tension	22-25 Ozs. Not Less Than 15 Ozs.
Cut-In Speed	1050-1200 R.P.M. at 13 Volts
Field Resistance	6.2 Ohms
Max. Controlled Charging Rate	
(Controlled by Current Regulator Winding)	19 Amperes — 13.5 Volts at 2000-2150 Generator R.P.M.

REGULATOR SPECIFICATIONS

Series	A and B	1500
Model	Lucas RB-106-1	RB-106-2
Regulator Relay		
Operating Voltage @ 68° and		
Generator R.P.M.	15.8 @ 1000	15.6-16.2 @ 1500
Air Gap	.012"-.020"	.015"
Point Gap	.006"-.017"	. . . . .
Cut-Out Relay		
Closing Voltage	12.7-13.3 Volts @ 1050-1200	12.7-13.3 Volts @ 1050-1200
	Generator R.P.M.	Generator R.P.M.
Cut-Out Voltage and Reverse Current	9-10 Volts, 3-5 Amps.	8.5-11 Volts, 3.5-5 Amps.
Air Gap	.011"-.015"	.025"-.030"
Point Gap	.002"-.006"	.000"-.010"

STARTING MOTOR SPECIFICATIONS

Make	Lucas
Model	M-35-G-1
Brush Spring Tension	15-25 Ozs.
Lock Test Amperage Draw	370-390 Amperes
Volts	7.3-7.7 Volts
Torque in Foot Pounds	9.3 Ft. Lbs.
No Load Test Amperage Draw	45 Amperes
Volts	12 Volts
R.P.M.	5800 R.P.M.

DISTRIBUTOR SPECIFICATIONS

Make	Lucas
Type	DM-2
Cam or Dwell Angle.	60° (+ or —3°)
Open Period	30° (+ or —3°)
Contact Point Gap	.014"-.016"
Contact Point Spring Tension Measured at Contacts.	20-24 Ozs.
Condenser Capacity	.2 Microfarads
Automatic Advance	
Centrifugal	
Distributor Degrees & R.P.M.	
A Series	0°-1° @ 500
	14°-16° @ 1900
B Series	0°-1° @ 380
	8°-10° @ 1500
1500 Series With Engine Number Prefix IH.	0°-1° @ 600
	7° @ 1700

ELECTRICAL SECTION

1500 Series With Engine Number Prefix 15-CNH (Car Serial #E-43116)	0°- 1°	@	300
	½°- 2½°	@	450
	6°- 8°	@	1130
	9°-11°	@	1500
	11°-13°	@	2400

Vacuum Advance

A Series	1°- 3°	@	6.5″ Hg.
	9°-11°	@	17″ Hg.
B Series	1°- 3°	@	6.04″ Hg.
	10°-12°	@	20.8″ Hg.
1500 Series With Engine Number Prefix IH.........................	0°- 1°	@	6″ Hg.
	12°	@	16″ Hg.
1500 Series With Engine Number Prefix 15-CNH (Car Serial #E-43116)	0°- 1°	@	5″ Hg.
	17°	@	10″ Hg.

MISCELLANEOUS SPECIFICATIONS

Timing, Breaker Points Open
 A Series
 1500 Series With Engine Number Prefix 15-CNH

 B Series and 1500 Series With Engine Number
  Prefix IH
Timing Mark Location
Firing Order
Spark Plug
Thread
Spark Plug Gap

7° B.T.D.C. (5/16″ B.T.D.C. Mark on Pulley)
5° B.T.D.C. (7/32″ B.T.D.C. Mark on Pulley)
7° B.T.D.C. at 480 Engine R.P.M. With Neon
Timing Light

11° B. T. D. C. (1/2″ B.T.D.C. Mark on Pulley)
Crankshaft Pulley and Timing Gear Cover
1, 3, 4, 2
Champion N-8 (Long Reach)
14 m.m.
.023″-.025″

LIGHT BULB CHART

Position	Trade Number
Headlamps	4430
Parking Lamps (Front)	1016
Tail Lamps	1016
High Beam Indicator	1447 or Lucas 987
Stop Light	With Tail Light
Directional Signal Front	With Parking Bulb
Directional Signal Rear	1141
Directional Signal Pilot	432 or Lucas 970
Radio Dial Light	53
Courtesy Light	57
Instrument Lights	1447 or Lucas 987
Low Oil Pressure Light	1447 or Lucas 987
No-Charge Indicator Light	1447 or Lucas 987
License Light	57

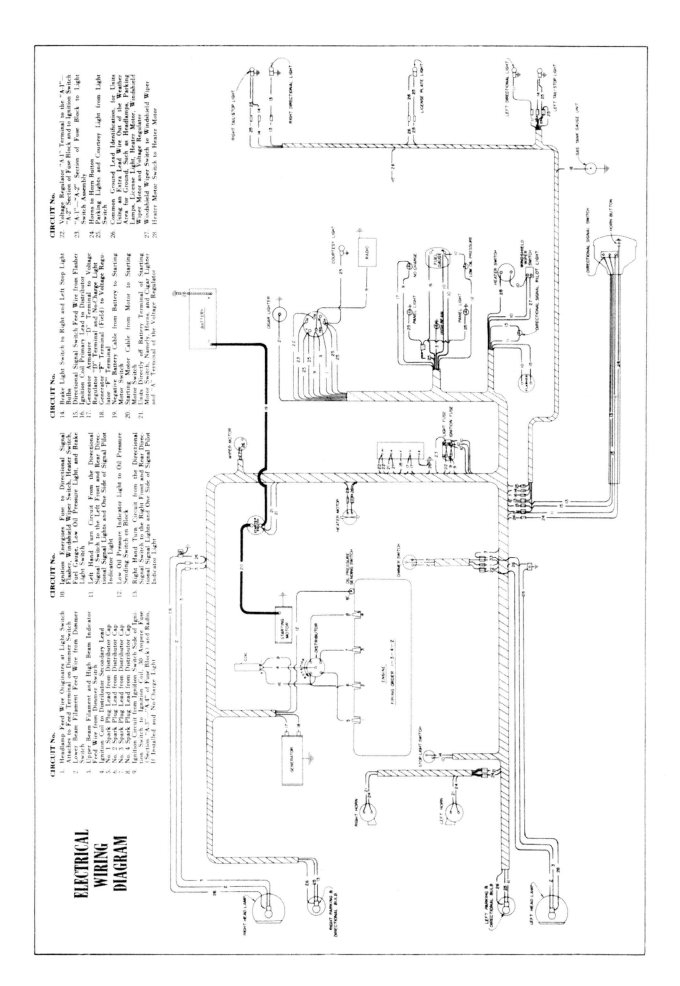

ELECTRICAL WIRING DIAGRAM

CIRCUIT No.
1. Headlamp Feed Wire Originates at Light Switch Attaches to Feed Terminal on Dimmer Switch
2. Lower Beam Filament Feed Wire from Dimmer Switch
3. Upper Beam Filament and High Beam Indicator Feed Wire from Dimmer Switch
4. Ignition Coil to Distributor Secondary Lead
5. No. 1 Spark Plug Lead from Distributor Cap
6. No. 2 Spark Plug Lead from Distributor Cap
7. No. 3 Spark Plug Lead from Distributor Cap
8. No. 4 Spark Plug Lead from Distributor Cap
9. Ignition Circuit from Ignition Switch Side of Ignition Switch to Ignition Coil (30 Ampere Fuse Section "A3"—"A4" of Fuse Block) and Radio, If Installed and No-Charge Light

CIRCUIT No.
10. Ignition Energizes Fuse to Directional Signal Flasher, Windshield Wiper Switch, Heater Switch, Fuel Gauge, Low Oil Pressure Light, and Brake Light Switch
11. Left Hand Turn Circuit From the Directional Signal Switch to the Left Front and Rear Directional Signal Lights and One Side of Signal Pilot Indicator Light
12. Low Oil Pressure Indicator Light to Oil Pressure Sending Switch on Block
13. Right Hand Turn Circuit from the Directional Signal Switch to the Right Front and Rear Directional Signal Lights and One Side of Signal Pilot Indicator Light

CIRCUIT No.
14. Brake Light Switch to Right and Left Stop Light Bulbs
15. Directional Signal Switch Feed Wire from Flasher
16. Ignition Coil Primary Lead to Distributor
17. Generator Armature "D" Terminal to Voltage Regulator "D" Terminal and No-Charge Light
18. Generator "F" Terminal (Field) to Voltage Regulator "F" Terminal
19. Negative Battery Cable from Battery to Starting Motor Switch
20. Starting Motor Cable from Motor to Starting Motor Switch
21. Ignition Circuit off Battery Terminal of Starting Motor Switch; Namely, Horns, and Cigar Lighter Units Directly off Battery Terminal of Starting Motor Switch and "A" Terminal of the Voltage Regulator

CIRCUIT No.
22. Voltage Regulator "A1" Terminal to the "A1" "A2" Section of Fuse Block and to Ignition Switch
23. "A1"—"A2" Section of Fuse Block to Light Switch Assembly
24. Horns to Horn Button
25. Parking Lights and Courtesy Light from Light Switch
26. Common Ground Lead Identification for Units Using an Extra Lead Wire Out of the Weather Area for Ground, Such as Headlamps, Parking Lamps, License Light, Heater Motor, Windshield Wiper Motor and Voltage Regulator
27. Windshield Wiper Switch to Windshield Wiper Motor
28. Heater Motor Switch to Heater Motor

Technical Service Manual

FUEL — CARBURETION —

EXHAUST SYSTEM

Fuel–Carburetion–
Exhaust

FUEL—CARBURETION— EXHAUST

FUEL TANK

A ten and one-half gallon fuel supply tank is provided. It is attached by straps to the under body behind the rear axle assembly.

The tank is connected to the fuel pump by a tubing coiled at the fuel tank outlet to allow for flexing. The tubing is routed along the right hand body side sill to the engine compartment across the front of the engine crossmember to the fuel pump on the left side of the engine. A flex-line connects the fuel line to the fuel pump.

AIR CLEANER

An oil bath air cleaner is supplied. It should be serviced every 5,000 miles, or more frequently when subjected to very dusty operation.

Service is by disassembly and cleaning in kerosene or similar solvent. Refill to proper level marked in reservoir with SAE 50 engine oil in warm weather operation and SAE 20 oil in cold freezing temperatures.

FUEL PUMP

An A. C. (English Manufacture) Type "T" mechanical diaphragm fuel pump incorporating a hand priming feature is used.

To remove the fuel pump, the air cleaner should be removed or loosened at the bottom and turned to expose the fuel pump area. Disconnect the fuel line at the carburetor and the flex-line at the pump. Remove the two nuts and lockwashers holding the fuel pump to the cylinder block and remove the fuel pump from the engine.

1. Fuel Pump to Carburetor Tube
2. Intake Manifold Drain Tube
3. Hand Priming Lever Handle
4. Fuel Pump
5. Fuel Pump Inlet Flex-Line

FIGURE 1—*Fuel Pump Location*

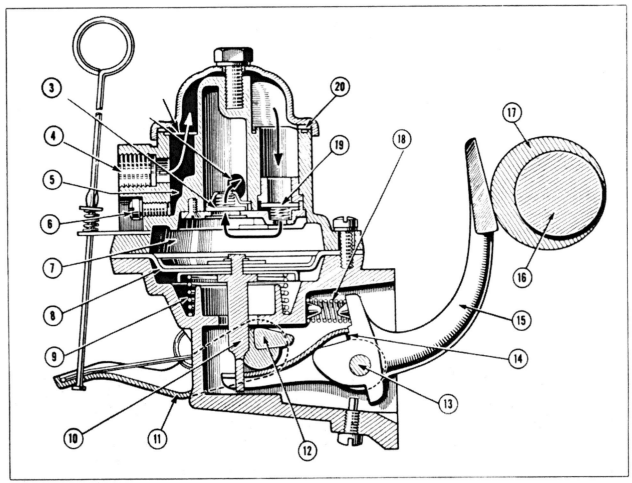

1. Filter Screen
2. Delivery Port
3. Discharge Valve
4. Inlet
5. Sediment Chamber
6. Sediment Chamber Drain Plug
7. Pump Chamber
8. Diaphragm
9. Diaphragm Spring
10. Diaphragm Pull Rod
11. Priming Lever
12. Priming Lever Cam
13. Pump Lever Pivot
14. Connecting Link
15. Fuel Pump Lever
16. Camshaft
17. Camshaft Eccentric
18. Anti-Rattle Spring
19. Inlet Valve
20. Cork Sealing Gasket

FIGURE 2—Fuel Pump Assembly

A diagramatic view of the fuel pump (Fig. 2) illustrates the construction and fuel flow through the pump when operating.

Test Data

The fuel pump operating pressure is from 1.5 to 2.5 P. S. I. measured at the carburetor inlet.

Rebuilding the Fuel Pump

Before disassembly of fuel pump, clean externally in solvent. Mark mating flanges of main body and valve body to aid in assembly.

Remove filter cover screw and washer. Remove filter screen and cork gaskets.

Remove screws holding valve body to main body and separate bodies. From the valve body, remove the valve retaining plate, valves, and gasket. To re-

move the diaphragm assembly from the main body, depress diaphragm and rotate 90° clockwise. Remove diaphragm and diaphragm spring.

Wash all parts in solvent and inspect. Discard all old parts which are replaced by parts supplied in repair kit.

Assemble pump in reverse of above procedure. To assemble the diaphragm, insert spring and depress diaphragm, with tab 120° to right of engine mounting flange (Fig. 3), until notches in diaphragm pull rod index with lever link. Rotate anti-clockwise 90° to lock pull rod in lever link.

CARBURETOR

A British manufactured Zenith downdraft carburetor is used. (Model VIG-8 on the A Series and Model 30 VIG-10 on all later series.)

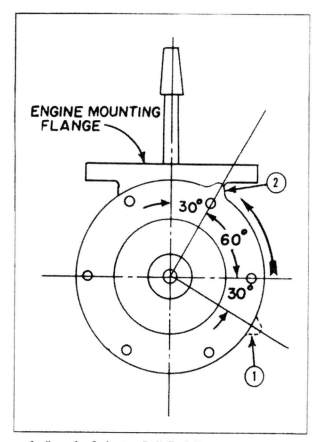

1. Start by Indexing Pull Rod Here
2. Rotate Tab 90° to Lock with Lever Link

FIGURE 3—*Installing Fuel Pump Diaphragm*

The principles of main and compensating jets supplemented with a vacuum controlled economizer and an accelerating piston plunger pump are utilized.

The float chamber (Fig. 6) contains the pump inlet valve (Item 8), the main jet (Item 9), the compensator jet (Item 10), the capacity well (Item 11), and the idle jet (Item 12).

The Float Circuit

A float level adjustment is not provided, the proper level being controlled by the design and size of the float and chamber. The float is free to move in the chamber which serves as a guide to the float movement.

Identification is given to the float top by stamping the word "top" on it. Upon disassembly of the carburetor, the float should be checked to see that no leaks or damage exist as incorrect fuel level would result.

Check the fuel valve seat assembly for dirt between the needle and seat.

Idle Fuel Circuit

Fuel from the fuel bowl flows into the passages below the main and compensating jets and into the

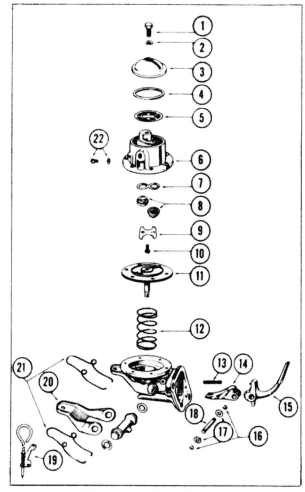

1. Valve Housing Cover Screw
2. Cover Screw Gasket
3. Valve Housing Cover
4. Filter Gasket
5. Filter Screen
6. Valve Housing
7. Valve Gasket
8. Inlet and Discharge Check Valves
9. Valve Retainer
10. Valve Retainer Screw
11. Diaphragm Assembly
12. Diaphragm Spring
13. Cam Lever Spring
14. Cam Lever Link
15. Cam Lever
16. Cam Lever Pin Clip
17. Cam Lever Pin Washer
18. Cam Lever Pin
19. Priming Pull Rod Assembly
20. Priming Pull Rod Lever
21. Priming Handle Spring
22. Drain Plug and Washer

FIGURE 4—*Exploded View of Fuel Pump Assembly*

idle jet well. With the throttle in the idle position, a low pressure area is created on the lower idle discharge port below the edge of the throttle valve plate. See Figure 5. This permits the atmospheric pressure upon the fuel in the float chamber to force fuel up through the idle jet (Fig. 5) which meters the fuel volume for idle speed operation.

A small air bleed above the emulsion block aerates the fuel in the idle passage above the idle jet. This

FUEL—CARBURETION—EXHAUST

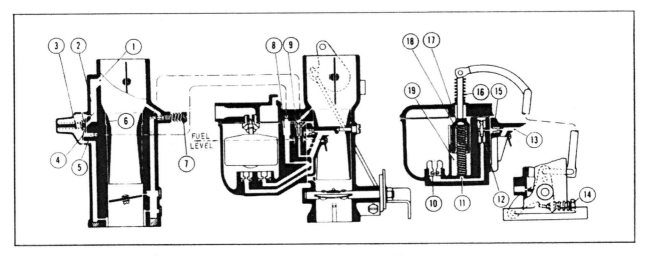

1. **Air Supply Passage to Capacity Well**
2. **Full Throttle Air Bleed**
3. **Economizer Valve Spring**
4. **Economizer Valve Diaphragm**
5. **Controlled Air Supply to Capacity Well**
6. **Part Throttle Air Bleed**
7. **Idle Mixture Adjusting Screw**
8. **Capacity Well**
9. **Idle Speed Jet**

10. **Accelerating Pump Inlet Valve**
11. **Pump Chamber Inlet Orifice**
12. **Pump Discharge Ball Check Valve**
13. **Main Nozzle**
14. **Idle Speed Adjusting Screw**
15. **Pump Discharge Jet**
16. **Pump Rod**
17. **Pump Piston**
18. **Pump Spring**
19. **Pump Chamber**

FIGURE 5—*Schematic Drawing of Carburetor Circuits*

fuel then flows down a channel to the idle discharge port at the carburetor flange. From here, it flows into the intake manifold.

The idle fuel mixture ratio is controlled by an adjusting needle (Item 7, Fig. 5) which regulates the amount of air entering the idle channel through the bleed in the carburetor air intake. Turning the needle in, or clockwise, richens the mixture and turning it out, or anti-clockwise, leans the idle mixture. The proper setting usually may be obtained with the needle from 0 to 1 turn from the closed, or rich, position.

As the throttle valve is further opened, a lower pressure begins to be effective at the upper idle circuit discharge port which is adjacent to the edge of the throttle valve plate. Idle circuit fuel flows then from two ports while the air pressure is in the process of being lowered around the main nozzle to bring the main and compensating fuel circuits into operation. This double port idle circuit serves to smooth the transition. See Figure 5.

Main and Compensating Fuel Circuits

When the throttle is opened sufficiently to cause enough differential of air pressure on the fuel in the main nozzle passage and the fuel in the float chamber, a flow of metered fuel begins from the main jet and compensator jet located at the bottom of the fuel bowl through separate passages over to the emulsion block. At the emulsion block, the two circuits join in a common passage up to the main nozzle and into the air stream at the narrow section of the venturi tube.

A bar is located at the edge of the main nozzle across the neck of the venturi tube. The purpose of this bar is to evenly distribute the fuel mixture across the venturi tube neck. The low pressure created below the bar in the air stream draws the fuel mixture from the main nozzle and pulls it across the venturi tube evenly each way from the center.

The capacity well, along with air from the idle and pump circuits, is an air bleed to help atomize fuel from the main and compensator circuits.

Economy Device

The economizer is a mechanism incorporated into the carburetor to adjust carburetor fuel flow to leaner proportions at part throttle cruising conditions. This device consists of a diaphragm assembly, valve and connecting passages, and controls the air bleed to the capacity well. Since the capacity well is a part of the main and compensating system, an increase in air bleed to this well results in a leaner mixture.

The higher vacuum (lower pressure) which exists under the throttle valve, at part throttle relative to full throttle, is employed to act on the diaphragm assembly opening a larger air bleed to the capacity well at part throttle resulting in leaner air fuel mixture ratios at part throttle.

In servicing the economizer, inspect for proper seating and functioning of the valve and make sure the passages to and from this valve are open. If this valve does not open at part throttle, it will result

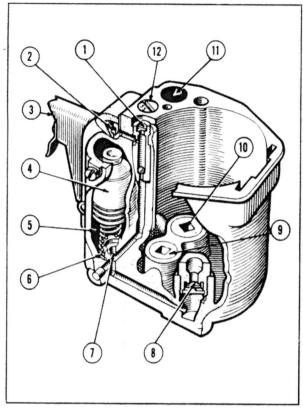

1. Pump Discharge Ball Check Valve
2. Pump Discharge Jet
3. Main Nozzle
4. Pump Piston
5. Pump Chamber
6. Pump Spring
7. Pump Inlet Orifice
8. Pump Inlet Valve
9. Main Circuit Jet
10. Compensator Jet
11. Capacity Well
12. Idle Speed Jet

FIGURE 6—*Carburetor Bowl Assembly, Sectional View of Pump Circuit*

in higher than normal cruising speed fuel consumption; if the valve should not seat and seal properly, it will result in lean full throttle operation.

Pump Circuit

A mechanical accelerating pump delivers a metered discharge of fuel whenever the throttle valve is opened for acceleration. This momentary enrichment of mixture assists the transition from lean part throttle mixtures to the normally richer full throttle mixtures.

Fuel for the accelerating pump fills the pump chamber through the pump inlet valve to the level of fuel in the bowl.

Linkage from the carburetor throttle shaft connects to the top of the pump piston. Any throttle opening pushes the pump piston down, the fuel pressure closing the inlet check valve. This pressure opens the pump discharge ball check and the

fuel is forced through the accelerating jet into the main nozzle and venturi. When the throttle is closed, the pump spring returns the piston to its original position with the pump chamber filled.

The pump discharge ball check falls back to its seat by gravity and prevents fuel pull over to the main nozzle and air bleed to the pump circuit.

NOTE: *The pump circuit above the ball check valve, the idle circuit, and the economizer controlled air bleed through the capacity well all act as air bleeds to the main and compensator circuits at fixed intermediate throttle positions (Fig. 5).*

Anti-percolation is derived from the venting to atmosphere through the upper section of the pump and idle circuits to the emulsion block.

The pump stroke length can be varied by two selections provided in the linkage by means of two holes in the throttle shaft arm. To obtain a longer pump stroke, the upper hole is used.

In servicing the accelerating pump system, carefully check the function of the inlet and outlet check valves. They should be free-acting and clean. The accelerating jet should also be checked for dirt.

Choke Circuit Operation

A manual choke control is provided with an automatic throttle pick-up and a choke valve release for acceleration when cold.

When the choke control is pulled out, the choke valve is closed and opens the throttle valve 1/32".

The adjustment of this choke spring tension is made by means of a grooved nut and drilled shaft. The nut attached to a coil spring is turned from the point of no tension on the spring to the left or counterclockwise one-half turn with the choke closed. A cotter key is used to secure the grooved nut in adjustment. Climatic conditions may require a change in this setting to greater tension.

As soon as the engine temperature warrants, the choke control should be pushed in opening the choke valve.

On extremely cold starts, the throttle may be pumped several times to force fuel into the intake manifold from the pump circuit. Pumping of the throttle *should never be done* to start a *hot* or *warm* engine.

CARBURETOR DISASSEMBLY AND ASSEMBLY

The carburetor should be emptied of fuel and cleaned externally before disassembly.

Figure 8 illustrates the complete carburetor which will assist in disassembly and assembly operations.

FUEL CARBURETION EXHAUST

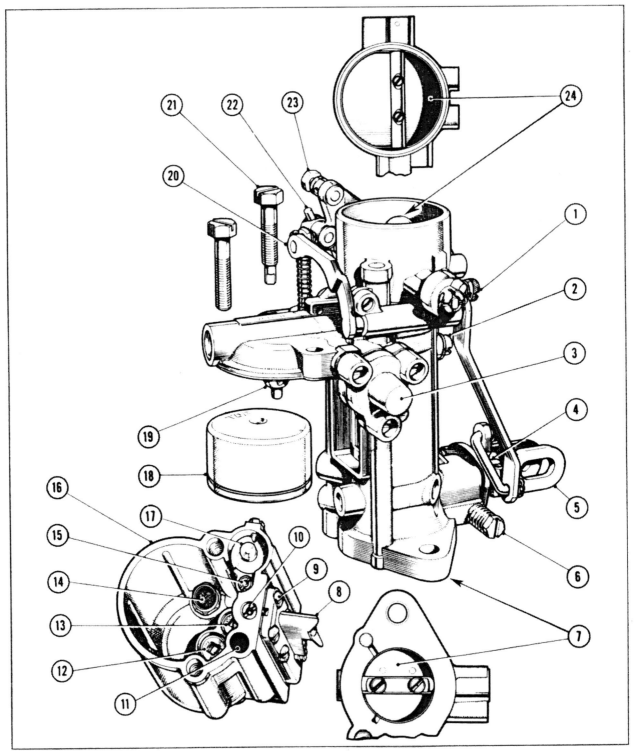

1. Idle Mixture Adjustment Screw
2. Carburetor Venturi Tube Set Screw
3. Economizer Valve Housing
4. Throttle Shaft Arm Attaching Nut
5. Throttle Shaft Arm
6. Idle Speed Stop Screw
7. Throttle Valve
8. Main Nozzle and Emulsion Block
9. Emulsion Block Attaching Screws
10. Idle Circuit Jet
11. Capacity Well Air Inlet Orifice Plug
12. Compensating Jet
13. Main Jet
14. Pump Circuit Inlet Check Valve
15. Pump Circuit Discharge Ball Check Valve Assembly
16. Carburetor Bowl Assembly (Less Float)
17. Pump Piston
18. Float
19. Float Needle Valve and Seat Assembly
20. Pump Control Lever
21. Jet-Key Type Main Body to Bowl Attaching Screw
22. Choke to Throttle Shaft Connecting Link
23. Choke Control Wire Swivel Set Screw
24. Choke Valve

FIGURE 7—*Carburetor Main Components*

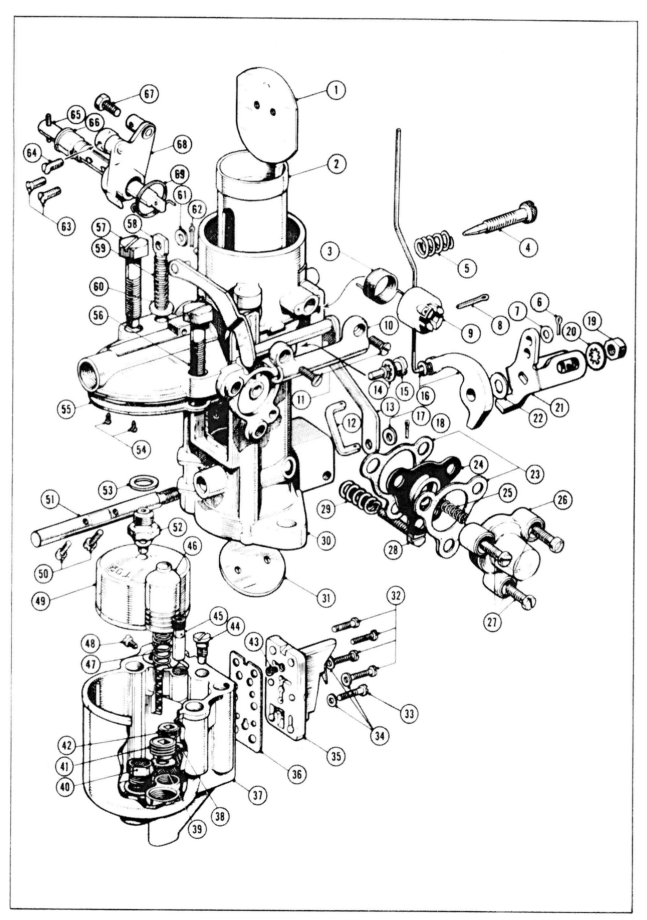

FUEL—CARBURETION—EXHAUST —

1. Choke Valve
2. Venturi Tube
3. Choke Spring (Automatic)
4. Idle Mixture Adjusting Screw
5. Idle Mixture Adjusting Screw Spring
6. Pump Control Link Cotter Pin
7. Pump Control Link Washer
8. Choke Valve Shaft Cotter Pin
9. Spring Carrier Grooved Nut
10. Pump Control Bearing Housing
11. Bearing Housing Attaching Screws
12. Pump Control Link
13. Pump Control Lever
14. Venturi Tube Set Screw Lockwasher
15. Venturi Tube Set Screw
16. Choke Fast Idle Control Linkage
17. Pump Control Link Washer
18. Pump Control Link Cotter Key
19. Throttle Shaft Arm Attaching Nut
20. Lockwasher
21. Throttle Shaft Arm
22. Throttle Shaft Arm Spacing Washer
23. Economizer Diaphragm Gaskets
24. Economizer Diaphragm
25. Economizer Diaphragm Spring
26. Economizer Valve Housing
27. Diaphragm Housing Screws
28. Idle Speed Stop Screw
29. Idle Speed Stop Screw Spring
30. Carburetor Main Body Assembly
31. Throttle Valve
32. Emulsion Block Attaching Screws (Short)
33. Emulsion Block Attaching Screws (Long)
34. Lower Emulsion Block Screw Washers
35. Emulsion Block

36. Emulsion Block Gasket
37. Carburetor Bowl
38. Main Jet Washer
39. Compensating Jet Washer
40. Pump Inlet Valve
41. Compensating Jet
42. Main Jet
43. Pump Discharge Jet
44. Idle Circuit Jet
45. Pump Circuit Discharge Ball Check Valve
46. Pump Piston
47. Pump Piston Spring
48. Pump Piston Locating Stop Screw
49. Float
50. Throttle Valve Screws
51. Throttle Valve Shaft
52. Float Needle and Seat Assembly
53. Float Needle and Seat Assembly Washer
54. Gasket Attaching Drive Screws
55. Carburetor Bowl to Main Body Gasket
56. Carburetor Bowl to Main Body Attaching Screw (Plain Type)
57. Carburetor Bowl to Main Body Attaching Screw (Jet-Key Type)
58. Pump Rod
59. Pump Rod Spring
60. Pump Rod Spring Washer
61. Pump Rod Pivot Washer
62. Pump Rod Pivot Washer Cotter Key
63. Choke Valve Attaching Screws
64. Swivel Screw
65. Choke Shaft
66. Choke Shaft Arm Bearing
67. Choke Control Wire Swivel Set Screw
68. Choke Shaft Arm
69. Choke Shaft Arm Spring

FIGURE 8—*Carburetor Assembly Components*

Separate the bowl assembly from the main body by removing the two bowl attaching screws. Carefully slide the bowl downward and away from the carburetor main body so as not to damage the emulsion block or main nozzle.

Remove the float from its chamber. This will expose the main and compensator jets at the bottom of the bowl. Note the square hole provided in the jets for ease of removal. One of the bowl-to-main body attaching screws is designed with a square shaft end. This is the jet-key for removing the main and compensator jets.

Remove the idle circuit jet with a suitable screw driver.

Remove the emulsion block from the fuel bowl. It is attached by five mounting screws. Loosen the center lowest screw first. Remove the other four screws. Then remove the lower center screw. You will notice that it acts as a puller for the emulsion block. The two lower screws are provided with washers.

The pump circuit discharge jet can be cleaned from the rear of the emulsion block without removing the jet.

Remove the pump inlet check valve and discharge ball check valve from the fuel bowl. Remove the pump piston locating stop screw and remove the pump piston and spring.

Remove the capacity well air inlet orifice plug.

Clean and inspect all parts. Blow out all passages with low air pressure.

Reassemble the bowl assembly in reverse to disassembly procedure replacing all jet gaskets, emulsion block gasket, and bowl gasket. Do not use any sealing materials on the gaskets. Install them as supplied.

Remove the three screws retaining the economy diaphragm housing to the carburetor main body. Carefully remove the housing, diaphragm and diaphragm spring assembly, and gaskets. Inspect all parts and clean thoroughly. Clean out the air passages to the capacity well.

Remove needle and seat assembly and clean passage and inspect.

Remove idle mixture screw and clean passages and discharge ports in main body. Inspect and replace the bowl assembly gasket after removing gasket retaining drive screws. A diagonal cutter or pair of pliers can be used to pull the drive screws retaining the gasket. If care is used in assembly, the gasket locating drive screws can be omitted.

Install a new needle valve and seat assembly and gasket.

Place float in bowl. Install bowl assembly and gasket using care to locate gasket properly.

Reassemble economizer diaphragm assembly using new gaskets and new diaphragm.

Install idle mixture screw spring and screw. Turn all the way in and then turn out about one-half turn.

Unscrew idle speed screw until throttle valve is seated.

Adjust choke to throttle arm shaft rod length at choke arm set screw with the choke closed for a 1/32" opening of the throttle valve. This will set the needed fast idle for cold starting. Reset idle speed stop screw to slightly open throttle valve.

Install carburetor on the car. Start and warm up engine. Adjust carburetor mixture for smooth idle operation with the idle speed stop screw set for a 625 R. P. M. engine speed. Road test for performance.

No alteration of the carburetion metering should be attempted unless the vehicle is to be used at high altitudes.

EXHAUST SYSTEM

A conventional engine exhaust manifold, exhaust pipe, muffler, and tail pipe comprise the main components of the exhaust system.

A combination intake and exhaust manifold gasket seals the intake and exhaust manifolds to the cylinder head. Both manifolds are removed as an assembly leaving them joined at the hot spot area. The exhaust manifold is drilled and tapped for two studs at an adapting flange for the attaching of the front exhaust pipe.

A copper backed asbestos lined gasket is used between the flanges on the A Series. Beginning with the B Series an exhaust pipe to manifold flange clamp is used.

A reverse flow muffler is used to silence the exhaust gas noises.

Exhaust Manifold Hot Spot

A hot spot is used to aid in vaporization and expansion of the fuel air mixture for better combustion.

The hot spot consists of a plate to which is attached a baffle spout to direct the exhaust gases onto the center of the plate. Two gaskets seal the hot spot below the carburetor between the intake and exhaust manifolds, which are attached at the hot spot with four (4) screws through the intake manifold, and into the exhaust manifold.

CARBURETOR SPECIFICATIONS

	A SERIES ZENITH NO. C-1386	B SERIES ZENITH NO. C-1466	1500 SERIES ZENITH NO. C-1528M	1500 SERIES (Hi-Comp.) ZENITH NO. C-1630
Main Jet	No. 92	No. 67	No. 72	No. 72
Compensator Jet	No. 60	No. 95	No. 97	No. 95
Idle Circuit Jet	No. 50	No. 50	No. 55	No. 55
Capacity Well Air Vent	No. 33	Open	Open	Open
Pump Discharge Jet	No. 50	No. 50	No. 60	No. 60
Needle and Seat Assembly	1.5 MM.	1.5 MM.	1.5 MM.	1.5 MM.

TECHNICAL SERVICE LETTER REFERENCE

Date	Letter No.	Subject	Changes information on Page No.

Technical
Service
Manual

Clutch

CLUTCH SECTION

The clutch is a single plate, dry disc type. A steel cover bolted to the flywheel contains the clutch drive plate, pressure plate, clutch levers, and springs (Fig. 1).

FIGURE 1—*Component Parts of Clutch*

The clutch drive plate is spring cushioned with a facing riveted to each side. The coil springs around the hub absorb the power shocks and cushion the driving mechanism. They are held in position by retaining wires.

The clutch throwout bearing is made of a graphite composition and is shrunk into the bearing retainer.

The clutch cover assembly consists of a pressed steel cover and a cast iron pressure plate loaded by six thrust springs. Mounted on the pressure plate are three levers which pivot on floating pins retained by eyebolts. Adjustment nuts are screwed on to the eyebolts and secured by staking. Fulcrums are installed between the lugs on the pressure plate and the outer ends of the release levers. Anti-rattle springs load the release levers, and retainer springs connect to the release lever plate (Fig. 2). No adjustment for wear is provided in the clutch itself. An individual adjustment is built into the clutch cover to adjust the height of the release levers. The adjusting nuts are staked into position and should never be disturbed unless the clutch assembly has been disassembled for the replacement of worn parts.

When the clutch pedal is depressed, the release bearing is moved toward the flywheel and contacts the release lever plate which is attached to the release levers. Each lever is pivoted on a floating pin retained by an eyebolt. The outer ends of the eyebolts extend

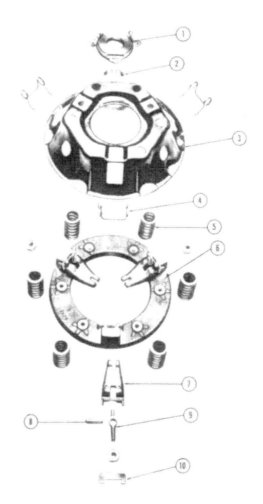

1. Release Lever Plate
2. Release Lever Plate Retainer Springs
3. Clutch Cover
4. Clutch Lever Anti-Rattle Springs
5. Clutch Cover Thrust Springs
6. Pressure Plate
7. Lever
8. Eyebolt Pin
9. Eyebolt
10. Fulcrum

FIGURE 2—*Exploded View of Clutch Assembly*

through the holes in the stamped cover and are fitted with adjusting nuts to secure the levers in the correct position.

CLUTCH PEDAL AND ADJUSTMENT

The clutch pedal and the brake pedal pivots on a shaft which is welded to the side sill. A lubricating fitting is provided on the inner end of the shaft to lubricate both clutch and brake pedals.

The clutch and brake pedals are disassembled from the shaft by removing the lubricating fitting, snap ring, washers, and spring.

The only adjustment necessary is to restore the free movement of the clutch pedal. This free movement must be maintained at $1/2''$ to $3/4''$.

As the driven plate facing wears, the free movement of the pedal will gradually decrease. This will eventually cause the throwout bearing to ride against the release lever plate preventing a full clutch engagement.

A SERIES

Adjustment is made by lengthening the rod between the pedal and spring loaded lever (Fig. 3).

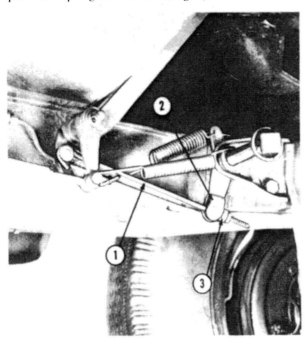

1. Adjustment Rod
2. Lever
3. Adjusting Nut

FIGURE 3—*Clutch Pedal Adjustment*

The $1/2''$ to $3/4''$ free movement in the pedal will give a minimum clearance of $3/32''$ to $1/8''$ between the graphite release bearing and the release lever plate, thus preventing constant contact of the release bearing on the lever plate.

Clutch linkage parts are illustrated in Figure 4.

The bracket is bolted to the side sill member and secures the clutch linkage in position.

B and 1500 Series

The clutch is operated by hydraulic pressure through a master cylinder and clutch throwout cylinder. The master cylinder is attached to the body side sill and the clutch pedal is connected to the master cylinder by an adjustable rod. (Fig. 5.)

Clutch pedal adjustment is made by shortening or lengthening the rod to obtain $1/2''$ to $3/4''$ free movement of the clutch pedal. No other adjustments are

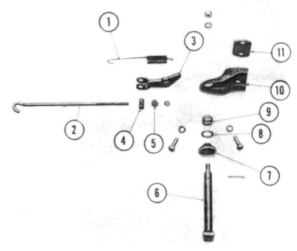

1. Return Spring	7. Rubber Boot
2. Adjusting Rod	8. Retaining Washer
3. Lever	9. Retaining Spring
4. Fulcrum	10. Bracket
5. Adjusting Nut	11. Bracket Shim Plate
6. Cross Shaft	

FIGURE 4—A Series—*Clutch Linkage*

FIGURE 5—*Clutch and Brake Master Cylinders —B and 1500 Series*

required. A bleed hole connection is located in the clutch throwout cylinder. Loosen connection approximately one half turn, then attach bleeder hose submerging end of hose in container with hydraulic brake fluid. Fill master cylinder to proper level and depress clutch pedal several times until all air bubbles in container cease. Tighten bleeder connection and recheck clutch master cylinder fluid level. The fluid level is marked on the cylinder.

FIGURE 6—*Clutch Throwout Cylinder*

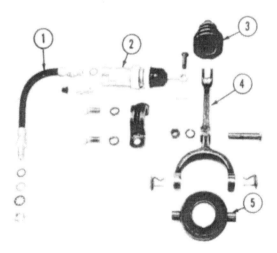

1. Clutch Release Hose
2. Throwout Cylinder
3. Rubber Boot
4. Throwout Lever
5. Throwout Bearing

FIGURE 7—*Hydraulic Clutch Release Components*

CLUTCH DISASSEMBLY

Always mark the clutch cover, flywheel, and pressure plate on original production assemblies before removing so that when they are reassembled, they will be in the same relative positions.

Loosen the cap screws a few turns at a time by diagonal selection until the spring tension is released. Remove the cap screws, lock washers, and clutch assembly from the flywheel.

The clutch cover and pressure plate are under spring

tension at all times. Therefore, care must be exercised when a clutch cover is disassembled.

Remove the three release springs and lever plate (Figs. 8 and 9).

FIGURE 8—*Removing the Release Lever Plate Springs*

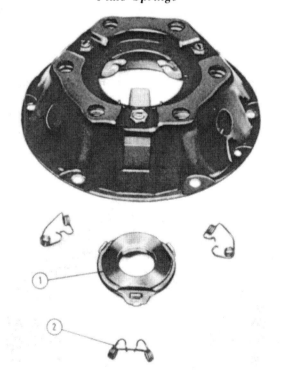

1. Release Lever Plate
2. Release Lever Spring

FIGURE 9—*Release Lever Plate and Springs*

Place the clutch cover in an arbor press with a hard wood block under the pressure plate. The wood block should not protrude beyond the circumference of the pressure plate. This will permit clearance for the cover when pressure is applied to the cover. Place a wood block across the top of the cover and compress until the release levers are free.

Then remove the adjusting nuts (Fig. 10).

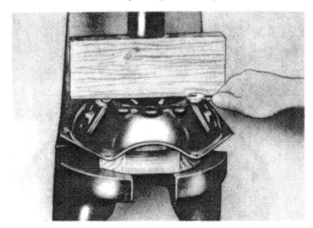

FIGURE 10—*Compress Springs to Remove Nuts*

Release the press slowly to prevent the springs from flying out.

> CAUTION: *When relieving the spring pressure, be sure that the cover does not stick on the pressure plate bosses.*

Lift the clutch cover off of the pressure plate, eyebolts, fingers, and springs.

Remove each release lever, by grasping the lever and eyebolt between the finger and thumb so that the inner end of the lever and the threaded end of the eyebolt are as near together as possible, keeping the eyebolt pin in position in the lever (Fig. 11).

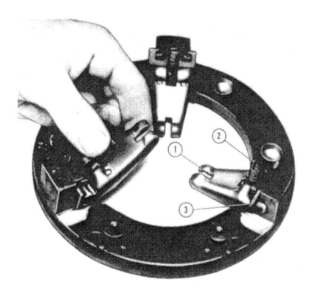

1. Lever
2. Eyebolt
3. Fulcrum

FIGURE 11—*Remove Levers*

The release lever fulcrum can now be lifted over the ridge on the lever and the lever, eyebolt, and the fulcrum can be removed.

CLUTCH PRESSURE SPRINGS

A thorough inspection of the pressure springs should always be made. They should be the same height and tested for spring tension. Should any of them show signs of weakness, all should be replaced.

CLUTCH PRESSURE SPRING SPECIFICATIONS

No. of Springs	6
Free Height	1-31/32"
Compressed Height	135# ± 5# at 1-13/32"
Total Load of 6 Springs	780# to 840# (Initial Engaged)

CLUTCH PRESSURE PLATE

Inspect the pressure plate to make sure that it is not cracked or scored. Check on a surface plate for a warped condition, as a pressure plate out of alignment will result in clutch chatter.

ASSEMBLY OF THE CLUTCH COVER

Prior to assembly, apply a small amount of lubriplate to each side of the pressure plate lug, eyebolt and pivot pin.

Lay the pressure plate on the block in the press. Assemble the lever, eyebolt, and pin holding the lever and eyebolt as close together as possible. With the other hand, grasp and insert the fulcrum in the slots of the pressure plate lug. Lower slightly and tilt the lower edge until it touches the vertical milled surface of the lug. Insert the lower end of the eyebolt in the hole in the pressure plate. The short end of the lever will then be under the hook of the lug near the fulcrum.

Slide the fulcrum upward in the slots of the lug. Lift it over the ridge on the short end of the lever and drop it into the groove in the lever (Fig. 12).

Assembly of Spring and Cover

After all levers are installed, place the clutch pressure springs in a vertical position on each spring boss. Check and insert the anti-rattle springs in the clutch cover and place the cover on top of the pressure plate assembly. The top of each pressure spring must enter its seat in the cover. Line up punch marks on cover and pressure plate for balance as shown in Figure 1.

Slowly compress the cover making sure that the eyebolts and pressure plate lugs are guided through the proper holes in the cover.

Hold the clutch under compression and screw the adjusting nuts down until they are flush with the tops of the eyebolts. Release the spindle of the press and remove the assembly.

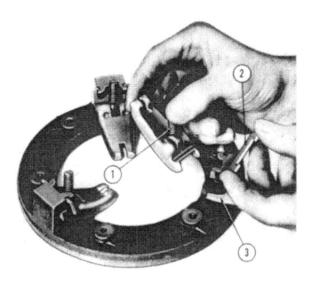

1. Eyebolt
2. Fulcrum
3. Pressure Plate Lug

FIGURE 12—*Install Levers*

Clutch Lever Height Adjustment

IMPORTANT: *Always inspect the release lever height adjustment when installing a new or relined clutch driven plate.*

Place clutch gauge plate J-5567 on the flywheel in the position normally occupied by the driven plate. Mount the cover assembly centering the gauge plate, lining up the three machined lands on the gauge plate directly under the levers (Fig. 13).

1. Machined Land
2. Gauge Plate

FIGURE 13—*Clutch Gauge Plate J-5567*

Tighten the cover screws one to two turns at a time by diagonal selection to avoid distorting the cover.

Each lever should be depressed several times before checking. This will seat the levers in their operating position (Fig. 14).

FIGURE 14—*Depressing Levers*

Turn the adjusting nut on each eyebolt until the tip of each lever is flush with the hub on the gauge plate. Depress each lever again and recheck with straight edge (Fig. 15).

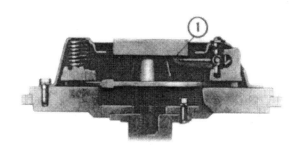

1. Flush With Hub

FIGURE 15—*Adjustment of Lever Height*

Satisfactory operation of the clutch is dependent on accurate adjustment of the release levers. After setting all three levers, the height of the levers should not vary over .005".

Locking Adjustment Nuts

After checking the lever heights, stake the adjusting nuts with a dull punch to lock them in place (Fig. 16).

1. Adjusting Nuts

FIGURE 16—*Locking Adjusting Nuts*

Install the clutch release lever plate on the tips of the release levers and then secure by means of the three retaining springs (Figs. 17 and 18).

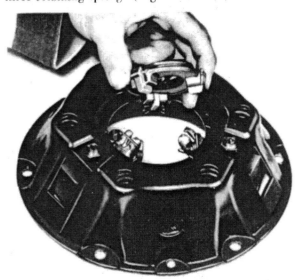

FIGURE 17—*Install Release Lever Plate*

FIGURE 18—*Install Clutch Release Lever Retaining Springs*

CLUTCH DRIVE PLATE

A new plate should be installed if the plate or cushion springs appear to be defective. The cushion springs should not be bent out of shape or flattened.

CLUTCH THROWOUT BEARING

A Series

To remove the clutch throwout bearing, remove the two retaining springs with a screw driver (Fig. 19).

FIGURE 19—*Remove Clutch Throwout Bearing Retainer Springs—A Series Shown*

After the springs are removed, lift the bearing away from the fork and slide it off the clutch shaft.

To remove the clutch operating shaft, remove nut and lock washer from throwout bearing fork taper pin and remove pin (Fig. 20).

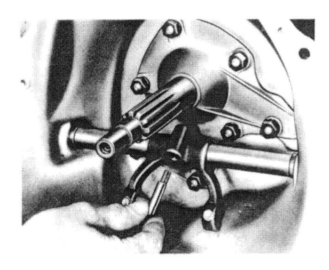

FIGURE 20—*Remove Throwout Bearing Fork Taper Pin—A Series*

Remove snap ring and flat washer from right side of clutch operating shaft. Then remove shaft from left side of case.

CAUTION: *Do not lubricate the graphite composition throwout bearing at any time.*

To replace the throwout bearing retainer springs, insert the straight end of the spring in the drilled hole in the throwout bearing retaining cup and snap the turned end of the spring into the concaved drilled portion of the fork (Fig. 21).

FIGURE 21—*Installing Throwout Bearing and Retainer Springs—A Series Shown*

B and 1500 Series

To remove the clutch throwout bearing, remove the two retaining springs with a screw driver.

After the springs are removed, lift the bearing away from the fork and slide it off the clutch shaft.

To remove the clutch throwout lever, disconnect the clevis pin from the clutch throwout cylinder. Then remove the throwout lever bolt and nut, and unscrew the bolt from the transmission housing. Remove the lever and rubber boot from the inside of the housing.

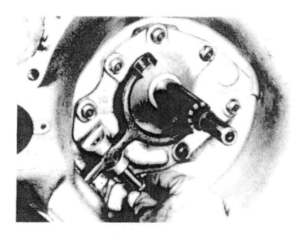

FIGURE 22—*Remove Throwout Lever Bolt— B and 1500 Series*

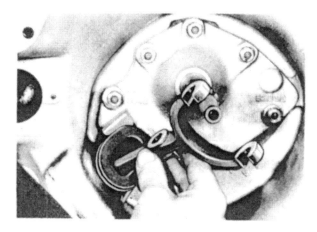

FIGURE 23—*Remove Throwout Lever and Boot —B and 1500 Series*

CAUTION: *Do not lubricate the graphite composition throwout bearing at any time.*

To replace the throwout bearing retainer springs, insert the straight end of the spring in the drilled hole in the throwout bearing retaining cup and snap the turned end of the spring into the concaved drilled portion of the throwout lever.

CLUTCH INSTALLATION

Inspect the condition of the flywheel as well as the pressure plate for any roughness. Check all flywheel stud nuts for tightness. Use a torque wrench and tighten stud nuts to 32 foot pounds.

Slide the clutch driven plate onto the transmission clutch shaft to make sure that it is free on the splines. If the splines on the transmission clutch shaft are burred, remove the burrs with a fine file or stone. If the movement of the clutch driven plate is not free on the splines, the result will be clutch drag and hard shifting of transmission gears.

Place the driven plate and clutch cover assembly on to the flywheel with the larger chamfered spline end of the driven plate hub towards the transmission. Install Clutch Aligning Tool J-1625 or a dummy shaft to align the driven plate. Tighten the cap screws one to two turns at a time by diagonal selection and tighten securely.

The weight of the transmission must be supported during installation in order to avoid strain on the clutch shaft and driven plate.

Refer to Transmission Section for installation of transmission.

Adjust clutch pedal for ½″ to ¾″ free movement.

Technical Service Manual

Transmission

(A Series)

TRANSMISSION SECTION

(A Series)

GENERAL DATA

Type: .... Synchro-Mesh
Gear Shift: .... Lever on Instrument Panel
Number of Gears: ...... Three Forward, One Reverse
Type of Gears: .... Helical Constant Mesh
Capacity: .... 3½ Pints (U.S.) Engine Oil
            For Summer, Use SAE
            No. 40
            For Winter, Use SAE
            No. 30
            Minus 10°F., Use SAE
            No. 20
Gear Ratios: .... First Speed 2.44:1
             Second Speed 1.54:1
             Third Speed .... Direct
             Reverse 3.49:1

TRANSMISSION REMOVAL

First disconnect one of the battery leads at the battery terminal and then the starter lead at the starter.

Remove the four top transmission to engine mounting bolts from the engine compartment.

Raise and support the car securely.

Install Engine Support Fixture, Tool J-5565 (Fig. 1)

1. Tool J-5565

FIGURE 1—*Engine Support Fixture*

Disconnect the propeller shaft at the rear axle companion flange; move the shaft forward off of the studs and pull the shaft from the transmission main shaft splines (Fig. 2).

Disconnect the rear crossmember at the rear transmission supports and side sill members. Slide the crossmember to the right and out over the exhaust pipe (Fig. 3).

Disconnect speedometer cable and shift rods from transmission levers. Remove the lower four transmission flywheel housing to engine bolts and remove starter.

FIGURE 2—*Removing the Propeller Shaft*

FIGURE 3—*Remove Crossmember*

Disconnect clutch linkage cross shaft by sliding rubber boot onto shaft, remove cotter pin, clutch and brake pedal pull-back springs. Then, slide the cross shaft through the hole in the bracket. Turn the transmission assembly counter-clockwise to release the universal end of the cross shaft from the clutch operating shaft (Fig. 4).

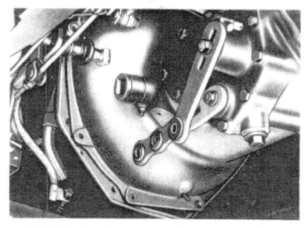

FIGURE 4—*Removing Clutch Cross Shaft*

Lower the rear engine support fixture approximately one and a quarter inches.

The transmission is then removed by moving the

complete transmission assembly toward the rear of the car to release the clutch shaft from the pilot bushing and clutch assembly (Fig. 5).

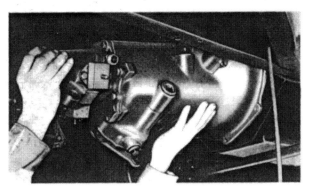

FIGURE 5—*Removing Transmission Assembly*

DISASSEMBLING THE TRANSMISSION

With the transmission assembly completely drained of its lubricant and set up on a transmission stand, the unit is ready for disassembly.

Clutch Throwout Bearing

To remove the clutch throwout bearing, remove the two retaining springs with a screw driver (Fig. 6).

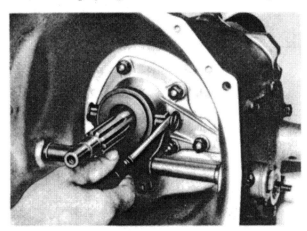

FIGURE 6—*Remove Clutch Throwout Bearing Retainer Springs*

After the springs are removed, lift the bearing away from the fork and slide it off the clutch shaft (Fig. 7).

Remove nut and lock washer from throwout bearing fork taper pin and remove pin (Fig. 8).

Remove snap ring and flat washer from right side of clutch operating shaft and remove shaft from left side of case (Fig. 9).

Transmission Disassembly

Remove the nuts and lock washers that retain the front transmission cover. The cover can be removed at this time; however, it is advisable to remove the cover when the countershaft is being removed (Fig. 10).

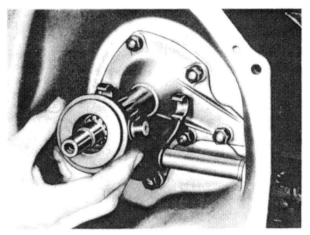

FIGURE 7—*Removing the Clutch Throwout Bearing*

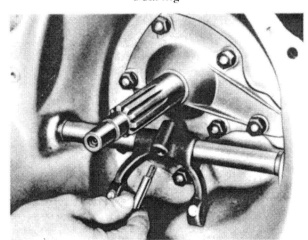

FIGURE 8—*Remove Throwout Bearing Fork Taper Pin*

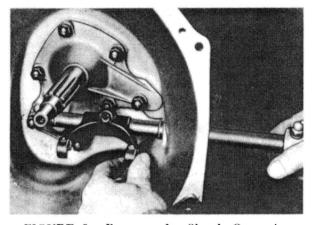

FIGURE 9—*Remove the Clutch Operating Shaft and Fork*

Remove the cap screws from the side cover and remove the cover and shifter shafts as an assembly (Fig. 11).

Remove the cap screws and pull off the rear cover. When removing the cover, it may be necessary to tap the transmission main shaft with a plastic hammer to release the rear cover from the rear bearing retainer (Fig. 12).

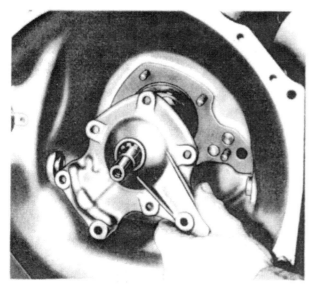

FIGURE 10—*Removing the Front Transmission Cover*

FIGURE 11—*Remove Side Cover and Shifter Shafts*

Tap the countershaft slightly forward to release and remove the front cover (Fig. 10).

Remove the snap ring from the second and high shifter rod located in front of the fork. Then tap the two shifter rods from the front of the transmission toward the rear to release the lock keys which keep the rods from turning.

Two dummy shafts can be fabricated from one half inch (½") round stock as shown in Figure 13

FIGURE 12—*Removing the Rear Cover*

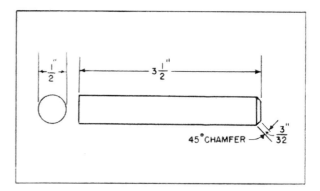

FIGURE 13—*Dummy Shaft Dimensions*

to retain the loaded balls and springs in the shifter forks.

Install the dummy shaft into the shifter forks from the rear. Keep the dummy shaft tight against the shifter rod as the rods are being removed. This will retain the loaded ball and spring in the shifter fork (Fig. 14).

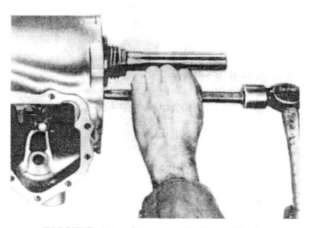

FIGURE 14—*Remove Shifter Rods*

When removing the second and third speed shifter rod, remove the spacing sleeve which is located on the rod behind the shifter fork.

With the shifter rods removed, the shifter forks can be lifted out of the case (Fig. 15).

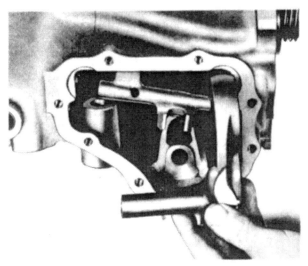

FIGURE 15—*Removing Shifter Forks*

Remove the reverse idler gear and bracket. The bracket is fastened to the case by a hexagon head set screw which also locks the shaft in position. Bend the lip on the lock washer, remove the bolt, and bracket. Then tap the reverse idler shaft out toward the rear of the case and remove the gear (Fig. 16).

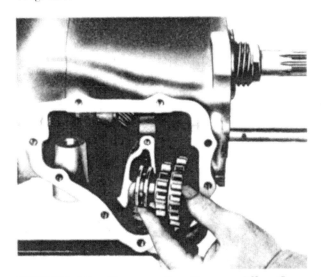

FIGURE 16—*Remove the Reverse Idler Gear*

With a soft metal drift and hammer, tap the countershaft forward. After the countershaft is removed, the countershaft gears and two thrust washers will drop to the bottom of the case. The countershaft gears cannot be removed from the case until the main shaft and clutch shaft assemblies are removed (Fig. 17).

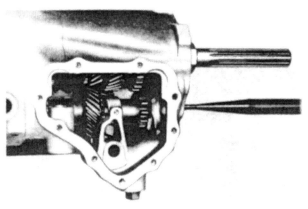

FIGURE 17—*Removing the Countershaft*

Remove the main shaft and gear assembly out of the case tipping the rear of the main shaft down slightly to pass over the countershaft gears (Fig. 18).

FIGURE 18—*Removing the Main Shaft and Gear Assembly*

Before removing the clutch shaft, tilt the countershaft gear so it clears the gear teeth on the clutch shaft. Then with a soft metal drift, drive the shaft forward and out of the transmission case (Figs. 19 and 20).

FIGURE 19—*Tap Out the Clutch Shaft with a Soft Drift*

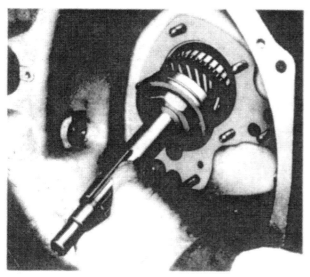

FIGURE 20—Lift Clutch Shaft Assembly Out of Case

Lift the countershaft gear and thrust washers out through the rear of the case (Fig. 21). The larger diameter thrust washer is located in the front of the transmission case. The smaller diameter thrust washer is located in the rear of the case and is supplied in various sizes to obtain the proper end play which is .001" to .003". If the end play exceeds .003", a new thrust washer should be fitted to correct this condition.

FIGURE 21—Remove the Countershaft Gear out of the Rear of the Transmission Case

Disassembly of Main Shaft Gears

Slide the second and third speed synchro-clutch gear off of the main shaft (Fig. 22).

Depress the spring loaded thrust washer lock pin with a pointed tool. Then turn the retaining thrust washer lock ring in line with the splines on the main shaft. Remove the washer, lock pin, and spring (Fig. 23).

FIGURE 22—Remove Synchro-Clutch Gear Assembly

FIGURE 23—Remove Thrust Washer Retaining Lock Ring

Remove the second speed gear, bronze bushing, and bronze thrust washer from the main shaft (Fig. 24).

FIGURE 24—Remove Second Speed Gear and Bushing

TRANSMISSION SECTION
(A Series)

Remove the first speed gear and bronze bushing from the main shaft (Fig. 25).

FIGURE 25—*Remove First Speed Gear and Bushing*

Remove the first and reverse speed sliding gear from the main shaft (Fig. 26).

The rear transmission ball bearing and speedometer drive gear are secured to the main shaft by means

FIGURE 26—*Remove First and Reverse Sliding Gear*

of a nut and lock washer. To remove these, place the main shaft in a vise after protecting the splines and finished surfaces with a shop cloth. Then bend the lips on the lock washer and unscrew the hexagon nut. Remove the main shaft from the vise. Then place the shaft with the rear ball bearing retainer on the vise, and tap the long splined end of the shaft with a plastic or lead hammer. This will release the shaft from the ball bearing and speedometer drive gear.

The component parts of the main shaft assembly are illustrated in Figure 27.

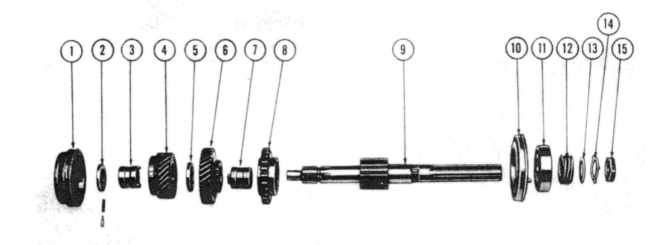

1. Synchro-Gear
2. Retaining Thrust Lock Washer, Spring, and Pin
3. Second Speed Gear Bushing
4. Second Speed Gear
5. Bronze Thrust Washer
6. First Speed Gear
7. First Speed Gear Bushing
8. First and Reverse Sliding Gear

9. Main Shaft
10. Rear Bearing Retainer
11. Rear Ball Bearing
12. Speedometer Drive Gear
13. Spacing Washer
14. Lock Washer
15. Hexagon Nut

FIGURE 27—*Component Parts of Main Shaft Assembly*

Clutch Shaft Disassembly

To remove the bearing from the shaft, bend the lip of the lock washer away from the nut. Place the shaft in a vise protecting the splines, and remove the nut which has a LEFT HAND THREAD. Place the bearing on the jaws of an open vise, resting the assembly on the snap ring, and tap the shaft downward.

> CAUTION: *Use only a soft hammer to prevent the end of the shaft from spreading.*

When installing a new bearing, use Tool J-2995 Bearing Installer; tighten the left hand nut securely and carefully bend the lock washer lips on two sides of the nut.

Disassembly of Rear Cover

The rear cover housing contains the dust shield, rear oil seal, breather and speedometer driven gear.

The dust shield is indented in three places into the machined groove of the rear cover housing. To remove the dust shield carefully, hacksaw the three indentations and tap the shield off of the rear cover. A new dust shield must be fitted when reassembled. When installing a new dust cover, it must be located evenly to eliminate interference with the propeller shaft (Fig. 28).

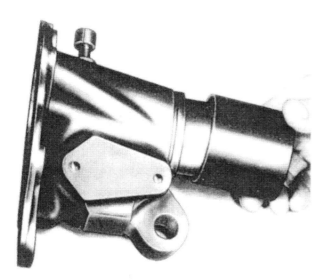

FIGURE 28—*Rear Cover and Dust Shield*

The rear oil seal is also indented in three places in a machined groove in the rear cover. Due to the oil seal cover being made of lighter material, it can be driven off without the use of a hacksaw. When installing a new oil seal, care must be exercised when indenting the oil seal cover in three places in the groove provided in the rear cover. This is to in-

sure proper seating of the cork gasket against the rear cover, otherwise a leak will occur if not properly installed (Fig. 29).

FIGURE 29—*Rear Cover and Oil Seal*

The speedometer driven gear is screwed into the cover with a fibre gasket provided for a seal. The breather can be removed from the cover with a screw driver.

The component parts of the complete transmission are illustrated in Figures 30 and 31.

Synchro-Clutch Gear Disassembly

The synchro-clutch gear consists of an inner and outer sliding gear held in position by five balls and springs located in the inner gear.

When separating the gear, place it in a shop cloth to prevent losing the balls and springs (Fig. 32).

CLEANING AND INSPECTION

Clean all parts thoroughly and examine parts for wear.

Should the cross shaft appear excessively loose in the bushings, new bushings should be installed. These bushings are a press fit into the case with the outer ends flush with the case. After installing new bushings, drill a hole in the bushing in line with the lubricating fittings.

Bearings

The front and rear transmission ball bearings may become worn after considerable length of service and should be renewed if looseness occurs between the inner and outer races.

Clutch Shaft and Main Shaft Bushing

This bushing is fitted with a maximum permissible

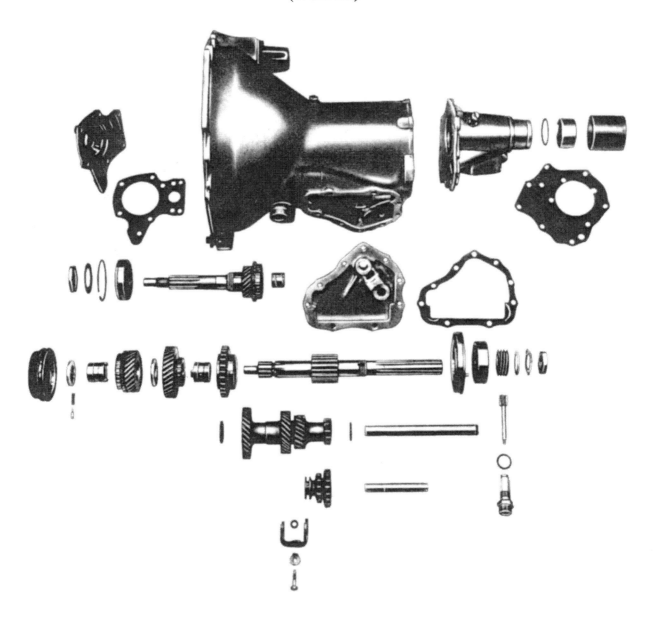

FIGURE 30—*Component Parts*
of Transmission

internal clearance of .003″ between the bushing and main shaft. If worn above this tolerance, the bushing and/or shaft should be replaced.

Second and Third Speed Bronze Bushings

The phosphor bronze bushings should not have any up and down movement. The fitted clearance should be within .00025″ to .00175″.

Countershaft Gear Thrust Washers

These thrust washers are designed to permit .001″ to .003″ end play clearance of the countershaft gears. The rear thrust washers are supplied in variable thicknesses to obtain the proper end play.

Countershaft Gear Bushings and Shaft

If the countershaft gear bushings and shaft show evidence of excessive wear, either or both must be replaced.

Synchronizing Clutch Gear Cones

The bronze cones are shrunk onto the clutch shaft and second speed gears, and if worn, the clutch shaft and/or second speed gears must be replaced.

Rear Oil Seal

The rear oil seal should only be replaced if it shows signs of leaking. If it becomes necessary to replace the oil seal, extreme care must be exercised upon installation.

ASSEMBLY OF TRANSMISSION

NOTE: *Lubricate all parts before assembly into case.*

TRANSMISSION SECTION
(A Series)

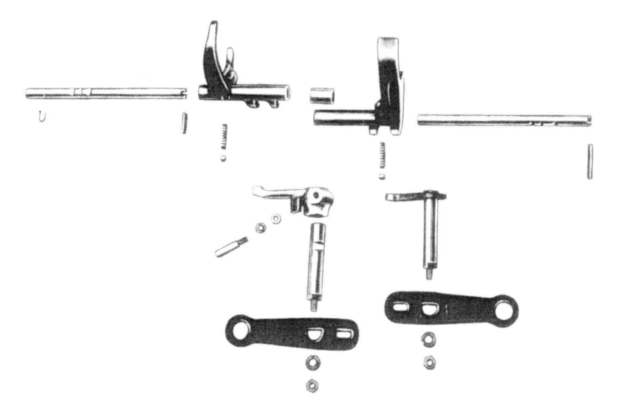

**FIGURE 31—*Component Parts
of Transmission***

**FIGURE 32—*Synchro-Clutch Gear
Disassembled***

Install the countershaft gears (Fig. 21), thrust washers, and countershaft. Check the end play clearance with a feeler gauge. If clearance is over .003"

or less than .001", replace the rear thrust washer to proper size to obtain clearance of .001" to .003" end play.

Remove the countershaft and insert a thin rod or transmission countershaft tool so that the countershaft gears and thrust washers will be positioned in assembly sequence, in the bottom of the transmission. This will allow clearance for replacing the main shaft gear assembly.

After the clutch shaft and front transmission bearing has been assembled, drive the clutch shaft into the front of the transmission case. This operation can be accomplished by using Tool J-2170 and an outer three-inch Timken bearing race. The bearing snap ring must fit flush in the recess of the case. Then insert the clutch and main shaft bushing in the clutch shaft. The maximum clearance between the main shaft and the bushing is .003".

Main Shaft and Gear Assembly

To reassemble the synchro-clutch gear, install Tool J-5568 aligning sleeve over the inner gear. Install each spring and ball through the drilled hole in the aligning sleeve using a punch to depress the spring and rotate the tool until all five springs and balls are inserted. Slide the outer gear over the inner gear and snap into place (Fig. 33).

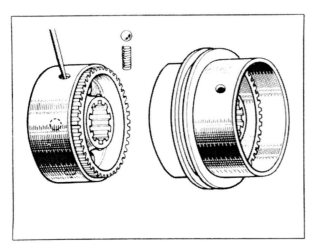

FIGURE 33—*Assembling Synchro-Clutch*

FIGURE 35—*Install the Reverse Idler Gear*

After the gears, rear bearing, and retainer are assembled to the main shaft, install the assembly from the rear of the case (Fig. 34). Start the shaft into the clutch shaft bushing and tap the rear end of the shaft with a plastic hammer until the rear bearing retainer becomes flush with the recess in the case.

The main shaft and clutch shaft should rotate freely. If binding occurs, tap the clutch shaft slightly which should alleviate this condition.

Install the countershaft with the lipped end to the front; the rear end should be flush with the case. The lipped end of the countershaft fits into a recess in the front cover which keeps the shaft from turning.

Install the reverse idler gear, shaft, and bracket (Fig. 35). After the bracket is secured, bend the lip on the lock washer against the hexagon head and the case.

Shifter Forks and Rods

The dummy shafts should be inserted in each

shifter fork to keep the preloaded spring and ball in place before assembly in the case.

Install the second and third speed shifter fork in the case placing the fork in the synchro-clutch gear groove and place the first and second speed fork over the teeth of the first and reverse sliding gear (Fig. 36).

Start the second and third shifter rod from the rear of the case and place the limit sleeve on the rod. Push the rod into the fork keeping the rail tight against the dummy shaft. Then holding the shifter fork toward the rear, slide the shaft through the fork and remove the dummy shaft. Install the snap ring in the groove at the front end of the shifter fork on the rod. Install the first and reverse shifter rod in a similar manner. Check to see if the balls engage the grooves in the rods. Then insert the locks in the slots at the rear of the case.

FIGURE 34—*Install the Main Shaft Assembly*

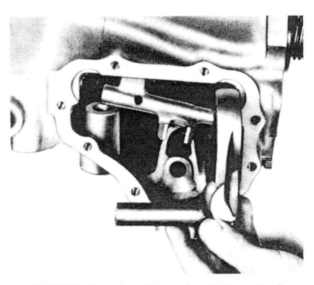

FIGURE 36—*Installing the Shifter Forks*

TRANSMISSION SECTION
(A Series)

Transmission Covers—Rear, Side, and Front

Align the dowel pin in the rear bearing retainer with the rear cover and install the rear cover, gasket, and speedometer driven gear.

Install the front cover and gasket. Then install the side cover assembly and gasket aligning the shifter shafts with the shifter forks. Install the shift levers.

Install the clutch operating shaft and throwout bearing assembly.

Lubrication of the Transmission

Check the lubricant level of the transmission every 1,000 miles. The transmission should be filled to the filler plug level on the right side. Drain and refill every 5,000 miles.

Transmission Capacity — 3½ pints (U.S.).
For Summer, use SAE No. 40 Engine Oil.
For Winter, use SAE No. 30 Engine Oil.
Minus 10°F., use SAE No. 20 Engine Oil.

TECHNICAL SERVICE LETTER REFERENCE

Date	Letter No.	Subject	Changes information on Page No.

Technical Service Manual

Transmission
(B and 1500 Series)

TRANSMISSION REMOVAL

First disconnect one of the battery leads at the battery terminal and then the starter lead at the starter.

Remove the four top transmission to engine mounting bolts from the engine compartment.

Raise and support the car securely.

Drain transmission lubricant.

Install Engine Support Fixture, Tool J-5565 (Fig. 1).

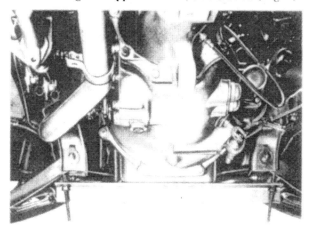

1. Tool J-5565

FIGURE 1—*Engine Support Fixture*

Disconnect the propeller shaft at the rear axle companion flange and pull the shaft from the transmission main shaft splines.

FIGURE 2—*Removing Propeller Shaft*

Remove the rear crossmember from the rear transmission supports and side sill members.

Disconnect the speedometer cable, and the shift rods from transmission levers.

Disconnect the clutch release cylinder from the transmission.

Remove the remaining four lower transmission to engine bolts and remove starter.

Lower the engine support fixture approximately one and a quarter inches and lift transmission toward the rear of the car, being careful not to leave the weight of the unit hang on the clutch shaft which could damage or bend the clutch drive plate.

FIGURE 3—*Removing Transmission*

DISASSEMBLING THE TRANSMISSION

With the transmission assembly completely drained of its lubricant and set up on a transmission stand, the unit is ready for disassembly.

Clutch Throwout Bearing

To remove the clutch throwout bearing remove the two retaining springs with a screw driver (Fig. 4).

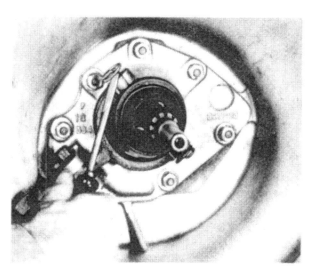

FIGURE 4—*Remove Clutch Throwout Bearing Retainer Springs*

After the springs are removed, lift the bearing away from the fork and slide it off the clutch shaft.

Remove the cotter and clevis pins from the release cylinder rod and remove the cylinder (Fig. 5).

Remove the pivot bolt from the front cover and throwout lever (Fig. 6).

Remove the throwout lever and rubber boot, lifting them out toward the inside of the transmission bell housing (Fig. 7).

TRANSMISSION SECTION
(B and 1500 Series)

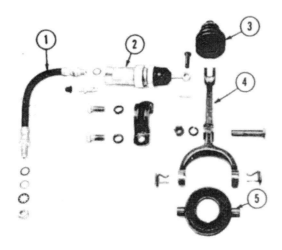

1. Clutch Release Hose
2. Throwout Cylinder
3. Rubber Boot
4. Throwout Lever
5. Throwout Bearing

FIGURE 5—*Hydraulic Clutch Release Components*

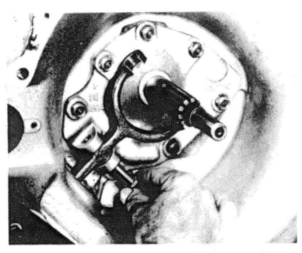

FIGURE 6—*Remove Throwout Lever Bolt*

FIGURE 7—*Remove Throwout Lever and Boot*

Transmission Disassembly

Remove the nuts and lock washers that retain the front transmission cover. The cover can be removed at this time. However, if it cannot be lifted off the studs, it is advisable to remove the cover when the countershaft is being removed (Fig. 8).

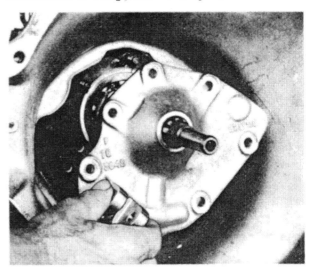

FIGURE 8—*Removing the Front Transmission Cover*

Remove the cap and flat head screws from the side cover and remove the cover and shift shafts as an assembly (Fig. 9).

FIGURE 9—*Remove Side Cover, Shift Shafts and Shifter Forks*

Remove the cap screws and pull off the rear cover. When removing the cover, it may be necessary to tap the transmission main shaft with a plastic hammer to release the rear cover from the rear bearing retainer (Fig. 10).

TRANSMISSION SECTION
(B and 1500 Series)

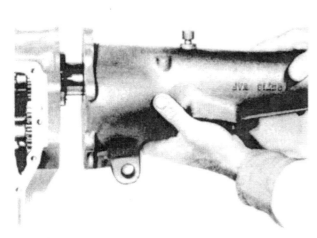

FIGURE 10—*Removing the Rear Cover*

Tap the countershaft slightly forward to release and remove the front cover if not removed previously.

Bend the lip on the reverse idler gear set screw locking washer and remove the set screw (Fig. 11).

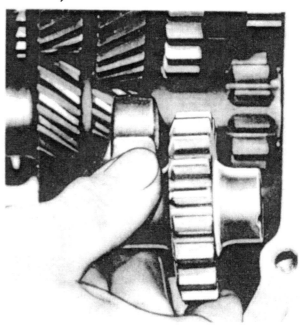

FIGURE 12—*Removing Reverse Idler Shaft and Gear*

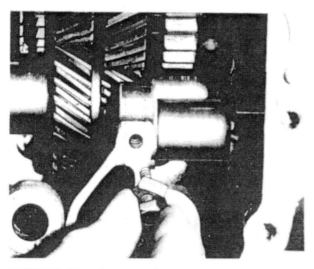

FIGURE 11—*Remove Reverse Idler Set Screw*

FIGURE 13—*Removing the Countershaft*

Tap reverse idler shaft to rear of transmission and remove reverse idler gear (Fig. 12).

With a soft metal drift and hammer, tap the countershaft forward. As the countershaft is removed the countershaft gear and two thrust washers will drop to the bottom of the case. The countershaft cannot be removed from the case until the main shaft and clutch shaft assemblies are removed (Fig. 13).

Remove the main shaft and gear assembly from the case tipping the rear of the main shaft down slightly to pass over the countershaft gears (Fig. 14).

Before removing the clutch shaft, tilt the countershaft gear so it clears the teeth on the clutch shaft. Then with a soft metal drift, drive the shaft forward out of the transmission case (Figs. 15 and 16).

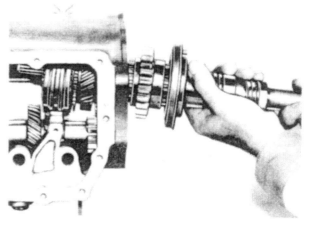

FIGURE 14—*Removing the Main Shaft and Gear Assembly*

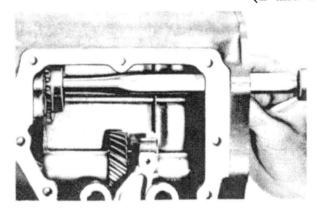

FIGURE 15—*Tap Out the Clutch Shaft With a Soft Drift*

FIGURE 17—*Remove Synchro-Clutch Assembly*

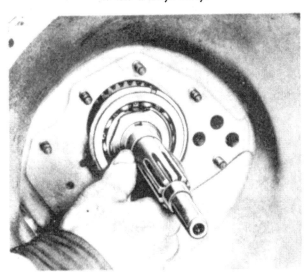

FIGURE 16—*Lift the Clutch Shaft Assembly Out of Case*

FIGURE 18—*Depress Thrust Washer Retaining Lock Pin*

Lift the countershaft gear and thrust washers out through the rear of the case. The larger thrust washer is located in the front of the transmission case. The smaller diameter thrust washer is located in the rear of the case and is supplied in various sizes to obtain the proper end play which is .003″. A new thrust washer should be installed if end play exceeds .006″.

Disassembly of Main Shaft Gears

Slide the synchro-clutch assembly off of the main shaft (Fig. 17).

Place the main shaft assembly in a vise protecting the shaft with a shop cloth.

Depress the spring loaded thrust washer lock pin with a pointed tool. Then turn the retaining thrust washer lock ring in line with the splines on the main shaft. Remove the washer, lock pin and spring (Figs. 18 and 19).

Remove the second speed gear and bronze bushing from the main shaft (Fig. 20).

FIGURE 19—*Remove Thrust Washer Retaining Lock Ring*

Remove the bronze thrust washer, first speed gear, and bushing from the main shaft (Fig. 21).

FIGURE 20—*Remove Second Speed Gear and Bushing*

FIGURE 22—*Remove First and Reverse Sliding Gear*

FIGURE 21—*Remove the Thrust Washer, First Speed Gear, and Bushing*

Remove the first and reverse sliding gear from the main shaft (Fig. 22).

The rear transmission ball bearing spacer sleeve, and speedometer gear are secured to the main shaft by means of a nut and lock washer. Place in a vise, protecting the shaft with a shop cloth, bend the lip of the lock washer away from the hexagon nut and unscrew the nut.

Remove the main shaft from the vise and slide the nut, washer, speedometer gear, and spacer off the shaft.

To remove the ball bearing from the shaft, replace the hexagon nut and tap the end of the shaft on a hard wood block.

Clutch Shaft Disassembly

To remove the bearing from the shaft, bend the lip of the lockwasher away from the nut. Place the shaft in a vise, protecting the splines, and remove the nut which has a left hand thread. Place the bearing on the jaws of an open vise, resting the assembly on the snap ring and tap the shaft downward.

CAUTION: *Use only a soft hammer to prevent the end of the shaft from spreading.*

When installing a new bearing, use Tool J-2995 Bearing Installer. Tighten the left hand nut securely and carefully bend the lock washer lips on the two sides of the nut.

Disassembly of Rear Cover

The rear cover housing contains the speedometer driven gear, breather, and rear oil seal.

The speedometer driven gear is screwed into the rear cover with a fibre gasket provided for a seal. The breather can be removed with a screw driver.

The rear oil seal is indented in three places in a machined groove in the rear cover. The rear oil seal can be removed by carefully cutting into the indented parts of the seal with a hack saw and then using Tool J-2619 and J-4830 to pull the seal from the cover (Fig. 23).

Care must be exercised when installing a new seal to indent the oil seal cover in three places, equally spaced, in the machined groove provided in the rear cover. This is to insure proper seating of the cork gasket against the rear cover, otherwise a leak will occur if not properly installed.

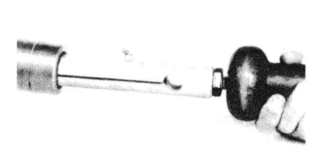

FIGURE 23—*Remove the Rear Oil Seal*
Using Tool J-2619 and J-4830

Disassembly of Synchro-Clutch Gear

The synchro-clutch gear consists of an inner and outer sliding gear held in position by three balls and springs located in the inner gear (Fig. 24).

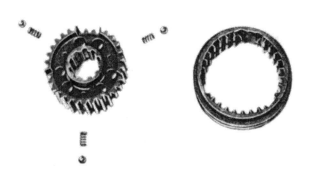

FIGURE 24—*Component Parts of Synchro-*
Clutch Gear

When separating the gear, place it in a shop cloth to prevent losing the balls and springs.

Disassembly of Countershaft Gear Needle Bearings

The countershaft gear contains three sets of needle bearings, two sets located at the large diameter gear, and one at the smallest diameter gear. They are held in place by snap rings with the rollers kept in place by retainers (Fig. 25). The snap rings are removed with a pointed tool.

Disassembly of Shift Shafts and Forks

After removing the shift levers place the side cover assembly in a vise and remove the first and reverse shift shaft (Figs. 26, 27 and 28).

FIGURE 25—*Countershaft Gear and Needle*
Bearings

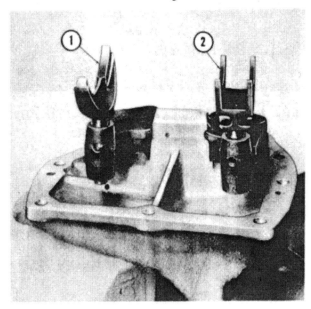

1. 2nd and High Shifter Fork
2. 1st and Reverse Shifter Fork

FIGURE 26—*Side Cover and Shift Shaft*
Assembly

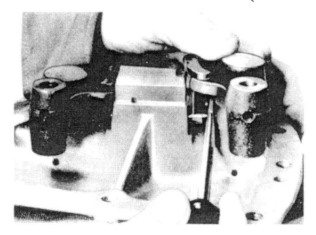

FIGURE 27—*Removing the First and Reverse Shift Shaft*

FIGURE 29—*Removing the Second and Third Speed Shift Shaft*

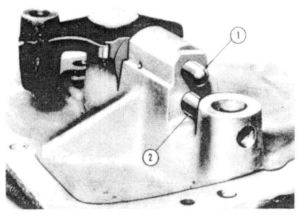

1. Interlock Plunger   2. Speed Finder Plunger

FIGURE 28—*First and Reverse Shift Shaft Removed*

Remove the speed finder plunger, spring, and shift interlock plunger. Then remove the second and third speed shift shaft (Fig. 29).

The side cover, speed finder assembly, and interlock plunger are illustrated in Figure 30.

If the shift shaft oil seals require replacement, care must be exercised when prying them out of the side cover. They can be replaced by pressing them into the side cover with the use of a 13/16″ socket (Fig. 43).

CLEANING AND INSPECTION

Clean all parts thoroughly and carefully examine parts for wear.

Bearings

The front and rear transmission ball bearings may become worn after considerable length of service and should be replaced if looseness occurs between the inner and outer races.

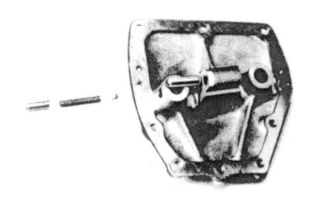

FIGURE 30—*Components of Side Cover, Speed Finders and Interlock Plunger*

Clutch Shaft and Main Shaft Roller Bearings

The clutch shaft and main shaft needle roller bearings, if worn excessively, should be replaced. The pilot end of the main shaft and the bearing hole of the clutch shaft should also be examined; if worn or pitted they should be replaced.

The main shaft outside diameter should be .5688″ to .5693″ at the needle roller bearing end.

The inside diameter of the clutch shaft should be .8065″ to .8072″ at the needle roller bearing end.

The outside diameter of the needle roller bearing should be .118″ ± .00025″. The minimum clearance is .001″ and the maximum .0025″.

TRANSMISSION SECTION
(B and 1500 Series)

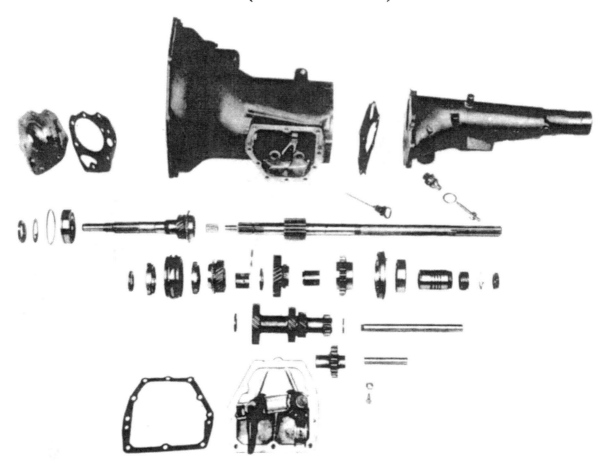

FIGURE 31—*Component Parts of Transmission*

Second and Third Speed Bronze Bushings

The phosphor bronze bushings should not have any up and down movement. The fitted clearance should be within .00025" to .00175".

Countershaft Needle Bearings and Shaft

If the countershaft needle bearings and shaft show evidence of excessive wear, the countershaft gear, bearings, and shaft must be replaced.

Synchro-Clutch Friction Rings

If the threaded portion of the friction rings show evidence of excessive wear, they should be replaced.

Rear Oil Seal

The rear oil seal should only be replaced if it shows signs of leaking. If it becomes necessary to replace the oil seal, extreme care must be exercised upon installation.

ASSEMBLY OF TRANSMISSION

NOTE: *Lubricate all parts before assembly into case.*

Synchro-Clutch Assembly

To reassemble the synchro-clutch gear, place the outer gear on a bench, then insert the three springs in the inner gear. Start the inner gear into the outer gear and set the three balls in place. Press the inner gear down and push the balls in place with a punch (Fig. 32). Then with a quick snap press the inner gear flush with the outer gear.

Countershaft Gear Assembly

Place the countershaft gear on the bench and install the shaft then the bearing races, needle bearings, and snap rings. See Figure 25.

Clutch Shaft Assembly

Install the ball bearing on the clutch shaft using Tool J-2995 Bearing and Snap Ring Installer. Install the lock washer and left hand nut and tighten securely. Bend lock washer over flat portion of nut and install snap ring in groove on ball bearing.

Main Shaft Assembly

Place the ball bearing on the main shaft and start the bearing by tapping it with the spacer sleeve (Fig. 33).

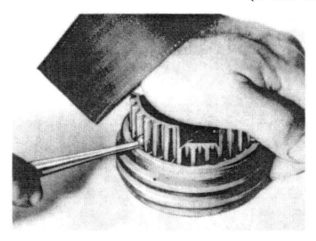

FIGURE 32—*Installing Balls and Springs in Center Gear*

FIGURE 34—*Installing Ball Bearing Retainer, First and Reverse Sliding Gear*

Install the first and reverse bronze bushing and gear (Fig. 35).

FIGURE 33—*Installing Main Shaft Ball Bearing*

FIGURE 35—*Install First and Reverse Bushing and Gear*

Install the bronze thrust washer fitting it flush against first and reverse gear (Fig. 36).

Install the second speed bronze bushing, spring and lock pin (Fig. 37).

NOTE: *When installing bronze bushing, align notch in bushing with lock pin hole in shaft. Then insert the bushing into the splined bronze thrust washer which locks both bronze bushings stationary on main shaft.*

Depress the lock pin and move second speed bronze bushing slightly forward over lock pin.

Carefully install second speed gear over the bronze bushing (Fig. 38).

Install the speedometer gear, lock washer, and nut on main shaft. Place main shaft in a vise, protecting shaft with a shop cloth, and tighten nut securely. This procedure will press the ball bearing in place. Bend locking washer on flat of hexagon nut being careful not to chip teeth on speedometer gear.

Install the rear ball bearing retainer and the first and reverse sliding gear (Fig. 34).

TRANSMISSION SECTION
(B and 1500 Series)

Install retaining thrust washer against second speed gear, sliding bronze bushing, gear, and thrust washer over lock pin. The thrust washer will then be lined up with the groove in the main shaft (Fig. 39).

FIGURE 36—*Installing Thrust Washer*

FIGURE 37—*Installing Spring and Lock Pin*

FIGURE 38—*Install Second Speed Gear*

FIGURE 39—*Installing Retaining Thrust Washer*

Locate a pointed tool in the drilled hole in the thrust washer and rotate the washer in alignment with the main shaft spline. The lock pin will snap into the groove of the washer locking it in place (Fig. 40).

FIGURE 40—*Locking Retaining Thrust Washer in Place*

Check end play clearance between the bronze thrust washer and second speed gear. This clearance should be .003″ to .006″ (Fig. 41).

NOTE: *The steel retaining thrust washer is supplied in variable sizes.*

Install synchro-clutch gear and friction rings. Lubriplate will hold the friction rings to the gear (Fig. 42).

FIGURE 41 — *Checking End Play Clearance*

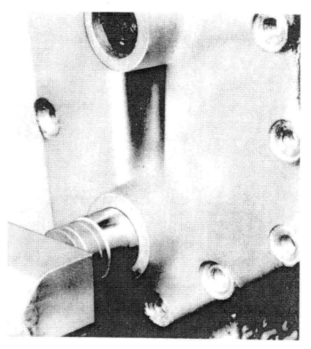

FIGURE 43—*Installing Shift Shaft Oil Seals*

FIGURE 42—*Install Synchro-Clutch Gear and Friction Rings*

FIGURE 44—*Installing the Second and High Shift Shaft*

Assembly of Shifter Fork Assembly

Should the shift shaft oil seals require replacement, remove them carefully to avoid mutilating the aluminum side cover.

Protect the inside of the cover by placing a shop cloth on the inner jaw of the vise and press the new seals into place using a 13/16" socket (Fig. 43).

Place the cover in the vise and install the second and high shift shaft (Fig. 44).

Insert the ball bearing in the lower drilled hole (Fig. 45).

Insert the speed finder spring and plunger (Fig. 46).

Insert the shift shaft interlock plunger (Fig. 47).

Install the first and reverse speed shift shaft and depress the speed finder plunger with the flat of a screw driver.

Install the shifter forks. The first and reverse shifter fork is machined the same on both sides, but the second and high must be installed with the wide portion of the forging facing the first and reverse fork (Fig. 48).

Assembly of Countershaft and Gear

Place the steel thrust washers on the countershaft gear using lubriplate to hold them to the gear.

FIGURE 45—_Installing the Ball Bearing_

FIGURE 46—_Installing the Speed Finder_
Spring and Plunger

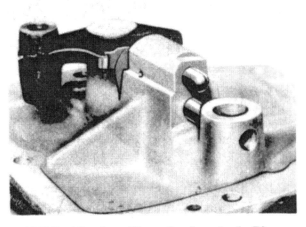

FIGURE 47—_Installing the Interlock Plunger_

FIGURE 48—_Install the Shifter Forks_

Set the gear in the transmission case through the rear of the case. Then install the countershaft. Check end play using a feeler gauge at the rear between the gear and small steel thrust washer. This tolerance should be .003″ to .006″.

Remove the countershaft leaving the gear and thrust washers lay in the bottom of the case.

NOTE: _The thrust washers will not slide away from the gear and case._

Install the main shaft and rear bearing assembly through the rear of the case using a rear cover cap screw temporarily to hold the assembly in the case.

Install the needle roller bearings in the clutch shaft assembly holding them in place with lubriplate or petrolatum.

Install the clutch shaft and front bearing assembly carefully, starting the roller bearings over the pilot of the main shaft. Tap the clutch shaft into place with Tool J-2995 until the snap ring on the outside diameter of the ball bearing seats against the case.

Align the countershaft gear and thrust washers and install the countershaft.

NOTE: _The cutaway portion of the counter shaft is toward the front. This cutaway portion protrudes from the front of the case and fits into the front cover which keeps the shaft from rotating._

Install the reverse idler gear and shaft, locking the shaft in place with the hexagon cap screw and locking tab washer. Bend the lip of the washer over the flat of the hexagon cap screw.

NOTE: _Make sure that the clutch and main shafts turn free; this can be accomplished by tapping the end of the clutch shaft with a plastic hammer._

TRANSMISSION SECTION
(B and 1500 Series)

Install the front cover and gasket.

Remove the cap screw from the rear cover which was temporarily used to hold the main shaft assembly in place and install the rear cover and gasket.

> NOTE: *The locating dowel pin on the rear ball bearing retainer will only fit into one of the drilled holes in the rear cover. Make sure that the correct location of the pin is attained before tightening the rear cover to the case. The countershaft should also be flush with the case before tightening the rear cover. This procedure is to insure against cracking the rear cover aluminum casting when tightening the rear cover to the case.*

Install speedometer gear assembly. When installing the shifter fork assembly and side cover, extend both shifter forks from the shift shafts. Set the first speed gear and synchro-clutch assembly in their neutral positions, then use lubriplate to hold the side cover gasket to the case and install the complete assembly (Fig. 49).

Install rubber boot on clutch throwout lever inserting lever through case from the inside. Then seat rubber boot in place on case; lubricate and install pivot bolt in front cover, making sure not to over tighten bolt which would cause throwout lever to bind, then lock securely with lock-washer and nut.

Install clutch throw-out bearing and retaining springs and fasten clutch throwout lever to release cylinder rod with clevis pin and cotter key.

LUBRICATION OF THE TRANSMISSION

Check the lubricant level of the transmission every 1,000 miles. The transmission should be filled to the filler plug level on the right side. Drain and refill every 5,000 miles.

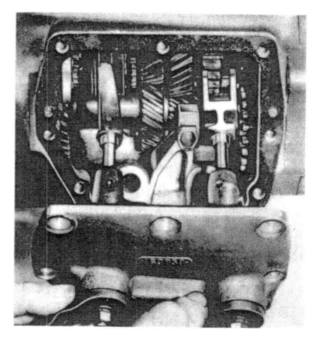

FIGURE 49—*Install Side Cover and Shifter Fork Assembly*

Transmission Capacity—5½ pints (U.S.).

For Summer, use SAE No. 40 Engine Oil.

For Winter, use SAE No. 30 Engine Oil.

Minus 10°F., use SAE No. 20 Engine Oil.

GEAR RATIOS

First Speed 2.44:1

Second Speed . . . 1.54:1

Third Speed . . . . Direct

Reverse 3.49:1

TECHNICAL SERVICE LETTER REFERENCE

Date	Letter No.	Subject	Changes information on Page No.

Technical
Service
Manual

Shifting System

SHIFTING SYSTEM SECTION

DISASSEMBLING THE SHIFTING MECHANISM

Remove the gear shift lever knob and gear shift lever nut (Fig. 1). After the nut is removed. push the lever toward the dash panel. This will loosen the chrome ball permitting it to slide from the lever.

1. Dirt Seal Spacer Retainer
2. Dirt Seal Spacers

FIGURE 2—*Remove Dirt Seal Spacer*

1. Gear Shift Lever Nut
2. Gear Shift Lever

FIGURE 1—*Gear Shift Lever*

Disconnect the gear shift rods from the operating levers at the bottom of the shifting mechanism by removing the cotter pins and lifting the rods out of the levers.

Remove the dirt seal spacer retainer from between the operating levers and remove the two halves of the spacer (Fig. 2).

Remove the two cap screws from the body bracket and remove the operating lever bearing housing.

The entire assembly can now be lowered into the engine compartment to facilitate further disassembly.

Remove the selector pin and remove the housing assembly from the operating shaft (Fig. 3).

Place the housing assembly in a vise and remove the large outer spring and spacer. This will permit the low and reverse, second and high operating levers, bronze fulcrum and inner spring to be removed.

The gear shift lever and operating shaft can now be removed from the passenger compartment. Note the position of the spring, pressure spring, and spring retainer on the gear shift lever (Fig. 4).

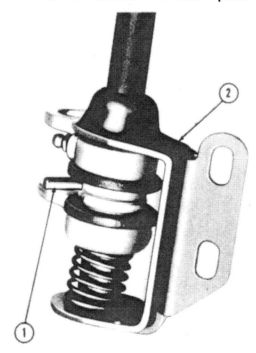

1. Selector Pin
2. Operating Lever Bearing Housing

FIGURE 3—*Remove the Selector Pin and Operating Lever Bearing Housing From the Operating Shaft*

The component parts of the shift assembly are shown in Figures 5 and 6.

ASSEMBLING THE SHIFTING MECHANISM

Place the operating lever housing in a vise. Apply a small amount of lubriplate to the bronze fulcrum and insert it in the housing.

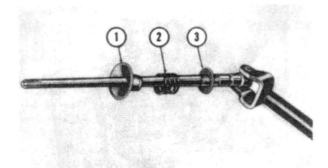

1. Spring Retainer
2. Pressure Spring
3. Spring Washer

FIGURE 4—*When Removing the Operating Shaft, Note the Position of the Spring Washer, Pressure Spring, and Spring Retainer*

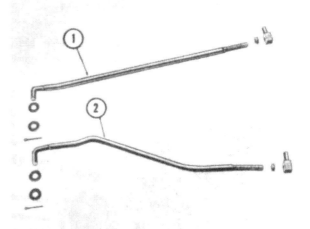

1. Second and High Shifter Rod
2. Low and Reverse Shifter Rod

FIGURE 6—*Shifting Rods*

Install the rubber dirt shield on both gear shift levers locating the metal side of the seal toward the selector pin groove. The metal side provides a hard bearing surface for the pin. Place the operating levers in the bearing housing and install the large outer spring and spacer against the low and reverse operating lever (Fig. 7).

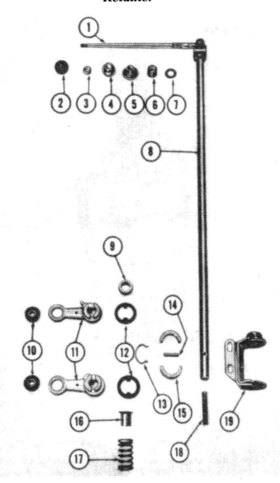

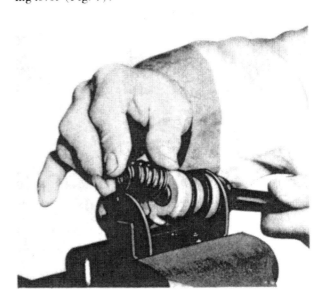

FIGURE 7—*Install Operating Levers and Spring*

Line up the holes in the operating levers and bronze fulcrum with the hole in the bearing housing to provide ease of assembly on the operating shaft.

Install the operating shaft and lever assembly through the hole in the floor board and rubber dirt seal.

Apply lubriplate to the small inner spring and install the spring in the end of the operating shaft. Then assemble the bearing housing to the operating shaft.

1. Gear Shift Lever	11. Operating Levers
2. Lever Ball	12. Dirt Seals
3. Lever Nut	13. Dirt Seal Retainer
4. Chrome Ball	14. Selector Pin
5. Spring Retainer	15. Dirt Seal Spacer
6. Pressure Spring	16. Spacer
7. Washer	17. Outer Spring
8. Operating Shaft	18. Inner Spring
9. Fulcrum	19. Bearing Housing
10. Grommets	

FIGURE 5—*Disassembly of Gear Shift Assembly*

Apply a small amount of lubriplate to the chrome ball; install the ball, lever nut, and the gear shift lever ball.

Fasten the bearing housing assembly on the body bracket.

The fastening bracket on the bearing housing has two elongated holes for alignment. These elongated holes provide adjustment to centralize the shifting lever between the steering wheel and instrument panel when the shifting lever is placed in the second and high speed position.

ADJUSTING THE SHIFTING MECHANISM

A 3/16″ (.1875″) diameter rod can be used as an aligning pin (Fig. 10).

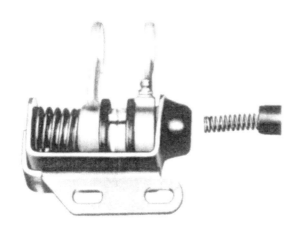

FIGURE 8—*Assemble Bearing Housing to Operating Shaft*

Turn the operating shaft so that the hole in the shaft will index with the notches in the operating levers and install the pin.

Install the two halves of the dirt spacers and secure by installing the dirt seal spacer retainer. When installing the dirt seal spacers, start each half by turning one end into the groove as shown in Figure 9.

1. Aligning Tool

FIGURE 10—*An Aligning Tool Is Used to Retain the Operating Levers in a Neutral Position While Adjusting the Shifter Rods*

With the aligning tool in position and the transmission levers in neutral, adjust the shifting rod trunnions to enter the grommets at the transmission levers. After the rods have been adjusted and connected to the transmission levers, remove the aligning tool. Lubricate the levers with pressure lubricant

LUBRICATION OF SHIFT MECHANISM

Lubricate operating levers with pressure lubricant every 5,000 miles.

Apply engine oil to grommets at shifter rods every 1,000 miles.

Remove nut and apply film of lubriplate to chrome ball every 10,000 miles.

FIGURE 9—*Install Dirt Seal Spacer and Retainer*

Install the gear shift lever spring washer, pressure spring and spring retainer on the gear shift lever and guide the lever through the hole in the instrument panel.

Technical Service Manual

Brakes–Wheels–Hubs–Drums

DESCRIPTION

A Girling Hydraulic Brake System is used. The front brakes have twin cylinders and floating shoes which insure automatic centralization of the brake shoes when in operation.

The rear brakes are of a single cylinder floating shoe non-servo lever type which also incorporates the hand brake mechanism.

HYDRAULIC SYSTEM

The hydraulic system should be kept free of dirt and moisture.

CAUTION: Keep mineral oils, gasoline, or kerosene out of the system as they cause rubber cups to soften and distort resulting in failure.

MASTER CYLINDER

Master Cylinder Removal and Disassembly

Disconnect the pressure pipe fitting from the cylinder and remove bolts from attaching bracket.

Disconnect piston push rod at clevis end, and brake pedal return spring.

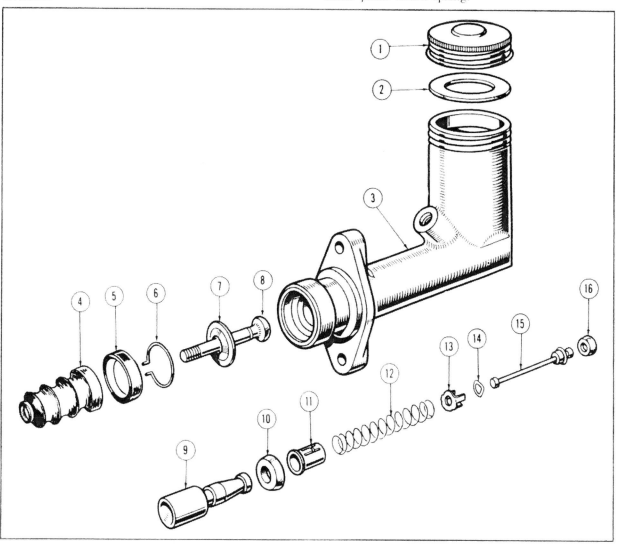

1. Cap	9. Piston
2. Gasket	10. Piston Seal
3. Cylinder	11. Spring Retainer
4. Dust Cover	12. Piston Return Spring
5. Ring	13. Valve Spacer
6. Retaining Clip	14. Spring Washer
7. Retaining Washer	15. Valve Stem
8. Connecting Link	16. Valve Seal

FIGURE 1—*Master Cylinder*

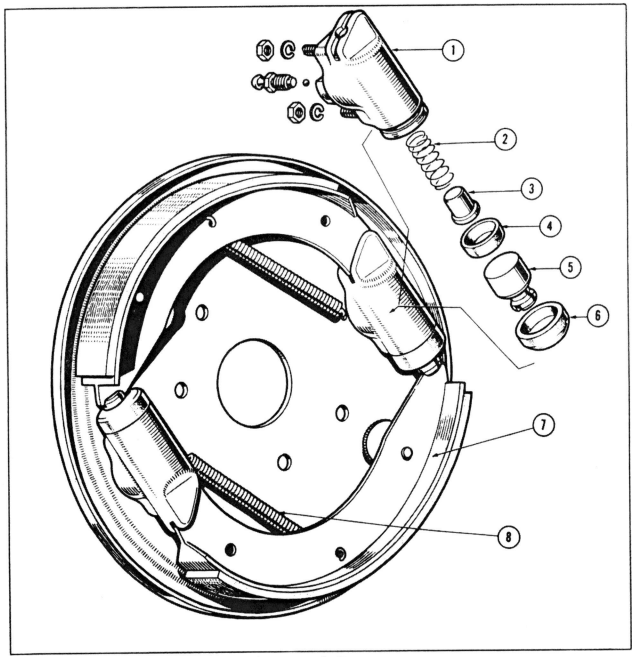

1. Wheel Cylinder	5. Piston
2. Spring	6. Dust Cover
3. Seal Support	7. Brake Shoe and Lining
4. Seal	8. Return Spring

FIGURE 2—*Front Brake Assembly*

Remove cylinder from the car and drain fluid. Pull back dust cover and remove retaining clip. The push rod and retaining washer can then be removed. At this time, remove the complete piston assembly.

The piston assembly can then be separated by lifting the spring retainer over the shoulder end of the piston. The piston seal can then be removed from the piston.

Depress the piston return spring allowing the valve stem to slide through the elongated hole of the spring retainer, thus releasing the spring ten-

sion, and remove the spring retainer, return spring, and valve.

Detach the valve spacer, spacer spring washer, and the valve seal from the valve head.

Examine all parts, especially the seals, for wear or distortion and replace with new parts where necessary.

Master Cylinder Assembly

Replace the valve seal so that the flat side is seated on the valve head. The spring washer should be

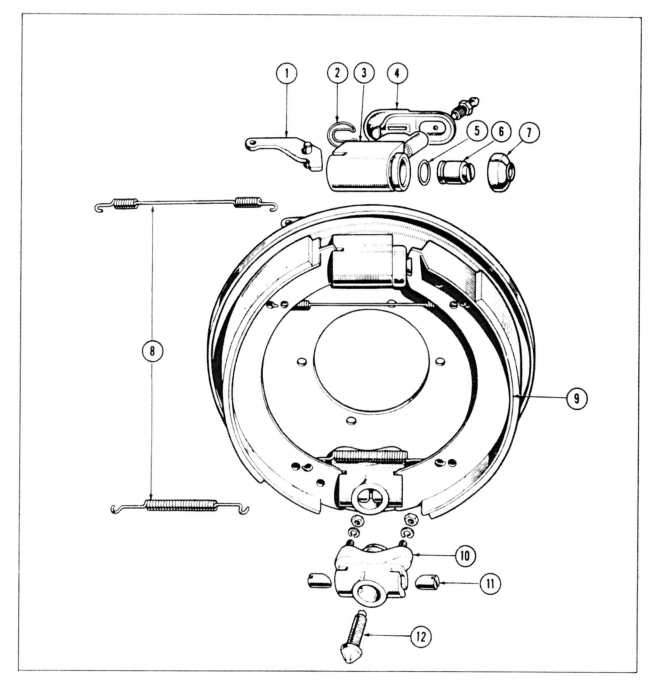

1. Pivot Pin and Lever
2. Retaining Clip
3. Cylinder
4. Dust Cover
5. Seal
6. Piston
7. Dust Cover
8. Return Springs
9. Brake Shoe and Lining
10. Adjuster Housing
11. Link
12. Wedge

FIGURE 3—*Rear Brake Assembly*

then located on the under side of the valve head, being held in position by the valve spacer, the projections facing the valve seal. Install the piston return spring in the center of the spacer. Insert the spring retainer into the spring and depress until the valve stem engages the elongated hole of the retainer.

Install new piston seal on the piston with the flat side seated against the face of the piston.

Insert the piston into the spring retainer; press the retainer in to insure proper installation.

Apply Brake Fluid to the entire assembly, and then insert the assembly into the bore of the cylinder. Replace push rod and retaining washer followed by the retaining clip. Lightly apply lubriplate to the area around the retaining washer and clip.

Replace the dust cover and reinstall cylinder.

WHEEL CYLINDERS

Front Wheel Cylinder

Each wheel cylinder consists of a light alloy body containing a spring, seal support, seal, steel piston, and dust cover (Fig. 2). Each shoe is located in a steel lined slot in the base of one wheel cylinder and expanded by the opposite piston.

Rear Wheel Cylinder

The rear wheel cylinder consists of a light alloy body containing a piston, seal, dust cover, and pivot pin and lever (Fig. 3).

The cylinder is attached to the backing plate by a spring clip allowing it to slide laterally insuring shoe to drum contact.

WHEEL BRAKE UNITS

Front Brake Assembly

The front wheel brake units consist of a backing plate assembly, two wheel cylinders situated opposite each other, and connected by a metal tube.

The bonded lining brake shoes rest on posts riveted to the backing plate and are held in position by two return springs. A felt washer to retain lubricant is installed on each riveted post.

Rear Brake Assembly

The rear wheel brake units consist of a backing plate assembly, one wheel cylinder, two bonded lining brake shoes, shoe return springs, and a wedge type adjuster. At the cylinder end, the primary shoe is located in a slot in the piston while the secondary shoe rests in a slot formed in the cylinder body. At the adjuster end, they rest in slots in the adjuster links. The shoes are supported by posts riveted in the backing plate. A felt washer to retain lubricant is installed on each riveted post.

REPLACEMENT OF BONDED BRAKE SHOES

For replacement purposes, factory bonded lining brake shoes are supplied. It is recommended that when installing replacement brake shoes, a new set of shoe return springs be also installed.

Front Brake Shoe Replacement

Remove wheels and brake drums. To remove the shoe and release return spring tension, lift one shoe out of the abutment slot of the wheel cylinder. Then release the other end from the wheel cylinder piston slot. Repeat the same procedure for the second shoe.

To prevent the wheel cylinders from expanding during this operation, use a suitable clamp or rubber band to hold them in place.

Check and lubricate adjusters for free operation. Turn the adjusters counter-clockwise to the full off position.

Lubricate the tips of the riveted rest posts and the operating and abutment ends of the new shoes. Fit the new return springs to the shoes. Place the hooked end in the shoe and the opposite end in holes in the backing plate near the abutment end of the same shoe. The shoes are replaced independently. Install drums and wheels. Adjust the brakes.

Rear Brake Shoe Replacement

Basically, the rear brake shoe replacement is the same as the front, the only difference being in the return spring location. When removing the shoes, lift one end out of the slot in the adjuster link and the other from wheel cylinder piston. Both shoes can then be removed with the springs.

Upon replacement, install new return springs to the shoes, the shorter spring at the adjuster end. Locate one shoe in the adjuster link and wheel cylinder piston slots, then pull the opposite shoe into position.

Adjust both service and parking brake assemblies.

BRAKE PEDAL ASSEMBLY

Brake Pedal Removal

Remove the brake pedal rod attaching bolt and remove the pedal rod. Detach the brake pedal return spring and remove clevis pin from master cylinder push rod. Then remove the brake and clutch pedal shaft grease fitting, retaining clip, washer, and spring. The brake pedal may now be removed from the car (Fig. 4).

BRAKE ADJUSTMENTS

Raise and support the car in a safe manner. The parking brake must be in a full released position.

Adjust the brake pedal free play to $\frac{1}{8}''$ by adjusting length of master cylinder push rod.

Front Wheel Brake Adjustment

Adjustments for lining wear can be made by means of two eccentrics located in the backing plate assembly. Fully release both eccentric adjusters on the outside of the backing plate by turning them counter-clockwise.

Then turn one of the adjusters clockwise until the brake shoe just touches the brake drum; then release the adjuster until the shoe is just free of

1. Clutch Pedal Return Spring
2. Clutch Pedal
3. Clutch Pedal Rod
4. Return Spring Bracket
5. Cushion
6. Brake Pedal Rod
7. Brake Pedal
8. Brake Pedal Return Spring
9. Clutch and Brake Pedal Covers
10. Pedal Shaft Spring
11. Washer
12. Lock Ring
13. Grease Fitting

FIGURE 4—*Brake and Clutch Pedal Assembly*

the drum. Repeat the process for the second adjuster.

Rotate the wheel to insure that the shoes are free of the drum.

Rear Wheel Brake Adjustment

With the hand brake fully released, turn the square end of the adjuster on the outside of each rear backing plate in a clockwise direction until a brake drag is felt. Then loosen two notches at which time the drum should rotate freely.

PARKING BRAKE

The parking brake actuates the rear brake shoes by means of a cable connected between the hand brake lever, and brake balance lever assembly which is attached to the left rear axle tube. Hand brake cross

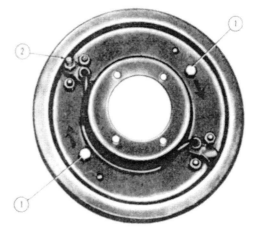

1. Brake Shoe Adjusters   2. Bleed Screw

FIGURE 5—*Front Brake Shoe Adjustments*

BRAKES — WHEELS — HUBS — DRUMS SECTION

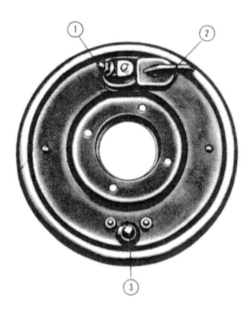

1. Bleed Screw   3. Brake Shoe Adjustment
2. Hand Brake Pivot Lever

FIGURE 6—*Rear Brake Shoe Adjusters*

rods are connected to the hand brake levers pivoted in the rear wheel cylinder bodies.

When operating the hand brake mechanism, the pivot lever expands the secondary brake shoe and the pivot moves the wheel cylinder body, and with it the piston, expanding the primary shoe.

Parking Brake Adjustment

Normal brake adjustments should be made at the brake shoe adjusters and not by the alteration of the parking brake cable.

The parking brake adjustment is made on the cable connector where it is attached to the hand brake lever. With the lever in the fully released position, remove inspection plate on side sill and disconnect the connector from the hand brake lever (Fig. 8).

Push back the rubber insulator on to the cable and loosen lock nut.

Rotate the connector and adjustment nut in a clockwise direction until cable slack is removed. Reinstall and check operation.

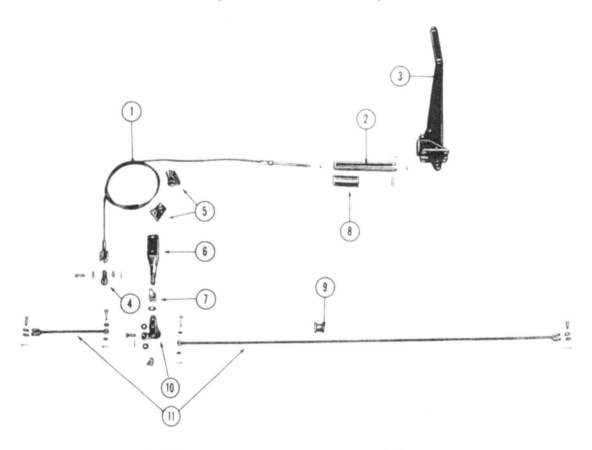

1. Cable
2. Connector
3. Parking Brake Lever Assembly
4. Link
5. Guide
6. Support
7. Carrier
8. Insulator
9. Ferrule
10. Lever
11. Rods

FIGURE 7—*Parking Brake Assembly*

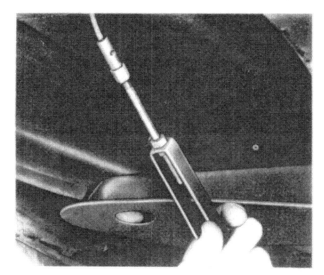

FIGURE 8—*Parking Brake Cable Adjustment*

NOTE: *When hydraulic pressure is applied, the primary shoe makes the initial contact to drum and when the hand brake mechanism is applied, the secondary shoe makes the initial contact. Therefore, when these two applications are made at the same time, the forces will oppose each other causing an instant back pressure on the brake pedal and will be noticeable by the operator.*

BRAKE SPECIFICATIONS

Type of Mechanism	Girling Hydraulic
Front	Twin Cylinder — Hydraulic
Rear	Single Cylinder — Non-Servo Lever Type
Total Foot Braking Area	76.8 Sq. Inch
Lining Size — Length x Width	
Front	7.68″ x 1.25″
Rear	7.68″ x 1.25″
Pedal Free Play	⅛″
Drum Diameter	8″
Front Wheel Cylinder	Single Acting
Rear Wheel Cylinder	Single Acting
Front Wheel Cylinder Bore	¾″
Rear Wheel Cylinder Bore	¾″
Master Cylinder Bore	¾″

WHEELS AND TIRES

Wheel Size	13″
Tire Size	5.20 x 13″
	5.60 x 13″
	at 1500 Series
	Car Serial Number
Tire Pressure Cold —	
Front	24 Lbs.
Rear	22 Lbs.

INFLATION PRESSURES

One of the most important factors in tire care is to maintain proper inflation. The recommended pressure for normal service is 24 pounds front tires; 22 pounds rear (cold).

The effect of three types of inflation pressure is shown in Figure 9.

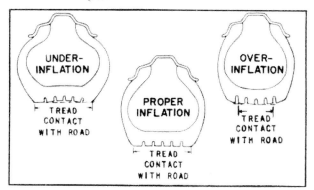

FIGURE 9—*Effect of Inflation Pressures*

The inflation pressure recommended by the tire manufacturer is the best pressure to use in order to maintain efficient balance, riding comfort, tire life, and smooth steering.

Whenever the air pressure is either greater or less than recommended, the balance of forces in the tire is upset; results are abnormal wear and premature failure.

ROTATION OF TIRES

To equalize tire wear, it is recommended that the tires be interchanged after the first 2,500 miles, then at 6,000 miles, and every 5,000 miles of service thereafter. Follow the rotation procedure as illustrated in Figure 10.

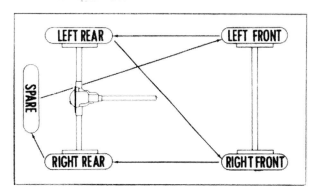

FIGURE 10—*Tire Rotation*

FRONT WHEEL BEARINGS

The inner and outer front wheel ball bearings are non-adjustable; the amount of thrust being determined by a collapsible spacer.

To check for wear, the wheel must be free of the ground. Rock the wheel sideways and any movement between the wheel and the backing plate denotes wear of the bearings. Should a very positive movement be apparent, the bearings need replacement.

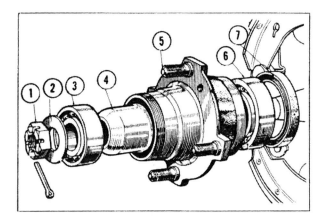

1. Nut   5. Front Hub
2. Washer   6. Inner Bearing
3. Outer Bearing 7. Seal
4. Spacer

FIGURE 11—*Front Wheel Bearings*

Disassembly

Remove the wheel and the countersunk screw holding the brake drum. Remove the brake drum.

Remove the cap, nut, and washer. Then remove the hub using a standard gear puller. The hub is withdrawn complete with the inner and outer bearings, spacer, and the seal.

Should the inner bearing race remain on the wheel spindle, it can be removed by carefully inserting a narrow chisel between the brake shoe and backing plate and lightly tapping the bearing race away from the shoulder on the spindle. When enough clearance is attained, a standard gear puller may be used to remove it the remaining distance.

With the hub removed, both the inner and outer bearing and spacer can be removed by gently tapping with a drift from the opposite ends of the hub.

Assembly

When assembling the hub, the inner bearing should first be inserted into the hub with the side marked "thrust" (thick side of bearing race) facing the spacer (Fig. 12).

Pack the bearing and hub with a recommended high grade wheel bearing lubricant; then insert the spacer so the domed end faces the outer bearing.

Replace the outer bearing so that the "thrust" side faces the spacer.

Use a soft metal drift to replace both bearings. Install the seal over the inner bearing so that the hollow side of the seal faces the bearing. The hub can now be replaced on the spindle. This is best done by using a steel tubing which will bear evenly on both the inner

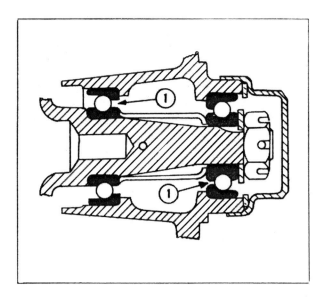

1. Thrust Side of Bearing

FIGURE 12—*Correct Installation of Bearings*

and outer races of the outer hub bearing. Tap the hub into position until the inner race bears against the shoulder on the spindle.

Install the flat washer and spindle nut. The spindle nut should be drawn up to 25 Foot Pounds torque. This will bring the inner races in contact with the spacer and provide the predetermined amount of preload. The cotter pin should then be installed. If the cotter pin holes do not line up with the castellations in the spindle nut, the nut should be backed off slightly.

Replace the brake drum and secure with the countersunk screw.

It is extremely important that the drum contacts the hub before the screws are tightened. If necessary, the drum may be pressed in position by tightening temporarily with two wheel nuts.

REAR WHEEL HUB AND BEARINGS

The rear wheel hubs are a pressed fit on the axle tubes and held in place by a lock washer and nut.

Removal

Drain the axle lubricant. Then remove the wheel and the drum locating screws. The drum can then be tapped off provided that the hand brake is released and the brake shoes are not adjusted so closely as to bind on the drum.

Remove the axle shaft retaining screw, which is exposed when the drum is removed. Draw out the axle shaft. Then remove the nut and lock washer from the axle tube. Remove the hub, rear wheel hub bearing, and seal assembly from the rear axle tube with a bearing puller (Fig. 14). Be certain that the pilot of the puller used on the housing tube will clear the inner race of the bearing when removing the hub.

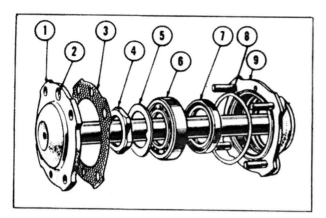

1. Axle Shaft
2. Axle Shaft to Hub Retaining Screw Hole Location
3. Gasket
4. Nut
5. Lock
6. Hub Bearing
7. "O" Ring
8. Oil Seal
9. Hub

FIGURE 13—*Rear Wheel Hub and Bearing Assembly.*

FIGURE 14—*Removing Rear Wheel Hub*

Assembly

If the oil seal has been removed for replacement, use a soft drift to install the new seal into position (lip towards the bearing) before the bearing is installed.

The hub ball bearing is not adjustable. It is essential, however, that the face of the outer race protrude .001″ to .004″ with the rear wheel hub gasket in place beyond the face of the hub when the bearing is pressed in the hub. This will insure that the bearing is definitely held between the abutment shoulder of the hub and the axle shaft flange.

During reassembly, the bearings and hubs should be packed with a high grade wheel bearing lubricant even though they receive some axle lubricant from the axle during operation.

Tool J-2995, Transmission Clutch Shaft Snap Ring Installer can be used to install the hub in position on the axle housing (Fig. 15). Then install the lock

FIGURE 15—*Installing Rear Wheel Hub with Tool J-2995*

washer and nut. Tighten the nut securing it by tapping down the lock washer on one of the flats of the nuts.

Replace the axle shaft locating it in a position that the two small holes of the flange and hub coincide. Then install the brake drum, aligning the small holes in the drum and axle flange.

It is extremely important that the drum contacts the axle flange before the screws are tightened. If necessary, the drum may be pressed in position by tightening two wheel nuts.

SPARE TIRE MOUNTING

The spare tire mounting is of a continental design (Fig. 16).

FIGURE 16—*Spare Tire Mounting*

Removal of the spare tire is conventional involving only the removal of the cap, lock, and hold down nuts.

Bolted to the rear deck panel is the spare tire mounting bracket, to which the spare tire is attached (Fig. 17).

FIGURE 17—*Spare Tire Mounting Bracket*

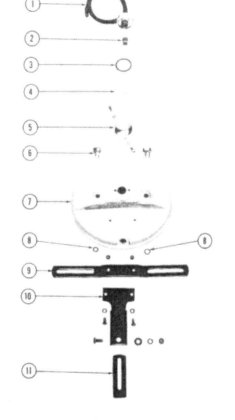

1. Lamp Base Assembly
2. Bulb
3. Gasket
4. Lens
5. Hood
6. Bolt
7. Spare Wheel Cap
8. Retainer Ring
9. License Plate Holder
10. Bracket
11. Clamp

FIGURE 18—*Spare Tire Cap, License Lamp, and License Bracket Assemblies*

SPARE WHEEL LOCK

The spare wheel lock assembly consists of a housing, locking bolt, spring and key cylinder.

It is installed on the upper spare wheel mounting nut (Fig. 16).

When in the locked position, the complete housing can be revolved around the mounting nut, thereby preventing removal.

Removing Cylinder From the Housing

Turn the key so that the groove in the key is in line with the cylinder to housing plunger. Cover the locking bolt hole to prevent the loss of spring or locking bolt when removing the cylinder. Press the locking plunger down with a section of stiff wire and remove the cylinder from the housing.

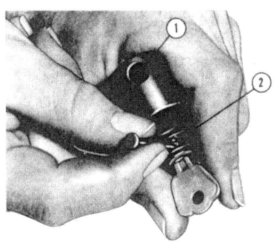

1. Locking Bolt Hole
2. Press the Locking Plunger with Stiff Wire

FIGURE 19—*Removing Cylinder from Housing*

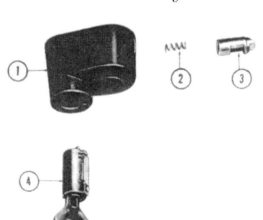

1. Housing
2. Spring
3. Locking Bolt
4. Key Cylinder

FIGURE 20—*Spare Wheel Lock Assembly*

Installing Key Lock Cylinder

Insert the spring and locking bolt into the housing with the notch toward the outside of the housing to allow the cylinder actuating cam to engage the locking bolt.

Compress the locking plunger on the cylinder and insert it into the housing. At the same time, compress the locking bolt so that the actuating cam can engage the notch in the locking bolt.

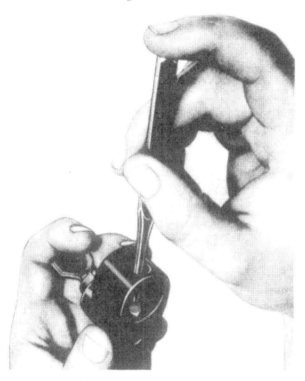

FIGURE 21—*Installing Lock Cylinder*

When the cylinder is in place, the key must be turned to lock the cylinder locking plunger into position in the housing.

JACK EQUIPMENT

Figure 22 illustrates jack equipment to enable tire and wheel changing.

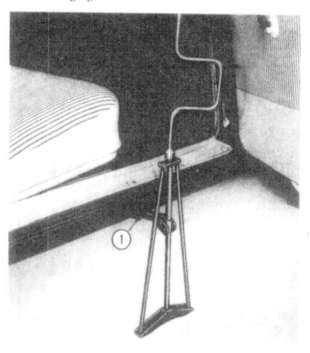

1. Jack Bracket

FIGURE 22—*Jack Equipment*

A jack bracket is welded to the left and right side sills below the door opening. The jack must be firmly inserted into the bracket preferably with the door in an open position, when the car jack is used.

IMPORTANT: *Set hand brake securely before jacking up car.*

TECHNICAL SERVICE LETTER REFERENCE

Date	Letter No.	Subject	Changes information on Page No.

Technical Service Manual

Rear Axle and Propeller Shaft

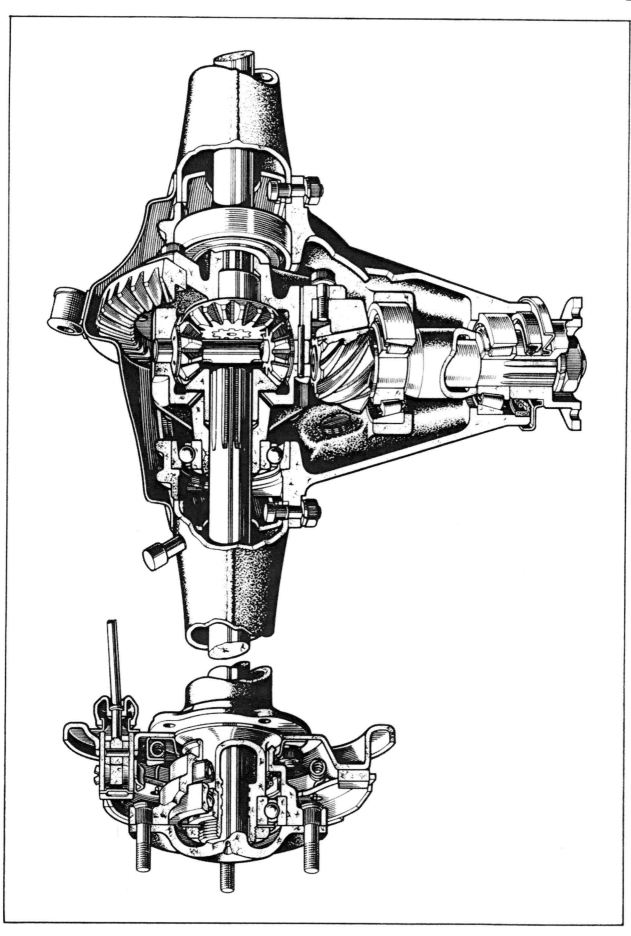

Rear Axle Assembly

REAR AXLE and PROPELLER SHAFT SECTION

REAR AXLE ASSEMBLY

A hypoid type drive is used to transmit power to the rear wheels. The axle is the ¾ floating carrier type. The differential carrier housing is the pedestal type, attached to the rear axle housing and removed as a unit.

LUBRICATION

The correct lubrication of the rear axle is of primary importance. It is essential not to overfill the rear axle with lubricant; consequently, after refilling, allow the excess lubricant to drain out of the filler hole before the plug is replaced. The filler plug is located in the differential gear carrier and the drain plug in the bottom of the case.

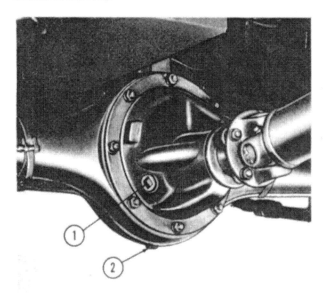

| 1. Filler Plug | 2. Drain Plug |

FIGURE 1—*Rear Axle Drain and Filler Plug Locations*

On a new car, the lubricant should be drained and refilled at 500 miles and subsequently every 6,000 miles. Do not, under any circumstances, mix various brands of lubricants. Use SAE 90 hypoid rear axle Lubricant. Oil capacity — 2¼ Pints (U.S.).

AXLE SHAFT REMOVAL

Jack up the car; remove the wheel.

Drain the axle prior to removing the axle shaft as this will prevent oil from leaking on the brake linings when the axle shaft is withdrawn.

Release the hand brake and make certain the linings are not binding on the drum.

Remove the drum locating screws. The drum can then be tapped off the hub.

Remove the axle shaft retaining screw which is exposed when the drum is removed, and pull out the axle shaft. The flange of the axle shaft may be tight on the studs; then it becomes necessary to pry it loose from the studs.

NOTE: *In all cases of axle shaft removal, install a new gasket between the hub and flange of the axle shaft upon reassembly.*

FIGURE 2—*Axle Shaft Removed*

REAR WHEEL HUB REMOVAL

Remove the wheel, drum, and axle shaft. The hub and bearing retaining nut is now accessible. This nut is locked in position by a keyed lock which is hammered down onto one of the flats of the nut.

Remove the hub with a bearing puller (Fig. 3). Be certain that the pilot of the puller used on the housing tube will clear the inner race of the bearing when removing the hub.

FIGURE 3—*Removing Rear Wheel Hub*

The hub, ball bearing, and oil seal are removed as a unit.

The bearing and seal can be tapped out of the hub with the aid of a soft drift.

REAR WHEEL HUB ASSEMBLY

If the oil seal has been removed or is being replaced, use a drift to install the new seal into position (lip towards the bearing) before the bearing is installed.

The hub ball bearing, which is not adjustable, is installed with the aid of a soft drift.

It is essential that the face of the outer race protrudes .001" to .004" beyond the face of the hub with the rear wheel hub gasket in place when the bearing is pressed in the hub. This insures that the bearing is definitely placed between the shoulder abutment in the hub and the flange of the axle shaft.

At time of assembly, the bearings and hubs should be packed with a high grade wheel bearing lubricant even though they receive some axle lubricant during operation.

Tool J-2995, Transmission Clutch Shaft Snap Ring Installer, can be used to install the rear wheel hub in position on the axle housing (Fig. 4).

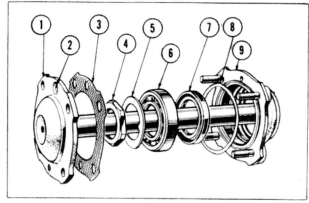

1. Axle Shaft
2. Axle Shaft to Hub Retaining Screw Hole Location
3. Gasket
4. Nut
5. Lock
6. Hub Bearing
7. Oil Seal
8. "O" Ring
9. Hub

FIGURE 5—*Rear Wheel Hub Assembly*

Remove the differential carrier from the axle housing (Fig. 6).

1. Differential Case to Axle Housing Studs

FIGURE 6—*Differential Carrier Housing Assembly in Rear Axle Housing*

Disassembly of Differential Carrier Assembly

The bearing caps are bored in position; therefore, note the number marked on the cap and housing half of the bearing seat to insure reassembling in exactly the same positions (Fig. 7).

The differential case assembly can be lifted or pried out of the differential carrier after the side bearing caps have been removed.

Measure total thickness of shims located behind the bearings for reference in reassembly. This amount has been established at the factory to provide a bearing preload of .002" and must not be disturbed.

FIGURE 4—*Installing Rear Wheel Hub With Tool J-2995*

REAR AXLE DISASSEMBLY

The differential gear carrier can be removed for service with the axle housing in place on the car.

Raise and support the rear of the body.

Remove the drain plug at the bottom of the axle housing and drain lubricant.

Remove the wheels, brake drums, and axle shafts.

Remove or disconnect the propeller shaft.

FIGURE 7—*Differential Bearing Cap Marks*

Pulling the Differential Side Bearings

A puller is used to remove the side bearing from the differential case (Fig. 8). When using this tool, be sure it pulls on the inner bearing race in such a manner that the rollers are free. If the puller bears on the roller cage, it will damage the bearing. Two recesses 180° apart are on the case to allow the claws of the tool to engage the inner race.

Removing the Ring Gear

Remove the cap screws that attach the ring gear to the differential case.

It is a good practice to mark the ring gear and case to retain the same location at reassembly.

Tap the ring gear from the case using a brass drift. Do not nick the ring gear face of the differential case (Fig. 9).

Removing the Differential Pinion Gears and Shaft

Use a drift 1/8″ in diameter at least 3″ long to drive out the lock pin that holds the differential pinion shaft in place (Fig. 10).

FIGURE 8—*Pulling Differential Side Bearing*

The pinion shaft can then be driven out with a brass drift.

Roll the differential pinion gears and thrust washers around on the side gears until they can be lifted out through the holes in the case. Then lift out the side gears (Fig. 11).

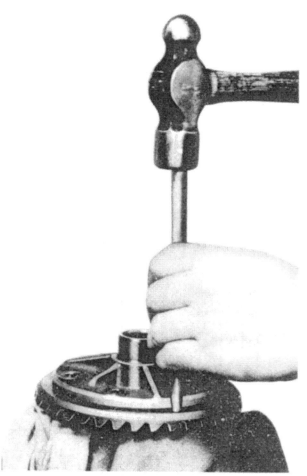

FIGURE 9—Tap the Ring Gear off the Differential Case with a Brass Drift

FIGURE 11—Removing the Differential Pinion and Side Gears

Removal of Rear Axle Companion Flange

Remove the rear axle companion flange nut.

Use a fibre hammer and tap gently to remove the companion flange from the drive pinion shaft.

Remove the oil seal.

Removal of Pinion Gear and Bearings

Tap the end of the pinion gear shaft lightly with a fibre hammer to free the front bearing cone from the shaft and remove the bearing (Fig. 12).

The pinion gear and rear bearing may be removed to the rear of the housing. Note the shims and pinion spacer. The shims determine the pinion bearing preload. The preload is adjusted at time of reassembly.

Removing Front and Rear Pinion Gear Bearing Cups

Use Tools J-5691-12 Front Pinion Bearing Cup Remover and J-5691-14 Rear Pinion Bearing Cup Remover installed on driver handle Tool J-872-5 to remove front and rear bearing cups as shown in Figure 13.

Removing Pinion Gear Rear Bearing

Use Tool J-358-1 with adapter plate J-5550 to remove the rear pinion bearing from the pinion shaft (Fig. 16).

FIGURE 10—The Pinion Shaft Lock Pin Being Driven Out of the Differential Case

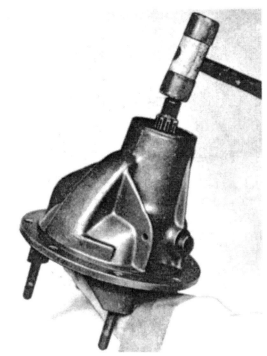

FIGURE 12—*Removing Pinion Shaft and Bearing*

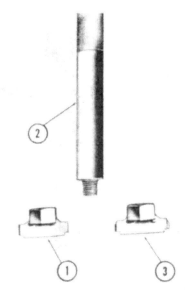

1. Front Pinion Bearing
   Cup Remover,
   J-5691-12
2. Driver Handle Tool
   J-872-5
3. Rear Pinion
   Bearing Cup
   Remover, J-5691-14

FIGURE 14—*Front and Rear Bearing Pinion Cup Remover*

FIGURE 13—*Removing Front Pinion Bearing Cup*

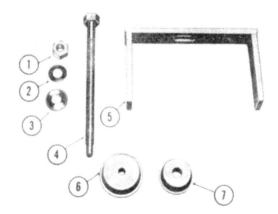

1. Nut
2. Washer
3. Thrust Bushing
4. Jack Screw J-5559-5
5. Bridge
6. Pinion Rear Bearing Cup Installer J-5559-10
7. Pinion Front Bearing Cup Installer J-5559-11

FIGURE 15—*Tool J-5559 Main Bearing Cap and Pinion Bearing Cup Remover and Installer*

INSPECTING DIFFERENTIAL PARTS

The Differential Pinion Shaft

Whenever one rear wheel is stuck and the other is spinning, the differential pinion shaft is subjected to strain. Inspect this shaft for scoring or other signs of wear.

The Differential Pinion Gears

Inspect the teeth of these gears for excessive wear or chipping. Fit a differential pinion shaft into the gear to check the hole for out-of-round or wear. Discard the thrust washers. New ones should be used during assembly.

The Differential Side Gears

Inspect side gears for worn, cracked, or chipped teeth. The gear should be a snug fit on the axle shaft

FIGURE 16—*Removing Rear Pinion Bearing With Tool J-358-1 and Plate J-5550*

FIGURE 17—*Ring and Pinion Gear Matched Set*

spline. Also inspect the fit of the side gear in the differential case bore. If any of the gears need replacement, pinion and side gears should be replaced as a set.

The Differential Case

Inspect side bearing surfaces for nicks or burrs. Small nicks or burrs may be dressed down with a stone or smooth file.

The Ring and Pinion Gears

Inspect the teeth of these gears for wear, cracks, or chipping. Then examine the tooth contact pattern to determine if the ring gear has been meshing correctly with the pinion gear.

If the tooth pattern indicates that the gears have not been meshing correctly, both should be replaced because it is impossible to adjust worn gears for quiet operation.

Whenever replacement of either gear is necessary, always replace both gears. These gears are run-in and lapped together at the factory as matched sets.

Inspect the ring gear attaching screws for elongation resulting from excessive tightening and replace any screws that are elongated.

The pinion and ring gears should be inspected to determine if they are a matched set. Numbers or marks are etched on the rear face of the pinion gear and the rear face of the ring gear (Fig. 17).

Pinion Bearings

Inspect pinion bearings, cones, cups, and rollers for excessive wear, over-heating, or scoring. If replacement is required, replace both the cone and the cup.

Inspection of Rear Axle Housing

The housing should be inspected for cracks, burrs, deep scratches, or nicks on the gasket or oil seal areas. A stone or smooth file can be used to remove nicks or burrs.

The bearing cup bores should be carefully inspected for burrs or nicks caused by bearing cup removal.

ASSEMBLING THE REAR AXLE

To insure a uniform method of adjusting rear axles, all specifications for correct adjustment are established on the basis of dry parts.

Assembling the Differential Gears

Install the side gears in the bores of the differential case.

Install the thrust washers behind the differential pinion gears and mesh the gears with the side gears so the holes are opposite and in line with each other (Fig. 18).

Roll the gears around until the gear holes are aligned with the differential pinion shaft hole in the case.

The pinion shaft is installed with the lock pin hole in line with the lock pin hole in the differential case.

Installing the Ring Gear

Prior to installing the ring gear, both the gear and the case should be inspected for nicks, burrs, grit, or particles that may prevent the ring gear from seating properly on the case.

FIGURE 18—*Installing Differential Side and Pinion Gears*

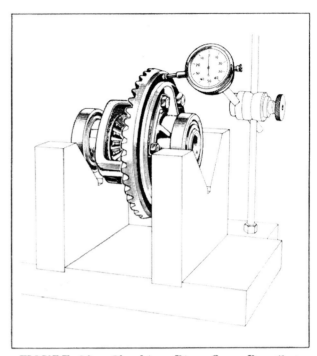

FIGURE 19—*Checking Ring Gear Run-Out*

Place the ring gear on the differential case; if using the same gear, align the marks to retain its original location.

Attach the ring gear to the case using a diagonal pattern in tightening the cap screws to 28-30 foot pounds torque.

At this point, the ring gear should be checked for alignment. Place the differential case with the ring gear mounted (torqued down) and bearings installed on a pair of vee blocks or the differential carrier. With the bearings setting in the vee blocks, the differential case can be rotated and the readings taken on the face of the ring gear with a dial indicator. The run-out should not exceed .002". If the run-out exceeds .002", the face of the case should be checked and if the run-out still exists, the case should be replaced. If the ring gear retains the run-out, the ring and pinion gears must be replaced as a set. Figure 19 outlines one method of checking run-out.

Lock the cap screws with the lock plates.

Installing Differential Side Bearings

Replace the original shim packs under their respective bearings.

The differential side bearing can be installed by using Tool J-2995, Clutch Shaft Snap Ring Installer. (Fig. 20). The side of the bearing marked "Thrust" is to be located towards the outside of the case.

In manufacturing a tolerance of the bearing housings is adjusted to give a .002" preload on the differential side bearings. This was done with the shims marked for reference in disassembly. Replace shims or new shims of same total.

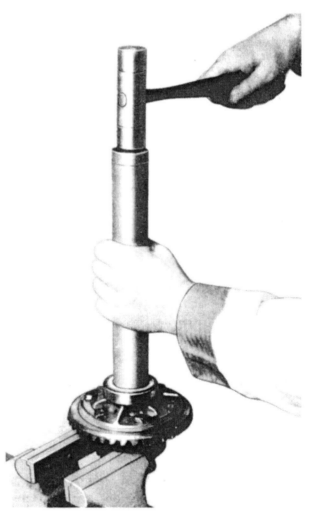

FIGURE 20—*Replacing Differential Side Bearings With Tool J-2995*

REAR AXLE AND PROPELLER SHAFT SECTION

Installing the Pinion Bearing Cups

The pinion bearing cups can be installed with Tool J-5559, Pinion Bearing Cup Remover and Installer. (Fig. 21).

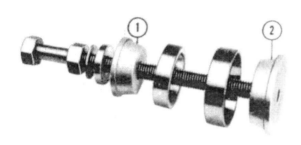

1. J-5559-2 Front Bearing Cup Installer
2. J-5559-1 Rear Bearing Cup Installer

FIGURE 21—*Tool J-5559 Pinion Bearing Cup Installer*

Center the rear cup in its bore and use J-5559-1, Rear Pinion Bearing Installer, which will seat in the inner angle of the cup. Center the front cup in its bore and insert the front pinion cup installer J-5559-2 into the inner angle of the cup. The cups can now be drawn into their respective bores to the cup shoulders. The cups should draw down straight due to the design of the tool which centers itself as the cups are drawn down.

FIGURE 22—*Installing Front and Rear Pinion Bearing Cups Using Tool J-5559*

Both pinion bearing cups should be fully installed and perfectly square against their respective shoulders in the housing.

PINION DEPTH ADJUSTMENT

To compensate for machining tolerances, the pinion and ring gear are tested at a standard cone setting and varied to attain the correct tooth contact pattern and quietness. The amount of this variation is etched on the rear face of the pinion gear as shown in Figure 17.

The pinion is marked either "zero", "plus", or "minus" the number of thousandths that the gear varies above or below standard. Thus the "plus" (+) figure means the pinion gear is farther from the center line of the axle than the standard and the "minus" (—) means closer to the center line.

When using a new ring and pinion set or a new rear pinion bearing, use a new adjusting washer. Adjusting washers are available from .116" to .130" in .002" variations.

Two methods of determining the correct thickness of the adjusting washer may be used.

Method No. 1

Rear axle drive pinion gauge J-2499 with bearing bore adapters and gauge point to fit this axle, makes selection of the correct adjusting washer a positive process (Fig. 23).

FIGURE 23—*Rear Axle Pinion Setting Gauge*

Place the rear pinion bearing cone in the bearing cup. Press the cone and revolve it to "set" the rollers.

Bolt the gauge plate over the bearing cone so it does not touch the housing at any point. The bolt runs down through the bearing and is secured at the pinion end of the housing by a cross piece and thumb screw.

Attach a dial indicator to the tool as shown. With

the indicator button on top of the gauge pin, set the dial indicator under tension at zero.

Install the tool with the adaptors squarely seated in the side bearing bores in the housing.

Swing the gauge point across the plate until the highest reading is obtained. This reading subtracted from the constant of .140″ will give the standard adjusting washer thickness for that housing.

Using this figure, add or subtract according to the marking on the pinion to determine the correct adjusting washer.

For example: When the gauge point is moved across the plate, a reading of .014″ is obtained; subtracting this figure from .140″ will give a standard of .126″.

That means using a standard "O" pinion, an adjusting washer of .126″ thickness would be required.

However, if the pinion marking reads minus two, then the pinion is .002″ too close to the ring gear center line. The .002″ must then be subtracted from the .126″ which would mean an adjusting washer of .124″ thickness is required.

Method No. 2

Rear Axle Drive Pinion Gauge J-5223 with bearing bore adapters to fit this axle may also be used.

Install front and rear bearing cups in the housing using the method previously outlined.

The thickness of the pinion depth washer is determined by the size of the washer removed on disassembly and in addition the plus or minus figure etched on the pinion. For example, if the original pinion was marked +2 and had a washer .124″ thick and the new pinion to be installed was marked −2, the new washer to be installed should be .120″ thick to bring the new pinion to its correct position.

Assemble the pinion depth adjusting washer selected as outlined above on the pinion shaft. Install pinion bearings, spacer, and pinion bearing preload shims on the pinion shaft as outlined in the following sections "Pinion Bearing Installation" and "Preloading Pinion Bearings." The bearings should be coated with rear axle lubricant.

Be certain the differential bearing bores in housing are clean. Mount discs of Pinion Setting Gauge J-5223 on gauge arbor and install gauge in housing bores (Fig. 24). Install differential bearing caps and tighten nuts finger tight.

The gauge block is held in place against the rear face of the pinion by the clamp screw. The gauge plunger pad can be moved to contact the gauge arbor by loosening the thumb screw in the end of the gauge block. After a clean contact is made, tighten the thumb screw.

Remove the gauge block. Use a two to three inch

FIGURE 24—Rear Axle Pinion Setting Gauge J-5223

FIGURE 25—Measuring Distance from Rear Face of Pinion Gear to Rear Axle Center Line

micrometer and measure the distance from end of anvil to top of plunger head as shown in Figure 25. This measurement represents the distance from the rear face of the pinion to the center line of the rear axle. This measurement should be 2.20″ for a correctly adjusted pinion with a zero "O" marking. A pinion marked +2, the measurement should be .002″ greater, or if marked −2, the measurement should be .002″ less.

If the micrometer reading shows the pinion setting is incorrect in relation to the given figures determined by use of the gauge set, the correct pinion depth adjusting washer must be installed. The washer previously selected must be removed and the newly determined washer installed.

Method No. 3

Note the inspection marks on the old and new pinion gears and measure the thickness of the old depth washer. Compare the inspection mark on the new pinion and use a depth washer to compensate for the difference.

For example: If the old pinion is marked minus two and the new pinion is marked plus two, there is a difference of .004″ in these two pinions. Therefore, the new depth washer must be .004″ thicker than the old one. If the old washer is .124″, the new one must be .128″.

Pinion Bearing Installation

Install the pinion depth adjusting washer on the pinion shaft next to the pinion gear.

Slide the large diameter of the bearing towards the teeth of the pinion gear. Use a length of suitable inside and outside diameter pipe and press the bearing tight against the gear.

Preloading Pinion Bearings

Rear axle pinion bearings are preloaded to compensate for expansion due to heat and loads of operation.

The preload is adjusted by selective shims installed between the front bearing and the spacer. The shims are available in .003″, .005″, .010″ and .020″ thicknesses.

Slide the spacer and the shims removed at time of disassembly on the pinion shaft.

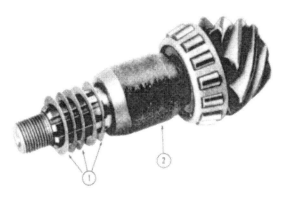

| 1. **Preload Shims** | 2. **Spacer** |

FIGURE 26—*Pinion Gear Assembly*

The pinion gear, bearing, spacer, and shims can be installed from the rear of the housing and the front bearing tapped into position from the front of the housing.

The propeller shaft companion flange can now be installed on the pinion shaft. Use a fibre hammer to gently tap the flange on the splines until it is possible to install the washer and pinion nut.

Do not install the oil seal prior to checking bearing preload. Tighten the pinion nut 140 to 150 foot pounds torque.

A tee handle wrench, socket, and a spring scale can be used to determine the amount of pinion bearing preload. The spring scale is attached to the tee handle at a distance of four inches from the center of the pinion shaft. Pull on the spring scale (Fig. 27), and note the reading in pounds on the scale as the pinion starts to move and multiply by four. This determines the number of inch pounds needed to turn the shaft. The specified pinion bearing preload is twelve to fourteen inch pounds. Three pound pull at four inches would indicate twelve inch pounds of preload. To eliminate the effect of gravity, turn the assembly so that the pulling effort is on a horizontal plane.

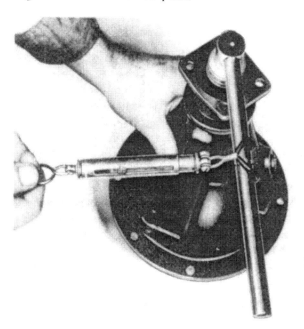

FIGURE 27—*Checking Pinion Bearing Preload*

Adjustment is affected by inserting or removing shims between the pinion bearing spacer and the front pinion bearing. Reduce or increase the degree of preloading till finally a drag of twelve to fourteen inch pounds is obtained.

Remove the propeller shaft companion flange as previously outlined; install the pinion oil seal which was excluded during the pinion bearing preload check. Replace the rear axle companion flange and tighten the companion flange nut 140 to 150 foot pounds torque.

Installing the Differential Assembly Into Carrier

Replace the differential assembly with the differential side bearings installed into the carrier and replace the bearing caps. The bearing caps are stamped on one side, and when fitting, this stamp should be on the same side as a corresponding stamp on the leg of the fixed bearing housing. This is extremely important as each bearing housing is machined with the cap in position.

The bearing caps must be correctly seated and the differential side bearings a tight fit in their respective housings. In all cases, tighten the bearing cap stud nuts to 50-55 foot pounds torque.

Adjusting Ring Gear and Pinion Back Lash

Back lash between the mesh of the ring gear and pinion should be between .005″ to .008″. The recommended amount of back lash is etched on the back face of the ring gear, for example: .008″ shown in Figure 17.

Measure the back lash by using a dial indicator against a tooth of the ring gear (Fig. 28). If the back lash is found to be too great or too small, adjustment may be affected by moving one or more shims from one side to the other. The shims are located behind the differential bearings (Fig. 29). The differential and bearings will have to be moved from the carrier each time the shims are transferred. Replace the unit and check the back lash each time the shims are moved.

Do not add or subtract any shims since a preload of .002″ was established at the factory. Shift shims from one side to the other until the recommended back lash is attained.

Inspecting and Adjusting Tooth Contact Pattern

Ideal tooth contact pattern is shown in Item A, Figure 30, where the mark is evenly spread over the profile and slightly nearer the toe than heel.

Paint eight or ten of the ring gear teeth with a light coat of red lead in oil.

Turn the ring gear until the painted section of the ring gear is in contact with the pinion gear. Turn the pinion while applying pressure to the ring either by a screw driver or drift between the ring gear and case. This causes the two gears to turn under load and impresses a pattern on the painted section of the ring gear (Fig. 30). This is the tooth contact pattern.

If all adjustments are correct, the tooth contact pattern will be distributed over the central part of the tooth as in Figure 30-A.

If the pattern is high on the ring gear, as in Figure 30-B, it means the pinion is too far from the ring gear. In that case, move the pinion toward the ring gear by placing a thicker washer between the pinion gear and bearing.

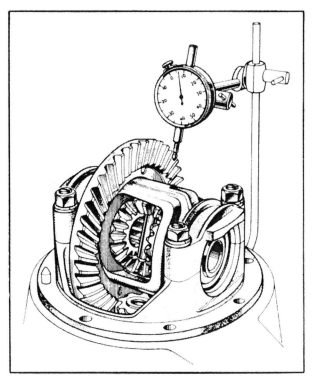

FIGURE 28—*Method Used to Check Ring and Pinion Gear Back Lash*

FIGURE 29—*Differential Side Bearing Shim Location Used to Adjust Back Lash*

If the pattern is low on the ring gear tooth, as in Figure 30-C, the pinion is too close to the ring gear. Then move the pinion away from the ring gear by placing a thinner washer between the pinion gear and bearing.

If the pattern is toward the small end or "toe" of the tooth, as in Figure 30-D, the ring gear is too close to the pinion. In that case, move the ring gear away from the pinion by putting a thinner shim on the left side and a thicker shim on the right.

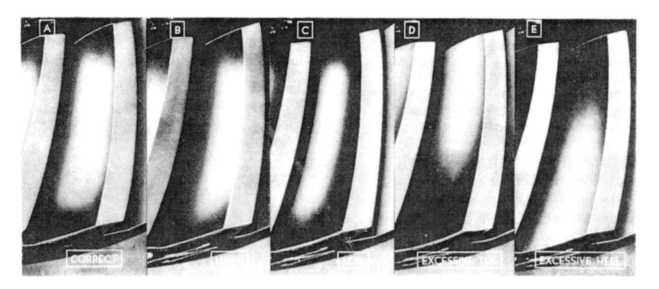

FIGURE 30—*Tooth Contact Patterns*

If the pattern is at the large end or "heel" of the tooth, as in Figure 30-E, the ring gear is too far from the pinion. Then move the ring gear toward the pinion by putting a thinner shim on the right side and a thicker shim on the left side.

When making toe or heel adjustments, be sure to keep the same total thickness of shims at the side bearings.

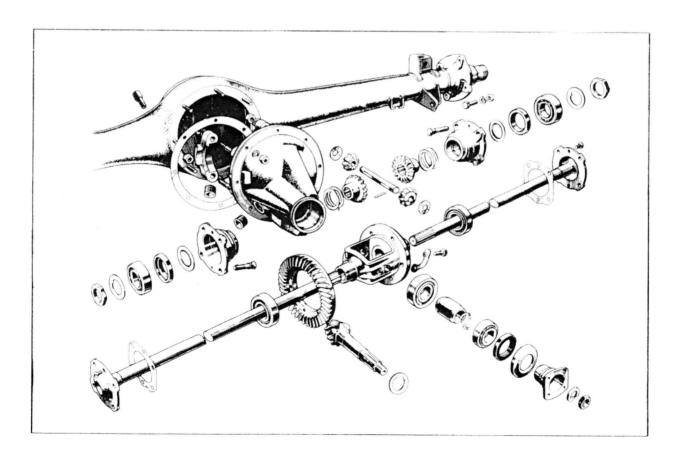

FIGURE 31—*Rear Axle Exploded View*

Replacing the Differential Carrier

Install a new gasket and replace the differential carrier in the rear axle housing. Tighten the nuts to the specified torque of 30 foot pounds.

Bolt the propeller shaft and companion flanges together and turn over the lock plate ends.

Install the axle shafts, brake drums, and wheels.

REMOVAL OF THE COMPLETE AXLE ASSEMBLY

Release the hand brake; disconnect the brake cable at the balance lever and the brake hose at the tee fitting.

Remove the propeller shaft bolts at the companion flange and disconnect the shock absorbers.

Remove the nuts under the spring retaining plate. These nuts screw onto the ends of the "U" bolts which hold the axle to the spring. Remove the "U" bolts. The complete axle unit can be removed.

REPLACING THE AXLE ASSEMBLY

Install the rear axle assembly indexing the center spring bolt with the axle spring bracket locating hole.

Install the "U" bolts, and connect the brake cable to the balance lever.

Install shock absorbers.

Connect the propeller shaft to pinion shaft.

Connect the brake hose and bleed brakes.

FIGURE 32—*Removing Complete Axle Assembly*

PROPELLER SHAFT

Description

The fore and aft movement of the rear axle is permitted by a sliding spline between the tubular propeller shaft and transmission main shaft.

The spline which slides onto the transmission main shaft is internal on the front yoke of the front universal joint (Fig. 33).

A dust cover on the forward end of the propeller shaft slides inside the dust cover on the rear of the transmission. Each universal joint consists of a cross, four needle roller bearings, and two yokes.

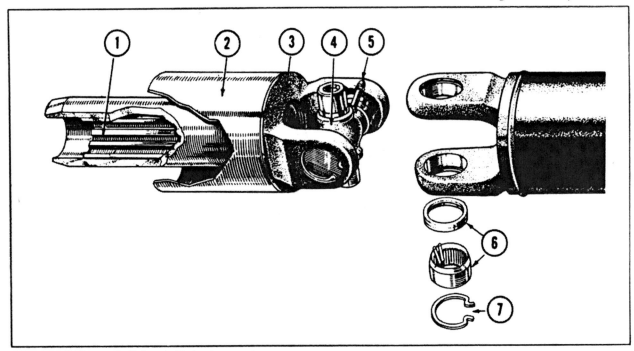

1. Internal Splined End of Propeller Shaft
2. Dust Cover
3. Front Yoke
4. Cross
5. Oil Nipple
6. Needle Bearing and Cup Assembly
7. Snap Ring

FIGURE 33—*Propeller Shaft and Universal Joint*

FIGURE 34—*Oil Chambers in the Cross of the Universal Joint*

Lubrication

An oil nipple is fitted to each cross of the universal joints to provide lubrication of the bearings (Fig. 33).

Do not use grease or chassis lubricant. Only Rear Axle Lubricant should be used. Figure 34 shows that the central oil chamber is connected to the four oil reservoirs and to the needle roller bearing assemblies. Lubricate at 10,000 mile intervals; use hand gun only.

Transmission oil lubricates the sliding splined joint between the propeller shaft and transmission. Before refitting the propeller shaft to the transmission, apply transmission lubricant to the splines.

Propeller Shaft Removal

Jack up the car. Remove the four bolts that attach the propeller shaft to the rear axle companion flange. This is shown in Figure 1.

Slide the propeller shaft forward on the spline of the transmission main shaft to allow the propeller shaft to be lowered and removed to the rear (Fig. 35).

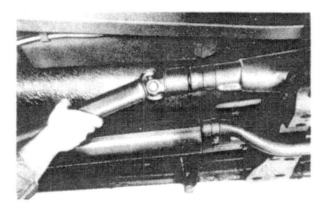

FIGURE 35—*Propeller Shaft Being Removed*

Disassembly of Universal Joint

Clean the area around the snap rings and bearing faces. Remove the snap rings by pressing the ends together and extracting them from the groove with a screw driver. If the rings do not come out easily, tap the bearing face to relieve the pressure against the ring.

Hold the shaft in one hand and tap the radius of the yoke with a lead or soft hammer. Turn the yoke over and extract the bearing.

To remove the yoke and cross, repeat the operation on the other bearings.

Inspection of Universal Joint

Should looseness or stress marks be observed in the bearing cases or cross journals, the universal joint should be replaced as no over-size journal or bearings are available.

The cup bearing races are a light drive fit on the yoke trunnions. The yokes should be replaced if the trunnion bearing holes are egg-shaped.

Replacing the Universal Joints and Yokes

Clean all drill holes in the journals of the cross and fill with rear axle lubricant. Spread lubriplate in the walls of the bearing race and install the needle rollers in place.

Install the cross in the yoke. Use a soft-nosed drift and tap the bearing in position. The bearings are a light drive fit in the yoke trunnions. The same operation is repeated for the other three bearings. The cross journal shoulders should be coated with gasket paste prior to installing the cork seal retainers to insure a good seal. Install snap rings in grooves.

If the joint appears to bind, tap lightly with a soft hammer to relieve any pressure of the bearings on the ends of the journals. All cork seals and retainers should be replaced upon rebuilding the universal joints.

Replacing the Propeller Shaft

Apply transmission lubricant on the propeller shaft, transmission main shaft, and transmission oil seal. Slide the propeller shaft onto the transmission main shaft.

The dust cover of the propeller shaft should fit inside the dust cover on the rear of the transmission.

Make sure the rear axle companion flange and yoke flange on the propeller shaft are clean to insure pilot indexing properly.

FIGURE 36—*Rear Spring Assembly Sequence*

SPRINGS

Coil springs are used in the front suspension and semi-elliptic in the rear. The rear springs when normally loaded form an inverse arch. Road noise transmission is minimized by insulating the springs from the body with rubber cushions and bushings.

Removing the Rear Springs

Raise and support the rear of the body.

Remove the rear spring clips from the axle tubes. Then remove the front bracket and the rear shackle from the body side sill.

SHOCK ABSORBERS

All shock absorbers, front and rear, are the direct acting, telescoping type. The end mountings are retained in rubber grommets.

The rear shock absorbers have an eye type lower mounting and a bayonet type upper mounting (Fig. 37).

All shock absorber mountings utilize a step shoulder to prevent over tightening the rubber grommets or bushings.

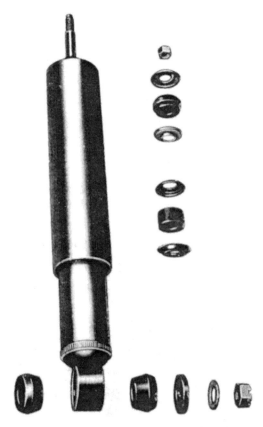

FIGURE 37—*Rear Shock Absorber Assembly Sequence*

REAR AXLE AND PROPELLER SHAFT SECTION

REAR AXLE TORQUE CHART

Description	Recommended Torque (All Parts Clean and Dry)
Ring Gear to Case Screw	28-30 Foot Pounds
Differential Bearing Cap Screw	50-55 Foot Pounds
Drive Pinion Nut	140-150 Foot Pounds
Drum to Hub Nut	40 Foot Pounds
Rear Brake Support Plate Screw Nut	22-28 Foot Pounds
Rear Wheel Hub to Axle Housing Tube Nut	125 Foot Pounds
Propeller Shaft Companion Flange Screw Nut	16-20 Foot Pounds
Differential Carrier to Axle Housing Stud Nut	30 Foot Pounds

REAR AXLE SPECIFICATIONS

Type	3 4 Floating, Unit Type
Drive Gear	Hypoid
Ring Gear and Pinion Back Lash	.005" to .008"
Ring Gear and Pinion Back Lash Adjustment	Shims
Pinion Shaft Bearing Tension	12-14 Inch Lbs.
Pinion Bearing Tension Adjustment	Shims
Differential Side Bearing Preload	Established in Machining Tolerance at .002"
Lubrication Capacity	2¼ Pts. (U.S.)
Type of Lubricant*	SAE 90 Hypoid
Rear Axle Ratio	4.55:1 (8.37) Model 540 to Serial Number E-11001
	4.55:1 (9-41) Model 540 beginning with Serial Number E-11001, also Model 560 to Serial Number E-26993
	4.22:1 (9.38) Model 560 beginning with Serial Number E-26993

*NOTE: DRAIN, FLUSH, AND REFILL AT 500 MILES ON NEW UNIT; EVERY 6,000 MILES THEREAFTER.

SPRING SPECIFICATIONS

Rear (Five Leaf)

Loaded Height — Top of main leaf 3/32" above the center line of the front and rear eyes at 422# when installed on axle tubes.

Rate Lbs. Per Inch

After Loaded

Height — 95# plus or minus 5# installed.

Technical Service Manual

Front Suspension-
Steering Gear

FRONT SUSPENSION STEERING GEAR SECTION

FRONT SUSPENSION

The front suspension is an independent linked parallelogram type. The left and right assemblies may be removed and serviced individually.

FIGURE 1—*Front Suspension Assembly (Right Side)*

FRONT COIL SPRING

Each front coil spring is located between the upper end of the steering knuckle pin and a seat in the wheelhouse panel.

Transmission of road noise through the front suspension coil springs is minimized by insulating the springs from the body with rubber cushions (Fig. 2).

Removing the Front Spring

Raise the front end of the car and support it at the body side sills.

Install *two* front coil spring compressors Tool KMO-735 or J-8081 enclosing nine coils. Compress the spring evenly until it may be removed from the car (Fig. 3).

FIGURE 3—*Removing the Front Spring Using Spring Compressor Set*

Installing the Front Spring

Install the spring compressors KMO-735 or J-8081 and compress the spring.

Assemble the spring cushions and seats on the spring and position the spring on the upper seat of the knuckle pin.

FIGURE 2—*Front Spring Assembly Sequence*

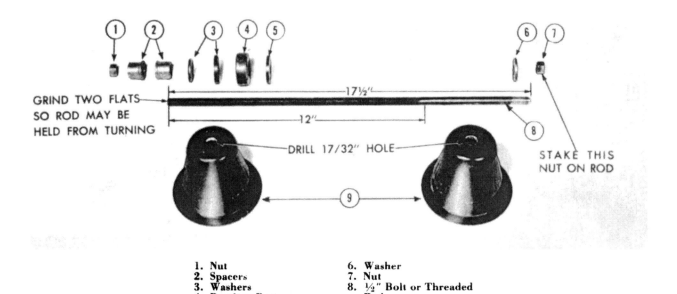

GRIND TWO FLATS
SO ROD MAY BE
HELD FROM TURNING

17½"

12"

DRILL 17/32" HOLE

STAKE THIS
NUT ON ROD

1. Nut
2. Spacers
3. Washers
4. Bearing, Part
   No. 17681
5. Washer

6. Washer
7. Nut
8. ½" Bolt or Threaded
   Rod
9. Upper Spring Seats,
   Part No. 3129499

**FIGURE 4—A Spring Compressor Tool
May Be Fabricated from These Parts**

CAUTION: *Lip of the spring seat must engage the knuckle pin seat to prevent the spring from slipping out of position.*

The spring may be compressed for installation or removal of the spring compressor tool with two upper springs seats, a ½" bolt or threaded rod, and other miscellaneous items shown in Figure 4.

SHOCK ABSORBERS

The shock absorbers are the direct acting, telescoping type. The end mountings of the shock absorbers are retained in rubber grommets.

The front shock absorber mounting is illustrated in Figure 1 and the assembly sequence is detailed in Figure 5.

The shock absorber bayonets utilize a step shoulder to prevent over tightening the rubber grommets or bushings.

UPPER AND LOWER CONTROL ARMS

The upper and lower control arms are complete assemblies. The inner ends of the control arms are attached to the mounting bracket with special bolts.

The control arms are insulated from the mounting brackets by rubber bushings installed in the sleeves of the control arms.

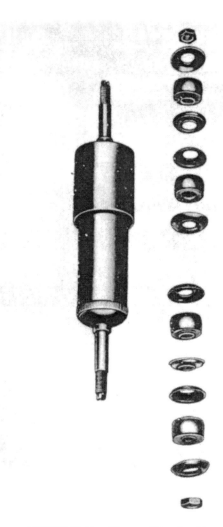

**FIGURE 5—Front Shock Absorber
Assembly Sequence**

The upper control arm is attached to the steering knuckle pin with a threaded pin (Fig. 6).

FIGURE 6—*Upper Control Arm Assembly Sequence*

The lower control arm is attached to the lower trunnion with a threaded pin (Fig. 7).

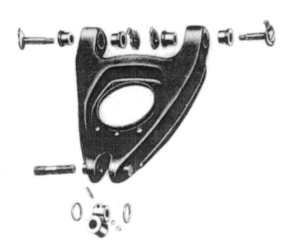

FIGURE 7—*Lower Control Arm Assembly Sequence*

Removing the Control Arms

Remove the wheel and spring; disconnect the tie rod from the steering arm and the shock absorber at the lower mounting. Then remove the two lower control arm mounting bolts. The front and rear rubber bushings are then removed through the large mounting bolt holes in the mounting bracket.

The nut on the lower end of the knuckle pin should then be removed.

Support the wheel spindle to prevent damage to the brake hose, and slide the lower control arm trunnion off of the knuckle pin.

The lower control arm may then be removed from the car.

The upper control arm is removed in the same manner as the lower. However, it is necessary to remove the wheel spindle and hang it in a position that will not damage the brake hose.

When reinstalling the control arms, application of lubriplate on the mounting bolt bushing area of the bracket will facilitate installation of control arms.

Install one side of the control arm; then using a large screw driver, pry against the control arm as shown in Figure 8 to compress the bushing. The remaining side may then be slipped into position.

NOTE: *Leaving the control arm mounting bolts loose will be of assistance in assembling the wheel spindle and lower trunnion on the knuckle pin.*

FIGURE 8—*Installing the Lower Control Arm*

Removing the Lower Trunnion From the Control Arms

The trunnion pin is locked in position by a tapered pin. Remove the nut from the lock pin and drive the pin out of the trunnion (Figs. 9 and 10).

The grease fitting on the trunnion end of the control arm must be removed to permit unscrewing the trunnion pin (Figs. 11 and 12).

When installing the trunnion pin, the cut-out on the pin must be aligned with the lock pin hole.

If a new trunnion pin is a loose fit in the control arm, the control arm should be replaced as the bushings are welded into place and the threads are then cut to insure correct alignment.

FRONT SUSPENSION STEERING GEAR

FIGURE 9—*Lock Nut for Trunnion Lock Pin*

FIGURE 11—*Removing Grease Fitting for Access to the Trunnion Pin*

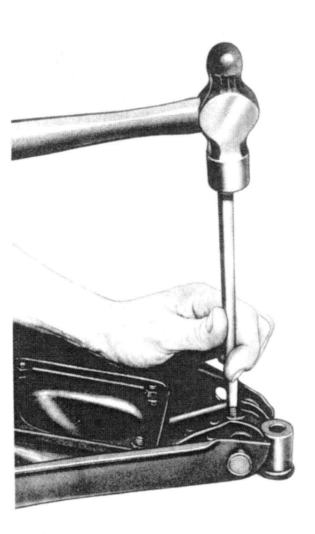

FIGURE 10—*Removing Trunnion Lock Pin*

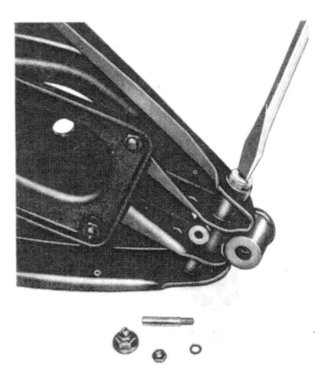

FIGURE 12—*Removing the Trunnion Pin*

STEERING KNUCKLE PIN AND SPINDLE

The steering knuckle pin incorporates the upper trunnion as an integral part. The knuckle pin is retained in the lower trunnion with a castellated nut.

The end play of the spindle is controlled by selective shims located between the lower end of the spindle and the lower trunnion (Fig. 13).

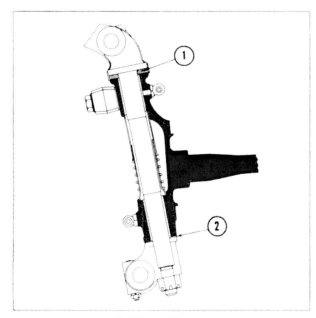

1. Thrust Washer
2. Selective Shim

FIGURE 13—*Sectional View of Knuckle Pin Assembly*

Two bronze knuckle pin bushings are pressed into the spindle to control the side play of the spindle.

A spring loaded telescoping type dust shield protects the knuckle pin from normal road dirt.

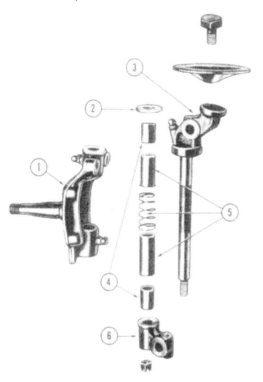

1. Spindle
2. Thrust Washer
3. Knuckle Pin
4. Upper and Lower Bushings
5. Dust Shield Assembly
6. Lower Trunnion

FIGURE 14—*Steering Knuckle Pin and Wheel Spindle Assembly Sequence*

Removing the Wheel Spindle

Remove the wheel, front spring, hub, and brake support plate. Disconnect the tie rod from the steering arm, and the shock absorber at the lower mounting.

Disconnect the lower control arm trunnion from the knuckle pin (Fig. 15).

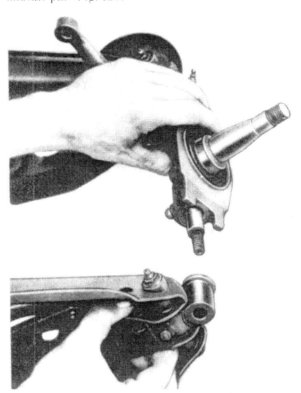

FIGURE 15—*Removing Lower Control Arm Trunnion From the Knuckle Pin*

The wheel spindle may now be slipped off of the knuckle pin (Fig. 16).

FIGURE 16—*Removing Wheel Spindle From the Knuckle Pin*

FRONT SUSPENSION STEERING GEAR

The thrust washer located between the top of the wheel spindle and the knuckle pin should be installed with the oil grooves up (Fig. 17).

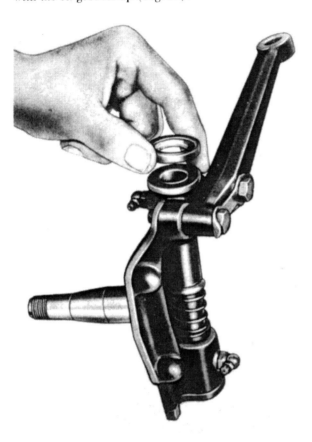

FIGURE 17—*Installing the Spindle Thrust Washer (Grooves Up)*

Selective shims installed between the lower shoulder of the spindle and the lower trunnion control the end play of the knuckle pin. These shims are supplied in .002″, .005″ and .010″ thicknesses.

These sizes will provide a range of adjustment to eliminate or minimize the end play of the spindle on the knuckle pin. The spindle must be a free turning fit with the lower knuckle pin nut tightened securely.

Replacing Knuckle Pin Bushings

A standard bushing driver may be used to remove and replace the knuckle pin bushings in the wheel spindle. Drive the new bushings in until the top of the bushing is flush with the top of each bore of the spindle. The lubricating holes must be aligned with the lubrication fitting holes.

Finish ream the bushings with piloted reamers. The upper bushing must be reamed to .6875″ to .6880″, and the lower .6250″ to .6255″. This will provide a clearance of .0005″ to .0015″ on the knuckle pin.

STEERING ARMS

The steering arms are designed to provide the correct toe-in for the straight ahead position and the correct turning angle (or toe-out) for turns.

Incorrect toe-out on turns is in many cases due to bent steering arms and is determined by inspecting the turning angles.

FRONT WHEEL ALIGNMENT

The caster and camber angles are predetermined at the time of manufacture and are, therefore, not adjustable in service.

Hard steering or abnormal tire wear, usually the result of incorrect front wheel alignment, may be the result of worn or damaged front suspension parts.

Where it is desired to check the front wheel alignment and normal alignment equipment is not satisfactory, it is possible to use portable floor turning plates and direct reading wheel hub gauges as illustrated in Figure 18.

NOTE: *To obtain correct readings, this method requires that set-up be made on a level floor area.*

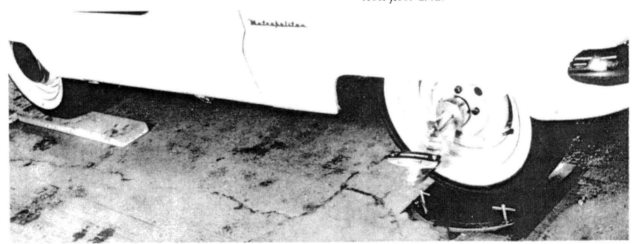

FIGURE 18—*Checking Front Wheel Alignment With Portable Equipment*

FRONT SUSPENSION STEERING GEAR

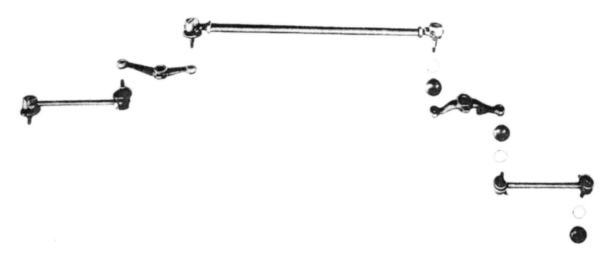

FIGURE 19—*Steering Linkage Assembly Sequence*

STEERING LINKAGE

The steering linkage is a bellcrank type incorporating an adjustable cross tube or rod to enable an adjustment of 0″ to 1/16″ toe-in (Fig. 19). Lock nuts are provided to prevent the cross tube or rod from turning with resultant change of adjustment.

Idler Assembly

The idler assembly consists of an idler body, attached to the body sill, idler arm shaft, and an idler arm (Fig. 20).

No adjustment of the idler arm shaft or idler arm is required.

Lubricate the idler assembly at 1000 mile intervals with chassis lubricant.

An idler arm shaft oil seal is installed in the lower end of the housing bore.

If a new idler arm shaft is loose in the idler housing, the housing must be replaced.

The idler arm may be removed from the shaft with a standard type two jaw puller.

The idler arm shaft is removed from the top of the housing after removing the idler housing cap.

STEERING GEAR

The steering gear is of the cam and lever type with a gear ratio of 13.5 to 1. The overall steering ratio is 21 to 1.

External adjustments are provided to eliminate all the play in the steering gear.

Raise the front wheels of the car and inspect the steering linkage ball joints, wheel bearings, and steering knuckle pin for looseness prior to making adjustments on the steering gear.

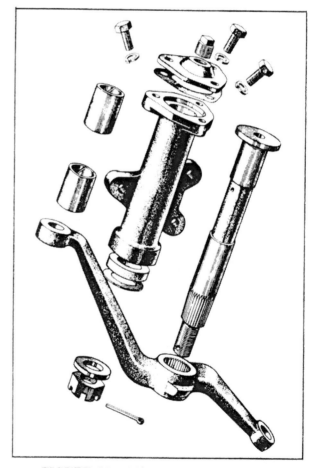

FIGURE 20—*Idler Assembly Sequence*

Cam Bearing Adjustment

Turn the steering wheel about one turn from the centered position and secure the wheel in this position to prevent any turning movement.

Steering cam bearing end play is determined by moving the front wheels sideways noting any end movement that may be felt between the steering wheel and jacket tube.

If end play is noted, the cam bearings require adjustment. Loosen the steering gear cover cap screws approximately one-eighth inch.

Separate and remove the top shim using a knife blade; do not damage the remaining shims or gasket. Retighten the cap and check for end play.

> CAUTION: *Remove one shim at a time to prevent adjusting the bearings too tight resulting in damage to the bearing races or hard steering.*

Steering Gear Alignment

Loosen the mounting bolts just enough to permit the gear to shift on the side sill and line up at the angle determined by the instrument panel bracket. Retighten the mounting bolts.

The steering gear alignment should be inspected prior to inspecting and adjusting the lever and cam mesh.

Lever and Cam Mesh Adjustment

Disconnect the steering linkage from the pitman arm.

Turn the steering wheel to the centered position to place the lever on the high point of the cam.

Loosen the lock nut on the lever adjusting screw located in the top cover of the steering gear.

Adjust the lever mesh to eliminate all play that may be noted at the pitman arm without causing a bind in the steering.

Steering Gear Removal

The radiator, carburetor air cleaner, intake manifold drain line and the top brace for the carburetor air cleaner must be removed to provide room for the steering gear removal.

Disconnect and mark the directional signal switch and horn wires at the plug-in type connectors in the engine compartment.

The shift rods should be disconnected from the gear shift operating levers.

Remove the steering gear support bracket from the inner wheelhouse panel, and steering gear.

The gear shift lever, shift shaft, operating levers and bracket may be removed as an assembly after removing the nut, ball, and gear shift knob from the gear shift lever.

Loosen the three set screws in the steering wheel hub and remove the directional switch and horn button assembly from steering wheel (Figs. 21 and 22).

> NOTE: *When removing this assembly, use care to prevent damaging the wire harness which must be pulled through the conduit tube in the steering gear.*

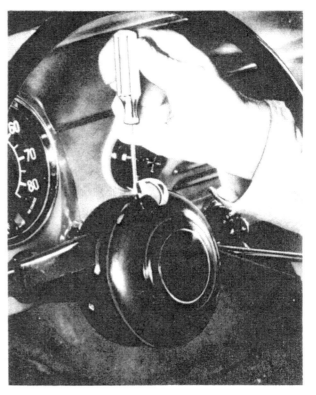

FIGURE 21—*Removing the Directional Switch and Horn Button Retaining Screws*

FIGURE 22—*Removing Directional Switch and Horn Button Assembly*

Remove the steering wheel using steering wheel puller J-1270-01 (Fig. 23).

Remove the steering jacket tube upper support cushion and retainer attaching screws.

Disconnect the left hand instrument panel to dash brace at the panel, and remove the lower left instrument panel attaching screw.

Remove the pitman arm nut. Note the location of the arm in relation to the cross shaft; mark the arm and shaft.

Remove the pitman arm using pitman arm remover J-5566-03. It is not necessary to disconnect the steering linkage from the arm.

FRONT SUSPENSION STEERING GEAR

FIGURE 23—*Removing Steering Wheel*

Remove the steering gear attaching bolts.

Move the steering gear housing toward the center of the car and pull it as far forward as possible.

Pull the instrument panel away from the dash until the upper end of the steering worm tube and jacket tube clear the hole in the panel.

Remove the gear shift lever mounting bracket, rubber cushion, cushion retainer, and jacket tube rubber grommet from the steering jacket tube.

Move the steering gear forward, guiding it around the engine manifolds and fuel pump, until the gear housing contacts the grille.

Lower the upper end of the jacket tube and slip it under the steering linkage cross tube and floor panel. Move the steering gear to the rear and lift the gear housing out of the engine compartment and from the car.

Disassembling the Steering Gear

Remove the steering gear cover plate; then the lever and cross shaft by tapping lightly on the end of the cross shaft (Fig. 24).

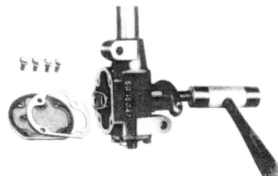

FIGURE 24—*Remove the Lever and Cross Shaft*

Remove the end cover, shims, and gaskets; do not lose or mutilate the shims.

Tap the cam tube at the steering wheel end to push the lower bearing race out of the housing (Fig. 25)

FIGURE 25—*Removing the Lower Ball Bearings*

NOTE: *The upper and lower ball bearings in the steering gear may be either the caged or loose ball type.*

Where it is desired to replace the upper worm ball bearings on a tube originally equipped with caged ball bearings, the caged bearing assembly may be cut from the tube and replaced with 14 loose ball bearings. The lower caged worm ball bearings may also be replaced with 14 loose ball bearings.

Procedure for proper assembly of the loose ball bearings will be found in following paragraphs "Assembling the Steering Gear."

Carefully remove the cam and tube from the housing. A metal dirt shield may be located above the upper race and must be cut off of the tube prior to removing the cam and tube.

Inspect the steering gear bearing races for wear or pits, the cam, and the cam follower peg of the lever for excessive wear. The lever cross shaft should be inspected for worn bearing surfaces, and the fit in the housing should be checked. The cross shaft oil seal should be inspected for proper contact on the cross shaft.

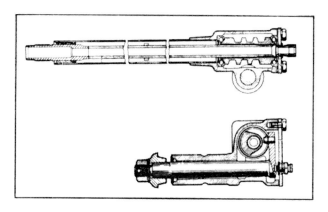

FIGURE 26—*Sectional Arrangement Drawing of Steering Gear*

FIGURE 27—*Steering Gear Assembly Sequence*

FIGURE 28—*Assembling the Upper Bearings*

Assembling the Steering Gear

Hold the steering cam and tube in a vertical position with the tube upwards. Using a thick grease, assemble the fourteen (14) ball bearings in place on the upper race of the cam (Fig. 28).

Install the upper bearing race in the housing.

Carefully slip the cam and tube into the steering gear housing until it seats in the upper bearing race (Fig. 29).

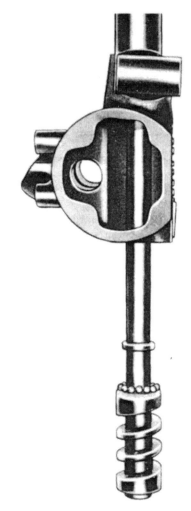

FIGURE 29—*Assembling Cam in Housing*

Using grease, assemble the lower ball bearings (14) on the lower bearing race and install in the lower end of the housing (Fig. 30).

Install the lower cover and shims. The cam bearings should be adjusted with shims installed between the cover and housing to eliminate end play without preloading the bearings.

After the cam has been adjusted, install the lever and cross shaft. The lever should be adjusted to eliminate play in the mid-position only, as the cam has a high point in the straight ahead position to compensate for normal wear.

FRONT COIL SPRING SPECIFICATIONS

Wire Diameter	.430''
Loaded Height	8½'' @ 569#
	± 16#
Rate Lbs. Per Inch	100# ± 3#
After Loaded Height	

FRONT WHEEL ALIGNMENT SPECIFICATIONS

Turning Angle	24½° + ½° — 0°
Kingpin Angle	6½°
Caster Angle	2° to 3° Pos.
Camber Angle	½° to 1½° Pos.
Toe-in	0'' to 1/16''

FIGURE 30—*Installing the Lower Bearings*

TECHNICAL SERVICE LETTER REFERENCE

Date	Letter No.	Subject	Changes information on Page No.

Technical Service Manual

Weather Eye System

WEATHER EYE SYSTEM

WEATHER EYE

The Weather Eye is designed to provide clean, fresh air for summer driving, and heated air for winter driving.

SUMMER DRIVING

The open cowl ventilator allows air to enter and circulate through the car. Drain tubes are provided in the vent.

During Summer operation, the water control valve should be in the fully closed position.

WINTER DRIVING

The Weather Eye is part of the engine cooling system and depends on normal engine operating temperature and air flow through the cowl ventilator to heat the interior of the car.

Fresh air enters the cowl ventilator and with the water control valve open, the air is heated as it passes through the heater core and circulated within the car at average driving speeds.

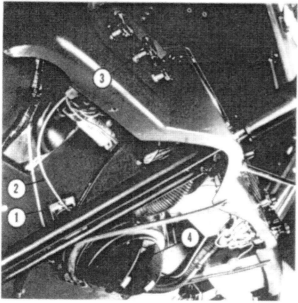

1. **Water Control Valve**
2. **Water Control Valve Cable and Conduit**
3. **Heater Switch and Water Valve Control (Knob "IN," Closed Position)**
4. **Air Deflectors**

FIGURE 1—*Weather Eye Controls*

A heater fan located in the center of the circular heater core may be utilized to circulate the heated air while driving in slow traffic.

DEFROSTING

Windshield defrosting is accomplished by the combination heater and defroster fan located in the center of the circular heater core.

Fresh air is rammed in through the open cowl ventilator while the car is in motion, or drawn in at idle or slow speed by the combination heater and defroster fan. It is deflected to the defroster ducts leading to air openings at the bottom of the windshield onto the glass.

WEATHER EYE WATER VALVE CONTROL AND SWITCH

The Weather Eye control switch is a combination electric rheostat switch and water valve control (Fig. 2).

FIGURE 2—*Heater Switch and Water Valve Control*

To open the water valve control, the control switch is pulled "OUT"; to close, it is pushed "IN." Moving the control valve to the full open position allows the full flow of water to pass through the heater core.

When the Weather Eye switch is turned to the first position to the right (clockwise) from the "OFF" position, the combination heater and defroster motor operates at high speed. The speed is decreased as the switch is turned gradually to the right.

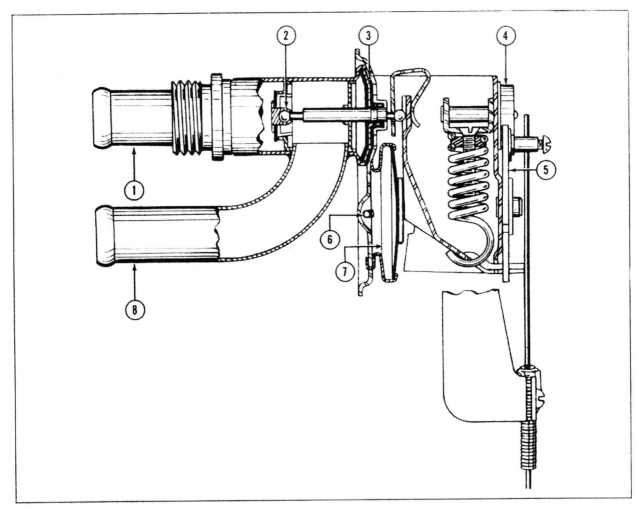

1. Valve Outlet Tube to Heater Core Tube
2. Water Valve and Metering Guide
3. Water Seal
4. Manual Control Roller
5. Operating Cam
6. Capillary Tube
7. Bellows
8. Water Inlet Tube from Cylinder Head

FIGURE 3—*Water Control Valve*

WATER CONTROL VALVE

The water control valve is operated manually and automatically which in turn controls the amount of fluid passing through the heater core. The thermostat incorporated in the valve has a flexible capillary tube leading from a small gas filled chamber and bellows to a position directly behind the heater core.

Automatic Control

With the water control valve in the complete "ON" or full "OFF" positions, the automatic feature will not operate.

Intermediate positions of the control knob will govern the automatic control.

The temperature of the air surrounding the capillary tube controls the volume of water flow through the heater core by thermostatic action. Passenger comfort will determine the correct control knob position. Depending on the position of the control knob, inside temperature is maintained at a desired level.

Weather Eye Removal

Open the water control valve to the full "OPEN" position. Drain a quart of coolant from the car.

The Weather Eye can be removed as a complete unit from the car.

On the inside of the car, disconnect the water control valve capillary tube, defroster hoses and ducts from the heater shroud (Fig. 4). Remove the two mounting screws to the dash panel at the top of the heater.

Disconnect the heater hoses from the heater core (Fig. 5).

Disconnect the heater motor wires. Remove the heater mounting screws (Fig. 6).

1. Defroster Hose, Left
2. Defroster Duct, Left
3. Water Valve Capillary Tube
4. Defroster Hose, Right
5. Defroster Duct, Right

FIGURE 4—*Parts to be Removed Inside the Car for Weather Eye Removal*

1. Cylinder Head Connector to Water Control Valve Hose
2. Cylinder Head to Water Control Valve Hose
3. Heater to Water Pump Hose
4. Water Control Valve to Heater Hose
5. Water Control Valve
6. Heater and Defroster Motor Wires and Connectors
7. Heater Hose to Water Pump Pipe.

FIGURE 5—*Weather Eye Hose Location*

1. Heater Hose Tubes
2. Mounting Screws
3. Heater Motor Wires and Connectors

FIGURE 6—*Heater Motor Wire and Heater Hose Connections*

The Weather Eye assembly is then removed as a unit by lifting it out of the opening in the dash panel (Fig. 7).

FIGURE 7—*Removing Weather Eye Unit*

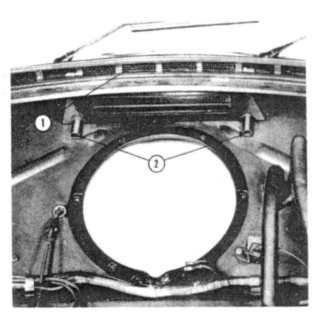

1. Cowl Vent Air Intake
2. Cowl Vent Air Intake Drain Tubes

FIGURE 8—*Weather Eye Cowl Vent*

WEATHER EYE DISASSEMBLY

Removal of Fan Housing

Remove the fan guard and adjustable air deflectors (Item 5, Fig. 9).

Three retaining clips inserted through the rubber seal hold the fan housing in position. Figure 10 illustrates the method used to remove the clips.

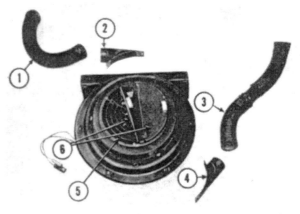

1. Defroster Hose, Left
2. Defroster Duct, Left
3. Defroster Hose, Right
4. Defroster Duct, Right
5. Fan Grille and Housing
6. Adjustable Air Deflectors

FIGURE 9—*Weather Eye and Defroster Duct Assembly*

FIGURE 10—*Removing Fan Housing Clips*

Removal of Heater and Defroster Fan

A collet type coupling holds the combination heater and defroster fan on the motor shaft (Fig. 12).

Removal of Heater Core

The heater core is maintained in position in the housing by a retaining plate that fits over the inlet and outlet necks of the core.

Removal of Heater and Defroster Motor

The motor and mounting bracket can be removed by removing the nuts from the studs on the outside of the housing (Fig. 14). The mounting bracket also holds the heater core in alignment in the housing.

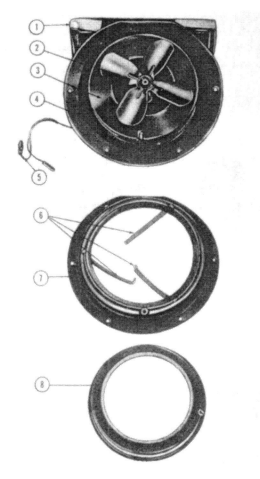

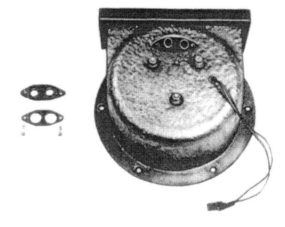

FIGURE 13—*Removal of Heater Core Retainer Plate*

1. Air Intake Conduit
2. Heater and Defroster Fan
3. Heater Core
4. Heater Housing
5. Heater and Defroster Motor Wires
6. Fan Housing Assembly Retaining Clips
7. Rubber Seal
8. Fan Housing

FIGURE 11—*Fan Housing and Attaching Parts*

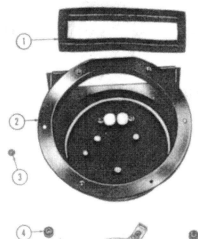

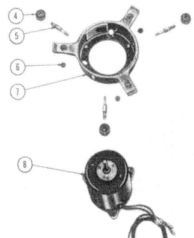

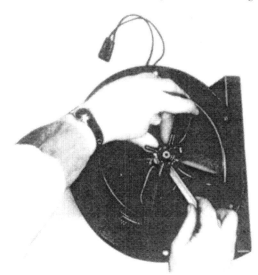

1. Conduit, Rubber
2. Housing
3. Motor Wire Grommet
4. Motor Mounting Grommet
5. Motor Mounting Stud
6. Heater Core Mounting Grommet
7. Heater Core and Motor Bracket
8. Heater and Defroster Motor

FIGURE 12—*Removing the Heater and Defroster Fan*

FIGURE 14—*Heater and Defroster Motor and Bracket Assembly*

WEATHER EYE SYSTEM

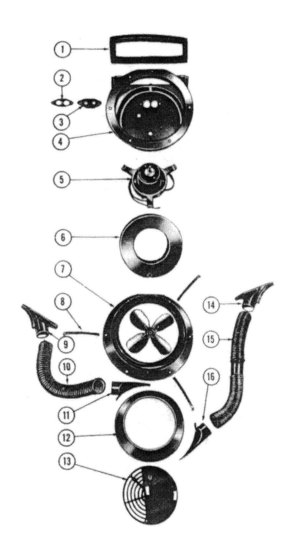

1. Cowl Air Intake Conduit, Rubber
2. Heater Core Retainer
3. Heater Core Retainer Gasket
4. Heater Housing
5. Motor and Mounting Bracket
6. Heater Core
7. Rubber Seal
8. Fan Housing Retaining Clip
9. Defroster Windshield Duct, Left
10. Defroster Hose, Left
11. Defroster Duct, Left
12. Fan Housing
13. Fan Guard and Adjustable Air Deflectors
14. Defroster Windshield Duct, Right
15. Defroster Hose, Right
16. Defroster Duct, Right

FIGURE 15—*Weather Eye Assembly*

WATER CONTROL VALVE REMOVAL

Disconnect the heater hoses from the water control valve.

Disconnect the capillary tube from its mounting on the fan housing assembly and the control cable and conduit from the valve. Then remove the water control valve from the dash panel.

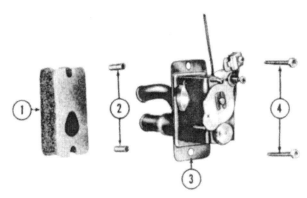

1. Water Control to Dash Sealer Gasket
2. Water Control Valve Mounting Spacers
3. Water Control Valve
4. Water Control Valve Mounting Screws

FIGURE 16—*Water Control Valve Assembly*

Water Control Valve Cable Adjustment

To correctly adjust the water control valve cable, the control knob on the dash must be in the "OFF" ("Pushed In") position and the water control valve cam must be in the "Closed" position prior to retightening the cable securely in the clamp.

REMOVAL OF WATER VALVE CONTROL AND SWITCH ASSEMBLY

Insert a small screw driver between the switch bracket and switch control stop collar as shown in Item 5, Figure 17. This will allow the control knob and shaft to be unscrewed from the threaded end of the control cable. Then pull the shaft and knob straight out.

The switch can be withdrawn from the instrument panel after the French mounting nut has been removed.

Disconnect the switch wires from the terminals and the cable conduit from the clamp (Fig. 17).

NOTE: *Upon installation, the control knob and shaft must be screwed completely into the threaded end of the cable. Then backed off two full turns to allow free operation of the heater switch.*

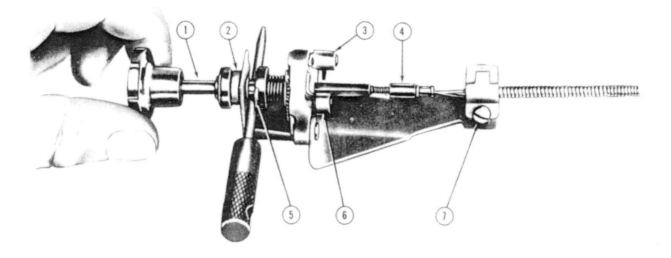

1. Control Switch Shaft and Knob Sweated Together
2. French Mounting Nut
3. Ignition Switch Terminal
4. Control Cable Threaded End
5. Switch Control Stop Collar
6. Heater Motor Wire Terminal
7. Control Cable Conduit Clamp

FIGURE 17—*Water Valve Control and Switch Assembly*

TECHNICAL SERVICE LETTER REFERENCE

Date	Letter No.	Subject	Changes information on Page No.

Metropolitan "1500" employs unitized body construction, a single all-welded structural unit combining great strength with a considerable saving of weight. This type of construction provides increased passenger safety with a longer, lasting, squeak-and-rattle-free all-steel body. Reduced weight improves power-to-weight ratio for responsive performance with high fuel economy.

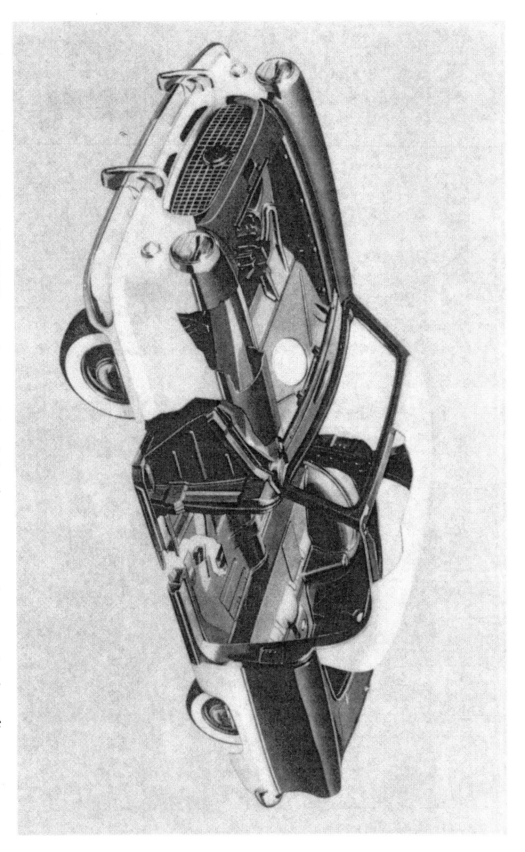

Technical
Service
Manual

Body

Technical
Service
Manual

BODIES — PANELS — SUBASSEMBLIES

Bodies–Panels–
Subassemblies

BODIES—PANELS—
SUBASSEMBLIES

FIGURE 1—*Convertible—Model 541*

FIGURE 2—*Hardtop—Model 542*

BODIES — PANELS — SUBASSEMBLIES

FIGURE 3—*Hardtop—Model 542*

FIGURE 4—*Convertible—Model 561*

FIGURE 5—*Hardtop—Model 562*

BODY IDENTIFICATION

Two body styles are available: the Convertible soft top and the Hardtop models. They are identified by individual chassis number and body number plates which are located on the right side of the dash under the hood (Figs. 6, 7, and 8).

The following Model and Series identification applies:

Model		Series	Starting Serial Number
541	Convertible	A	
542	Hardtop	A	E-1001
541	Convertible	B	
542	Hardtop	B	E-11001
561	Convertible	1500	
562	Hardtop	1500	E-21008

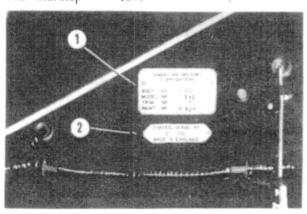

1. Body, Model, Trim, and Paint Numbers
2. Chassis Serial Number

FIGURE 6—*Location of Identification Number Plates*

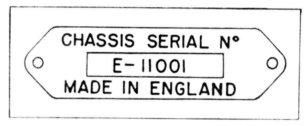

FIGURE 7—*Chassis Serial Number Plate (Number Prefixed by letter "E")*

The body number plate (Fig. 8) illustrates the body, model, trim, and paint numbers.

Whenever reference is made to the body, the body and model numbers as well as the chassis number must be given. The trim and paint numbers must be supplied in addition when reference concerns either of these items.

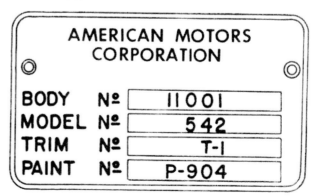

FIGURE 8—*Body Number Plate*

When reference is made to paint, the paint code number as shown on the body number plate and the color of the paint required must be given.

This information is required because some cars are painted two-tone and unless the color name is given, it would not be known which color is desired.

For example:

Paint No. P-904.

This would indicate the complete car was painted in one color (Canyon Red).

Paint No. P-903-7.

This would indicate the lower color was No. P-903 (Spruce Green) and the upper color No. P-907 (Mist Gray).

INDIVIDUAL PANELS AND ASSEMBLIES

The single unit construction of both the Convertible and the Hardtop models are the same. The parts of the underbody, floor, and frame unit of these models are interchangeable.

The body frame with its "U" shaped side sills, braces, reinforcements, and supports become box section units when the body floor panels and side panels are welded to both flanges of each "U" shaped structural member.

It also provides a means for replacement of only the damaged part or sections of such parts as required, which is less expensive than repairing and reinforcing.

In cases where a complete side is distorted beyond satisfactory repair by single units, it is suggested that a uniside assembly be considered.

Figure 12 illustrates the individual parts of this assembly before they are welded into one unit.

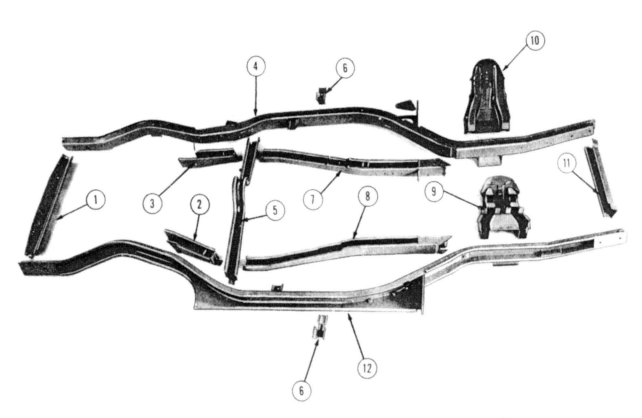

1. Rear Crossmember
2. Rear Spring Front Eye Hanger Gusset, Right
3. Rear Spring Front Eye Hanger Gusset, Left
4. Floor Side Sill, Left
5. Intermediate Crossmember
6. Jacking Bracket
7. Channel Reinforcement, Left
8. Channel Reinforcement, Right
9. Front Suspension Mounting Bracket Assembly, Right
10. Front Suspension Mounting Bracket Assembly, Left
11. Front Crossmember
12. Floor Side Sill, Right

FIGURE 9—*Individual Parts of Body Frame Assembly as Serviced*

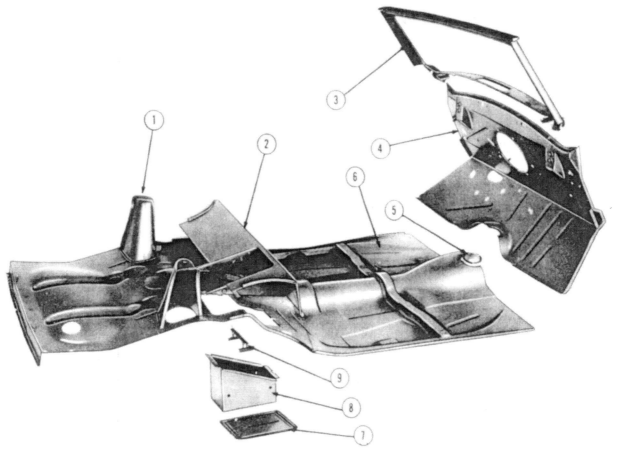

1. Shock Absorber Housing
2. Rear Seat Riser
3. Cowl Panel Assembly
4. Dash and Toe Board Assembly
5. Transmission Oil Filler Cover Plate
6. Brake Master Cylinder Access Hole Cover
7. Battery Box Cover
8. Battery Box
9. Battery Hold Down

FIGURE 10—*Individual Assemblies of Body Floor*

Most of the front end and body panels below the belt line are interchangeable on the Convertible and Hardtop models. However, in all cases, consult the Parts Catalog for this information.

REPLACEMENT OF NEW PANELS

In cases of damage to the various panels of the body, where replacement will be required, careful examination should be made as to the extent of the damage to determine which panels will be required for replacement.

In most cases the weld joints of one panel to another are visible and it can be easily determined how they may be separated for installation of a new panel.

There are, however, three locations in the body where all of the weld joints are not visible. These are

the roof panel, floor side sill section under the doors, and rear deck center panel. The following cross section views for each of these sections should be carefully reviewed before replacement of the roof panel, rear deck center panel, or any of the body side sill panels.

FLOOR SIDE SILL PANELS UNDER DOORS

As illustrated in Figure 13, the top weld joint of the body side sill panel reinforcement to the body floor flange and the body side sill panel are both visible. However, at the bottom of the body side sill panel reinforcement, the weld joint is on the inside of the body side sill panel and is not visible.

Where damage has only affected the body side sill panel, the following procedure will apply:

BODIES — PANELS — SUBASSEMBLIES

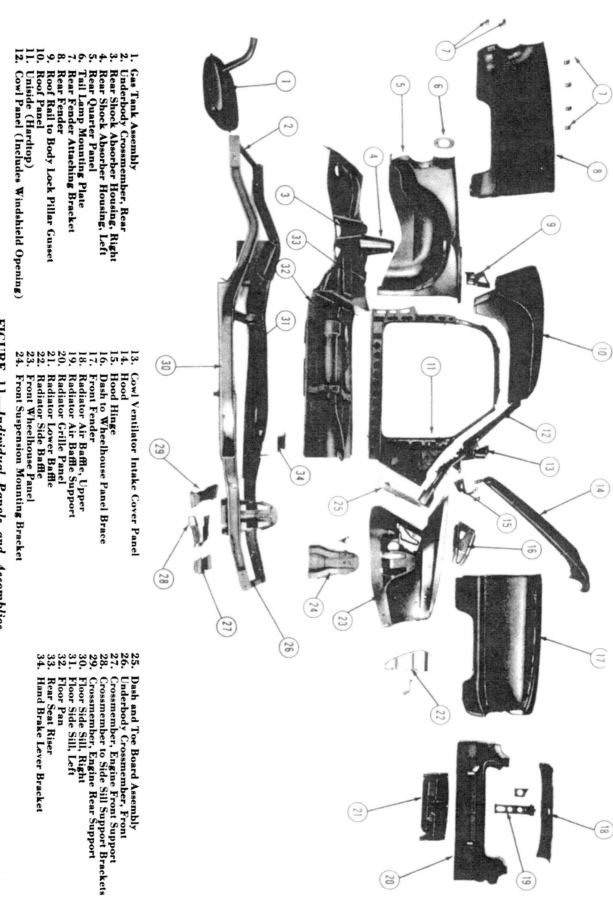

1. Gas Tank Assembly
2. Underbody Crossmember, Rear
3. Rear Shock Absorber Housing, Right
4. Rear Shock Absorber Housing, Left
5. Rear Quarter Panel
6. Tail Lamp Mounting Plate
7. Rear Fender Attaching Bracket
8. Rear Fender
9. Roof Rail to Body Lock Pillar Gusset
10. Roof Panel
11. Uniside (Hardtop)
12. Cowl Panel (Includes Windshield Opening)

13. Cowl Ventilator Intake Cover Panel
14. Hood
15. Hood Hinge
16. Dash to Wheelhouse Panel Brace
17. Front Fender
18. Radiator Air Baffle, Upper
19. Radiator Air Baffle Support
20. Radiator Grille Panel
21. Radiator Lower Baffle
22. Radiator Side Baffle
23. Front Wheelhouse Panel
24. Front Suspension Mounting Bracket

25. Dash and Toe Board Assembly
26. Underbody Crossmember, Front
27. Crossmember, Engine Front Support
28. Crossmember to Side Sill Support Brackets
29. Crossmember, Engine Rear Support
30. Floor Side Sill, Right
31. Floor Side Sill, Left
32. Floor Pan
33. Rear Seat Riser
34. Hand Brake Lever Bracket

FIGURE 11—*Individual Panels and Assemblies*

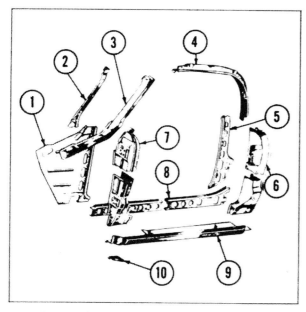

1. Cowl Side Panel Assembly
2. Front Body Upper Pillar Reinforcement
3. Front Body Upper Pillar
4. Side Roof Rail and Drip Moulding
5. Body Lock Pillar Reinforcement
6. Body Lock Pillar
7. Body Hinge Pillar
8. Body Side Sill Panel Reinforcement
9. Body Side Sill Panel
10. Body Side Sill Top Front Filler

FIGURE 12—*Uniside Assembly, Left
(Individual Parts of Uniside Before
Welding into One Unit)*

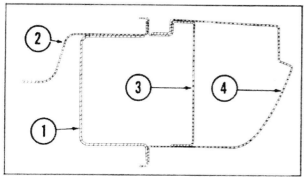

1. Floor Side Sill
2. Body Floor
3. Body Side Sill Panel Reinforcement
4. Body Side Sill Panel

FIGURE 13—*Cross Section View of Body
Floor Side Sill Assembly Under Door
Openings*

Removal Procedure

Drill out spot-welds or cut the body side sill panel from the body side sill panel reinforcement at top (Fig. 14) and bend panel down so it may be cut from the bottom side of the reinforcement leaving the reinforcement welded to the lower section of the body side sill panel and its weld joint to the bottom of the floor side sill lower flange intact.

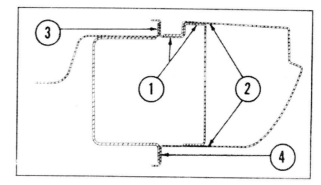

1. Spot-Welds at Joint of Body Side Sill Panel to Body Side Sill Panel Reinforcement at Top
2. Location to Cut Body Side Sill Panel from Reinforcement for Replacement of Body Side Sill Panel
3. Spot-Welds Body Side Sill Panel Reinforcement to Body Floor Flange
4. Spot-Welds Body Side Sill Panel to Body Floor Side Sill Flange

FIGURE 14—*Locations to Cut Panel and
Welds for Replacement of the Body Side
Sill Panel or the Panel and Reinforcement*

Installation Procedure

Install new panel at top of reinforcement and to lower outside edge of old body side sill panel, clamping this panel with "C" clamps in proper position.

Drill holes and weld the new panel at top, bottom side, and at bottom flange (Fig. 15).

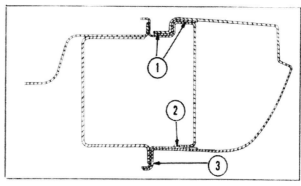

1. Drill Holes and Weld Body Side Sill Panel to Body Side Sill Panel Reinforcement at Top
2. Drill Holes and Weld New Body Side Sill Panel to Old Side Sill Panel and Reinforcement
3. Drill Holes and Weld New Body Side Sill Panel Flange to Old Side Sill Panel and Floor Side Sill Welded Flange

FIGURE 15—*Weld Locations When
Replacing Body Side Sill Panel*

BODY SIDE SILL REINFORCEMENT

Where damage to the body side sill panel (Item 4, Fig. 13) has extended into the reinforcement (Item 3) and both panels require replacement, the following procedure will apply:

Removal Procedure

Drill out the spot-welds in the reinforcement to body floor flange at top (Item 3, Fig. 14) and body side sill panel to floor side sill lower flange (Item 4).

Installation of New Panels

Properly fit body side sill panel reinforcement (Item 3, Fig. 13) into body side sill panel (Item 4, Fig. 13) and weld at top (Item 1, Fig. 15) then at lower side (Item 2, Fig. 15) and along lower edge reinforcement to body side sill panel.

Now clamp this assembly to the top and bottom flanges of the floor side sill and weld at Items 3 and 4, Figure 14.

ROOF PANEL

The weld joints of the roof panel to the body are visible at the front over the windshield and on the sides over the doors.

The welding flange of the roof panel is formed to point to the outside of the body in the drip moulding and over the rear window. When it is welded to the rear window upper rail, the weld joint of these two panels form a flange for the rear window glass sealer rubber which is visible when the rear window is removed.

Cross section views of each of these locations are shown in Figures 16, 17 and 18.

The rear side of the roof panel between the door opening and the rear window opening is butt welded to the top of the rear quarter side roof extension panel. This weld joint is not visible from the outside.

In cases of damage, where the roof panel is to be replaced, the old roof panel must be removed from the body in such a manner that the body main rails are not damaged. The complete new roof panel can then be installed and welded properly.

Roof Panel Removal Procedure:

Remove rear window glass assembly.
  Remove headlining.
  Remove seal in drip moulding to expose the weld joints.
  Drill spot-welds holding roof flange to drip moulding (Figs. 19 and 20).
  DO NOT DRILL through drip moulding.
  Before drilling, measure and mark the spot-welds at three-inch intervals. Drill through roof flange and drip moulding using 5/16" drill on all marked spot-welds. On other spot-welds, use 1/4" drill and drill only through weld flange of roof panel.
    NOTE: *These marked, drilled-through holes at three-inch intervals will be used to weld the new roof panel flange to the drip mould-*

ing by puddle welding from the bottom side of the door openings.

Clean, then file or grind to provide a smooth contacting surface, on the body main rails for the new roof panel.

Set the new roof panel on body main rails in proper alignment. Then at the rear side quarters, mark the extension panel to provide a proper fit to the roof panel for welding.

Remove the roof panel and cut the extension panels on body to these markings.

Preparing New Roof Panel for Installation

Refer to Item 1, Figure 19. These are the locations where the roof panel weld flange was originally welded to the body, therefore, the new roof should be rewelded at the same locations.

Carefully drill 5/16" holes in welding flange at location of Item 1, Figure 19, at three-inch intervals completely across front of roof. These holes will be used to puddle weld the front of the roof to the windshield header drip moulding.

Installing Roof to Body

Set new roof on body and properly align to windshield header and rear window upper rail, using "C" clamps to hold the roof in place at each corner and center at the front and rear.

Now align sides of roof panel into drip moulding.

Use a small block of wood to serve as a spacer between the roof panel and the drip moulding clamping it into position.

Weld front of roof to windshield header by puddle welding at Item 1, Figure 19.

Weld sides of roof panel by puddle welding through holes in drip moulding at Item 1, Figure 20.

Then at rear window flange, drill holes and puddle weld at Item 3, Figure 18, at three-inch intervals.

  CAUTION: *Use wet asbestos putty on roof panel and move to each location when welding. This will prevent excessive heat which causes wrinkles on metal.*

  Do not weld continuously by starting at one end and continuing to the other. This causes too much heat in one area. Keep welds at least twelve inches apart, then fill in welds after metal cools.

After painting, seal the edges of the roof panel flange to the drip rails at the front and both sides of body.

Brush red rubber cement on inside surface of roof panel and install new roof insulation material.

Install headlining material.

Install rear window glass assembly.

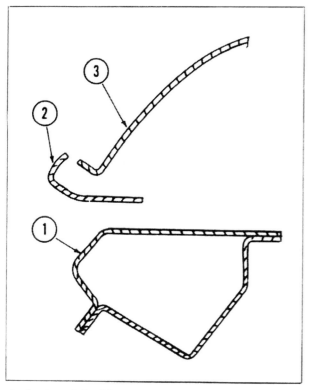

1. Section of Cowl Panel Assembly at Top of Windshield Opening Welded to Windshield Header Reinforcement
2. Drip Moulding
3. Roof Panel

FIGURE 16—*Cross Section View of Windshield Header Assembly to Which Roof Panel is Welded at Front*

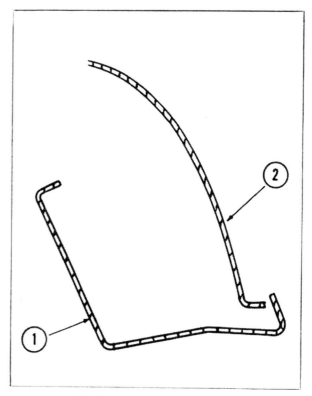

1. Side Roof Rail and Drip Moulding
2. Roof Panel

FIGURE 17—*Cross Section View of the Side Roof Rail and Drip Moulding to Which Roof Panel is Welded at Sides*

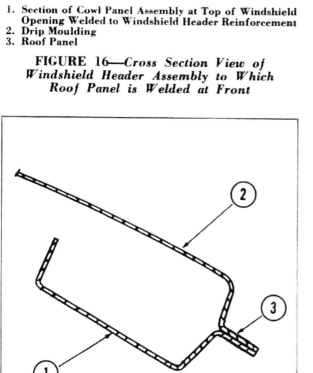

1. Rear Window Upper Rail
2. Roof Panel
3. Weld Joint of Roof Panel to Upper Rail Forming Flange for Rear Window Glass Sealer Rubber

FIGURE 18—*Cross Section View of Rear Window Opening at Top*

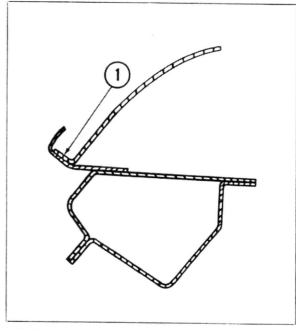

1. Location of Front Spot-Welds to be Drilled Out

FIGURE 19—*Removing Roof Panel at Front Over Windshield Opening*

BODIES — PANELS — SUBASSEMBLIES

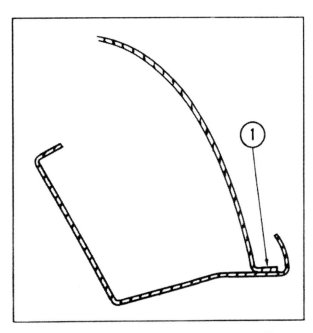

1. Location of Spot-Welds to be Drilled Out to Remove Flange of Roof Panel

FIGURE 20—*Removing Roof Panel from Drip Moulding on Sides of Body*

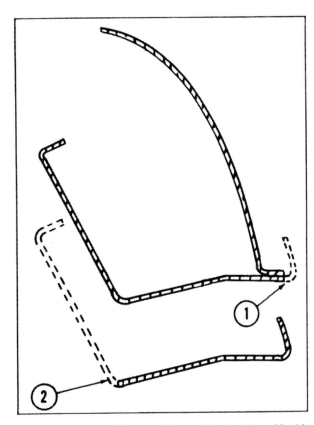

1. Location to Cut Damaged Gutter Section from Moulding
2. Location to Cut Flange from Service Drip Moulding

FIGURE 21—*Removing Gutter Section from Drip Moulding and Preparing Service Drip Moulding for Installation*

SIDE DRIP MOULDINGS

The side drip mouldings as shown at Item 1, Figure 17, serve as a base support to which the roof panel flange is welded. It will be supplied for service as shown.

In cases of damage to this part where replacement is required, the following removal and installation procedure will apply:

Side Drip Moulding Removal Procedure

Use hacksaw and cut gutter section from moulding as shown at Item 1, Figure 21.

Preparing Drip Moulding for Installation

On service replacement, cut off the inner flange (Item 2, Fig. 21).

Drill 5/16" holes in moulding from front to rear, spaced at eight-inch intervals, one inch from the outside edge of gutter.

Installing Drip Moulding

Loosen headlining on side of body.

Clamp moulding to body in proper position as shown in Figure 22.

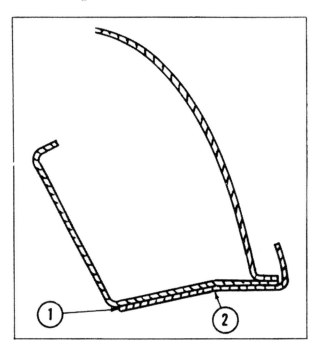

1. Spot-Weld End at Eight-Inch Intervals
2. Puddle Weld Through Holes in New Drip Moulding

FIGURE 22—*Installing New Drip Moulding Over Section of Old Drip Moulding*

Puddle weld at each hole (Item 2, Fig. 22), then weld at edge (Item 1) between the spots puddle welded.

CAUTION: *Pack wet asbestos putty between main rail and roof panel and move it at each weld. This will prevent heat from damaging metal or paint and prevent fire damage to roof insulation and sealing material.*

DOORS OR DECK COVER

The construction of these units consists of all reinforcements welded to the inner and outer panels before they are flanged and spot-welded together.

They are available for service in prime coat, ready to be installed and aligned to the body; then painted and have the hardware, trim, etc., transferred from the damaged parts.

HOOD

The hood is of a one-piece construction with two single arm operating hinges. With the hood raised, it may be secured in the open position by inserting the hood prop rod into the right hood reinforcement rod bracket (Fig. 23).

Hood Alignment

The screw holes in the hood hinge arm and attaching hood brackets are elongated to allow clearances to correctly align the hood to the body and front fenders (Fig. 24).

FIGURE 24—*Hood Hinge and Bracket Assembly*

Align the hood by loosening the bracket to hood cap screws and hinge arm to bracket screws. Move the hood in direction desired. Retighten and check alignment.

Hood Control

The hood release control is located just inside the center of the grille (Figs. 25 and 26).

1. **Hood Reinforcement Rod and Prop Bracket**
2. **Reinforcement Rod**
3. **Prop Rod**
4. **Hood Prop Rubber Stop**
5. **Adjusting Screws**

FIGURE 23—*Hood Hinge, Reinforcement Rod, and Prop Rod Assemblies*

FIGURE 25—*Hood Lock Release Control— A and B Series*

FIGURE 26—*Hood Lock Release Control—*
1500 Series

To release the hood, reach in behind the grille and
trip the hood lock lever. This releases the hood lock,
allowing the hood to release against the safety catch
(Fig. 27).

To prevent the hood from opening accidentally, the
safety catch must completely engage the formed inside
flange of the hood.

Apply lubriplate to all friction areas.

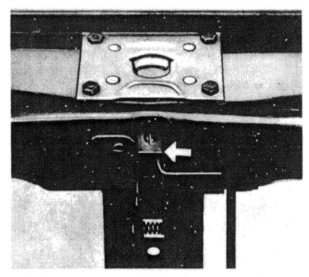

FIGURE 27—*Hood Lock Safety Catch*

RADIATOR GRILLE

The A and B Series grille is of a one-piece construction
attached at the sides to the grille panel assembly and
supported at the center with a bracket attached to the
grille panel and radiator air baffle (Fig. 28).

FIGURE 28—*Radiator Grille—A and B Series*

The 1500 Series grille is made up of five individual
pieces: the center or inner grille, the lower frame,
right and left side frames, and the upper frame which
is fastened to the front of the hood.

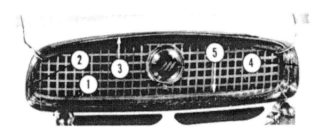

1. **Inner Grille**	4. **Grille Frame, Left**
2. **Grille Frame, Right**	5. **Grille Frame, Bottom**
3. **Grille Frame, Top**	

FIGURE 29—*Radiator Grille—1500 Series*

The inner grille is fastened at the bottom to the
grille panel with two machine screws which can be
removed through the air louvres in the grille panel.

The bottom grille frame fastening nuts are also accessible through the air louvres.

The grille upper fastening screws are visible when
the hood is raised.

The side grille frame fastening nuts are accessible
from under the fender.

FRONT FENDERS

The front fenders are of one-piece construction. They
are attached by means of bolts to the wheelhouse panel,
side sill, and grille panel, and welded to the body pillar.

Front Fender Removal

Remove the head and parking lamp assemblies.

If the car is radio-equipped, disconnect antenna
lead and remove antenna.

Remove all attaching bolts from the **wheelhouse
panel,** grille panel, and side sill assemblies.

Remove bumper assembly and back bar on the side
from which the fender is to be removed.

The fender flange is spot-welded to the door pillar
post (Fig. 30). Therefore, remove the door to facilitate drilling out the spot-welds.

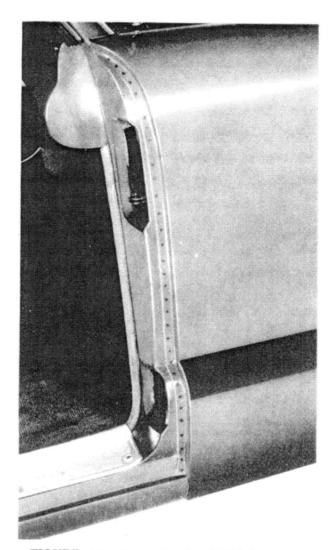

FIGURE 30—*Front Fender Weld Locations*

Drill out the fender to front body pillar spot-welds.

CAUTION: *When drilling out the spot-welds, do not drill beyond the thickness of the fender metal.*

The fender to grille panel joint is leaded or brazed on the later models and must be cut. This joint is bolted under the fender.

Installing a New Front Fender

Clean the surfaces where the fender and body pillar contact each other. They must be smooth and clean. Apply a suitable rust preventative to the mating surfaces.

Drill ¼" holes 3" apart in the new fender flanges where they are to be welded to the body pillar.

Place the new fender in position using drifts to align the fender. Install the fender to wheelhouse panel and fender to grille panel attaching bolts, plus the two side sill attaching bolts.

Check for correct alignment and tighten.

Clamp the rear flange of the fender to front body pillar. Recheck for alignment.

Puddle weld or braze the fender flange to body pillar at the previously drilled holes.

Lead in the fender to grille panel joint.

Brush Body Joint Sealer into the fender to body joints under the fender. Refinish fender and reinstall bumper, headlight, and parking lamp assemblies.

REAR FENDERS

The rear fenders are of one-piece construction and are spot-welded to the rear quarter body lock pillar, wheelhouse panel, belt rail, and rear deck center panel. Due to attaching flange differences, special service fenders will be supplied for the Hardtop and Convertible models.

Rear Fender Removal Procedure: Hardtop

Remove the rear window glass assembly and belt rail moulding.

Convertible

Remove the top and hold down clips from the belt rail.

Hardtop and Convertible

Remove bumper and back bar assembly from the side from which the fender is to be removed. Remove tail lamp assembly. Remove attaching fender bolt to side sill.

As shown in Figure 31, scribe a line approximately 2" from the edge of the attaching flange.

FIGURE 31—*Rear Fender Removal*

With this line as a guide, cut the fender completely off the body.

This operation is necessary to gain access to the spot-welds connecting the fender to the bead and rear deck panel.

BODIES — PANELS — SUBASSEMBLIES

Drill out all the spot-welds attaching the fender flange to the rear quarter lock pillar (Fig. 32). Pull flange away from the lock pillar.

CAUTION: *When drilling out a spot-weld, drill through one thickness of metal only.*

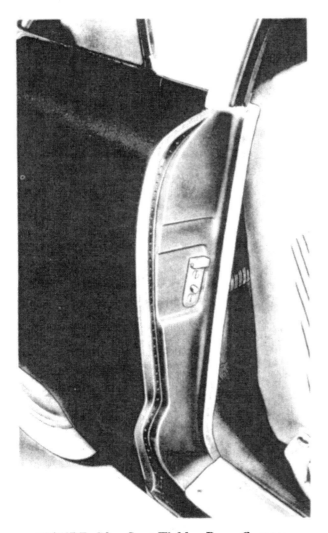

FIGURE 32—*Spot-Welds, Rear Quarter Lock Pillar*

Figure 33 shows how the fender is attached at the belt line to the roof panel extension and wheelhouse panel.

On the Hardtop model, do not remove the section of fender flange remaining on the belt rail from the lock pillar to the rear window. This flange will be used for added support when installing the new fender.

On the Convertible model (Fig. 34) use a No. 10 drill and drill out spot-welds at the belt rail area, the joint of the fender and wheelhouse panel from the lock pillar to the fender and deck panel bead. Pull the flange away from the body.

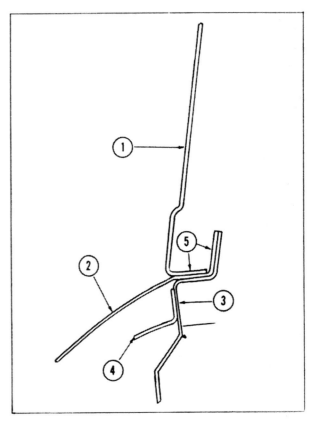

1. **Roof Panel Extension**
2. **Fender**
3. **Wheelhouse Panel**
4. **Lock Pillar**
5. **Spot-Welds**

FIGURE 33—*Rear Fender and Roof Panel. Hardtop Model Only*

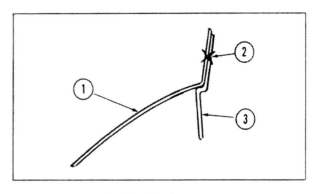

1. **Rear Fender**
2. **Spot-Welds**
3. **Wheelhouse Panel**

FIGURE 34—*Rear Fender and Wheelhouse Panel Spot-Welds. Convertible Model Only*

Figure 35 illustrates the fender and wheelhouse panel attaching flanges and spot-welds on the Hardtop model in the rear window opening between the roof panel extension and joint of fender and rear deck center panel. Use a No. 10 drill and drill out the spot-welds. Pull the fender flange away from the body.

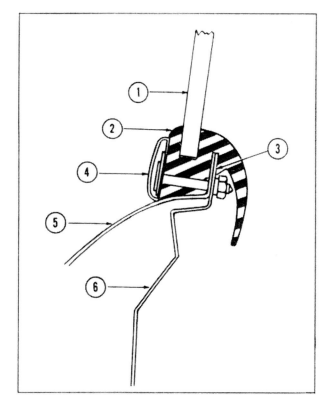

1. Rear Window
2. Rear Window Glass Rubber Channel
3. Spot-Welds
4. Lower Moulding
5. Rear Fender
6. Wheelhouse Panel

FIGURE 35—*Fender to Wheelhouse Spot-Welds. Hardtop Model Only*

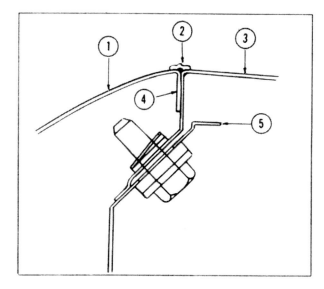

1. Rear Fender
2. Bead
3. Rear Deck Center Panel
4. Spot-Welds
5. Wheelhouse Panel

FIGURE 36—*Rear Fender, Bead, Rear Deck Center Panel*

As shown in Figure 36, the rear fender is spot-welded to a bead and rear deck center panel flange. Using a No. 10 drill, drill out the spot-welds through the thickness of the fender and bead. Remove flange from body.

With a No. 10 drill, drill out the spot-welds attaching the tail lamp mounting plate to the fender.

Below the tail lamp, the fender and deck panel flanges are spot-welded together; use a No. 10 drill and drill out the spot-welds. Remove the remaining part of the flange from the body.

From the inside of the trunk compartment, remove the six deck panel to wheelhouse panel attaching screws (Fig. 37).

Remove and discard the six speed nuts from the rear deck panel.

Installing a New Rear Fender: Hardtop

The Hardtop model requires a slightly different procedure than the convertible model because the steel stamp-

FIGURE 37—*Deck Panel to Wheelhouse Panel Attaching Screws*

ing of the roof top overlays the original fender weld at the belt line. Therefore, it is necessary to scribe a line on the new service fender at the point where the fender and the roof extension panel would meet (Fig. 38).

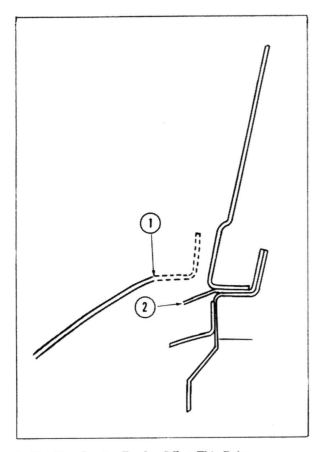

1. Cut New Service Fender Off at This Point
2. Old Fender Flange—Cut Off at This Point. Bend Slightly Downward

FIGURE 38—*Attaching Service Fender to Roof Extension Panel*

With a cutting tool, cut this flange off the new fender from the body lock pillar to the rear window. Bend the old fender flange that was left on the body slightly downward so that the new fender will be supported at this point.

Hardtop and Convertible

Clean all metal to metal contact surfaces. They must be smooth and clean. Apply a suitable rust preventative to the mating surfaces of the service fender bead and to where it will contact the rear deck panel flange, also the fender flange below the tail light opening.

Install six new speed nuts on the attaching brackets welded to the service fender.

Fit and align the new fender to body. Then apply a thin coat of body sealer to the mating surfaces of the fender and rear deck center panel. Clamp the fender (Fig. 39) in position, and install fender attaching bolts to the wheelhouse and deck panel.

Install fender to side sill attaching bolt.

With the fender in position and correctly aligned,

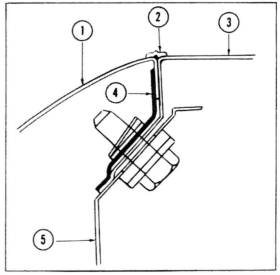

1. Fender
2. Bead Welded to Fender
3. Rear Deck Center Panel
4. Mounting Strap Welded to Fender
5. Wheelhouse Panel

FIGURE 39—*Attaching Service Fender to Wheelhouse Panel*

weld the new fender to the wheelhouse panel from the lock pillar back to the fender and deck panel bead.

On the Hardtop model at the belt line below the roof panel extension, butt weld and fill in at the joint where the new fender and old fender flange overlap each other. At the rear window opening, weld the fender to the wheelhouse panel.

Weld the tail light support plate in position.

Clamp the front flange of the fender to the lock pillar. Drill $1/4''$ holes approximately $2\frac{1}{2}''$ apart through the fender flange only from the belt moulding line down to the side sill.

Puddle weld the fender flange to the lock pillar at each hole.

Braze the top and lower corners to the body lock pillar.

Paint the fender and reinstall tail light and bumper. Brush Body Joint Sealer into all joints under the fender.

On the Hardtop model, install the rear window glass assembly.

On the Convertible model, install top and hold down clips to belt rail.

REAR DECK CENTER PANEL

The top edge of the rear deck center panel is welded to the body belt rail. This union forms a mounting flange for the rear window glass and rubber assembly on the Hardtop models. It is visible when the rear window glass assembly is removed.

On the Convertible models, this union forms a mounting flange for the back curtain portion of the fabric top.

BODIES — PANELS — SUBASSEMBLIES

The lower edge of this panel is welded to the bottom side of the body frame rear crossmember.

The sides of this panel have an extended flange, which serves a dual purpose. The fender flange is welded to the top portion combining the center panel and both rear fenders into one assembly. The lower portion of this flange is bolted to the rear wheelhouse panels which serve to fasten the sides of the center deck panel and the top edges of the fenders to the body.

In the original assembly of these bodies, the fenders are welded to the center deck panel, making one unit, then welded and bolted as an assembly to the body.

In service, this method of unit replacement would not be satisfactory unless all the parts included in this assembly were damaged beyond repair.

Therefore, a special rear deck center panel and right and left rear fender has been made available for service, whereby either right or left fender or the center deck panel can be replaced individually without disturbing the other parts.

These service parts will be provided with mounting straps and brackets whereby the individual part can be bolted on, or in cases of damage to both fenders and rear deck center panel requiring replacement of all three parts, the three service parts can be bolted and tack-welded together and be installed as one unit.

Rear Deck Panel Removal: Hardtop Model

Remove the rear window glass assembly and belt rail moulding.

Convertible Model

Remove the top and hold down clips from the belt rail.

Hardtop and Convertible

Remove spare tire and spare tire mounting bracket from the deck panel.

    Remove bumper and back bar assembly.

    Remove tail lamp assemblies.

Using a No. 10 drill, drill out spot-welds attaching the bottom flange to the rear body crossmember.

As shown in Figure 40, scribe a line approximately 1″ from the edge of the rear deck panel flange.

Using a cutting tool, cut the rear deck panel completely away from the body.

Figure 36 illustrates the production deck panel flange spot-welded to the bead and fender flange, from there the deck panel flange extends down and is bolted to the wheelhouse panel. Do not drill these spot-welds out. Using a cutting tool, cut off the bead and deck panel flange at point designated in Figure 41. Cutting the flange and bead at this point will allow the production fender to maintain its correct position.

FIGURE 40—*Rear Deck Center Panel Removal*

Using a No. 10 drill, drill out spot-welds holding tail lamp mounting plate, also welds below the tail lamp on the deck panel to fender flange.

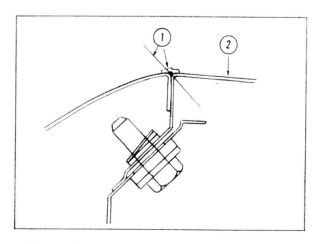

1. **Cut Bead and Deck Panel Center Flange at This Point**
2. **Rear Deck Center Panel**

FIGURE 41—*Removing Rear Deck Center Panel Flange*

The rear deck panel is spot-welded to the belt rail on both models. Using a No. 10 drill, drill out these spot-welds and pull the remaining deck panel flange away from the body.

Installing a New Rear Deck Center Panel

The service rear deck center panels are supplied with a bead and six outer brackets welded to the flange on each side (Fig. 42).

From the inside of the trunk compartment (Fig. 37), remove individually the screws holding the original deck panel flange to the wheelhouse panel and attach inner upper and lower brackets and reinstall bolts (Fig. 42).

Clean all metal to metal contact surfaces. They must be smooth and clean. Apply paint or suitable

BODIES — PANELS — SUBASSEMBLIES

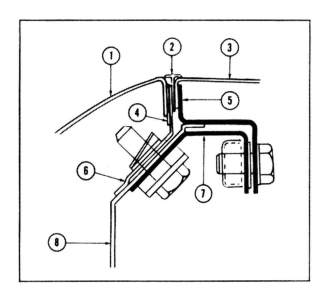

1. Rear Fender
2. Service Bead
3. Service Deck Panel
4. Original Bead Flange
5. Outer Service Bracket
6. Original Deck Panel Flange
7. Inner Service Brackets
8. Wheelhouse Panel

FIGURE 42—*Attaching Service Deck Panel*

rust preventative to the mating surfaces of the fenders and center deck panel.

Apply a thin but complete coat of Body Sealer to the service rear deck panel bead to where it will contact the fender flange, also the deck panel flange below the tail lamp mounting plate where it contacts the fender flange.

Install and align new rear deck panel to body. Clamp the front end to the body belt rail and lower end to the rear body crossmember.

Attach the inner and outer brackets from inside the trunk compartment (Fig. 42).

Weld the front flange to the body belt rail, and the tail lamp mounting plates to the rear deck panel. Then weld the lower flange to the rear body cross-member.

Paint the panel and reinstall tail lamp, bumper, and spare tire assemblies.

On the Hardtop model reinstall the rear window glass assembly.

On the Convertible model reinstall the top and hold down clips to the belt rail.

Removal of Rear Fenders and Rear Deck Center Panel

To remove the rear fenders and rear deck center panel as an assembly, cut the fender at the belt line below the roof extension panel as shown in Figure 38.

Drill and mill out the spot-welds at the belt rail, wheelhouse panels, center body pillars, and rear cross-

member. Then remove the bolts attaching this assembly to the wheelhouse panels from the inside of the trunk compartment.

NOTE: *The above operations are outlined in detail in preceding paragraphs.*

Installing New Rear Deck Center Panel and Fenders

Service fenders and rear deck center panel are supplied with beads attached. It will, therefore, be necessary to remove the beads from both sides of the service rear deck center panel whenever both the center deck panel and fenders are to be replaced.

To assure proper alignment, install and align the new service rear deck center panel to the body. Weld the front flange to the belt rail and temporarily attach the bottom flange to the bottom side of the rear crossmember with sheet metal screws until fenders are aligned to panel.

Install new service fenders according to previous instructions. Figure 43 illustrates how the service rear fenders are attached to the rear deck center panel.

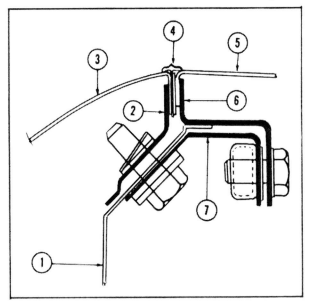

1. Wheelhouse Panel
2. Mounting Strap Welded to Fender
3. Fender
4. Bead Weld to Fender
5. Service Rear Deck Center Panel
6. Outer Service Mounting Bracket Welded to Center Panel
7. Inner Service Mounting Bracket

FIGURE 43—*Cross Section of Service Rear Fender, Rear Deck Center Panel, and Wheelhouse Panel Mounting*

Dependent on the extent of body damage, it may only be necessary to cut away damaged sections and replace them with a tailored cut section of a new panel. Operations of this type save considerable time and material.

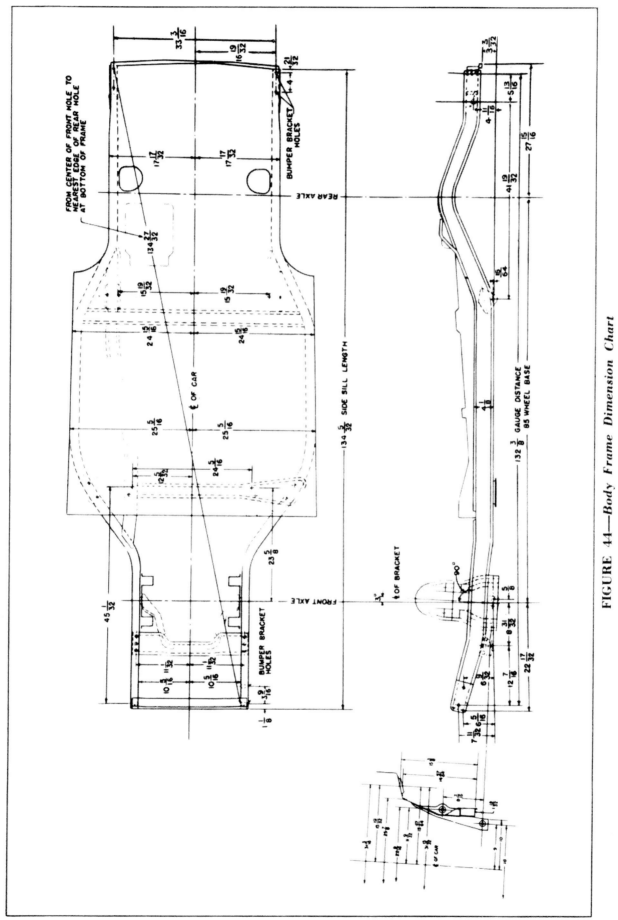

FIGURE 44—Body Frame Dimension Chart

Technical Service Manual

Door and Rear Quarter Trim, Hardware and Glass

DOOR and REAR QUARTER TRIM, HARDWARE and GLASS

IDENTIFICATION OF DOOR PARTS

The Hardtop and Convertible doors are interchangeable.

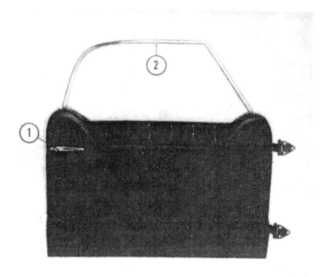

1. Door Key Lock Mounted in Outside Door Handle
2. Door Glass and Frame Assembly

FIGURE 1—Outside View Right Door— A and B Series

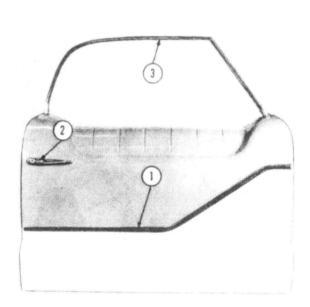

1. Door Moulding
2. Outside Door Handle and Key Lock Assembly
3. Door Glass and Frame Assembly

FIGURE 2—Outside View Right Door— 1500 Series Without Ventilator Assembly

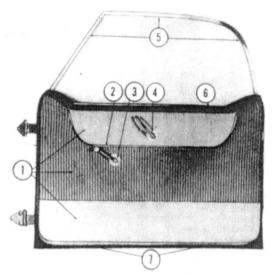

1. Trim Panel
2. Trim Panel Trim Moulding
3. Window Regulator Handle, Escutcheon, and Base
4. Remote Control Handle Escutcheon and Base
5. Door Glass and Frame Assembly
6. Door Finish Moulding
7. Door Sealer Rubber

FIGURE 3—Inside Trim Parts—A and B Series

FIGURE 4—Inside Trim Parts—1500 Series Without Ventilator Assembly

OUTSIDE DOOR HANDLE

The outside door handle is a plunger release type handle. It is fastened to the door outer panel by a

DOOR AND REAR QUARTER TRIM, HARDWARE AND GLASS

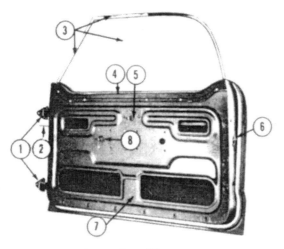

1. Upper and Lower Door Hinges
2. Door Check
3. Door Glass and Frame Assembly
4. Door Finish Moulding
5. Door Remote Control and Screws
6. Door Lock
7. Door Glass Stop Bracket Screws
8. Door Window Regulator and Mounting Screws

FIGURE 5—*Parts Assembled—A, B, and 1500 Series Door Without Ventilator Assembly*

FIGURE 6—*Parts Assembled—1500 Series Door With Ventilator Assembly*

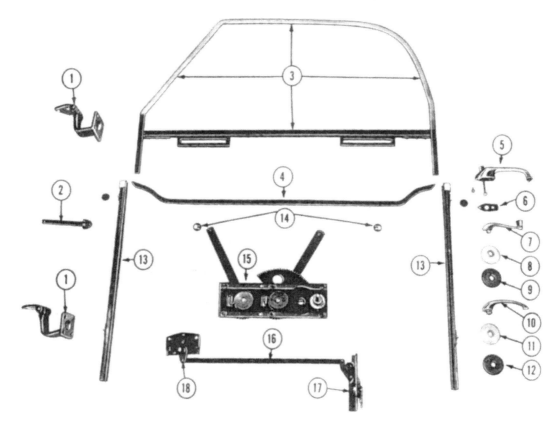

1. Upper and Lower Door Hinges
2. Door Check
3. Door Glass, Frame, and Bottom Channel Assembly
4. Door Finish Moulding
5. Outside Door Handle
6. Door Handle to Door Gasket
7. Door Window Regulator Handle
8. Plastic Escutcheon
9. Sponge Rubber Tension Washer
10. Remote Control Handle
11. Plastic Escutcheon
12. Sponge Rubber Tension Washer
13. Door Glass Slide Channels
14. Regulator Arm to Bottom Glass Channel Retainers
15. Door Window Regulator
16. Door Lock and Remote Control Link
17. Door Lock
18. Remote Control

FIGURE 7—*Parts Removed—A, B, and 1500 Series Without Ventilator Assembly*

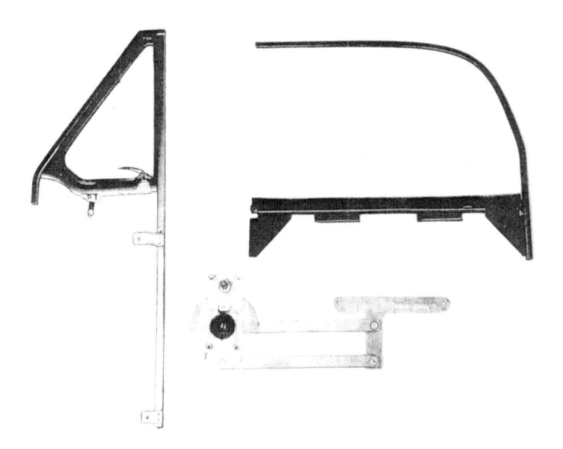

FIGURE 8—*Assemblies Removed—1500 Series Door With Ventilator Assembly*

stud and nut and a shoulder bolt concealed by the door sealer rubber' and door trim panel (Fig. 9).

Prior to Serial Number E-48848, only the right door handle contains a key lock cylinder. The left door handle can only be locked by the remote control handle.

Outside door handles with key locks in both right and left door handles were incorporated in production at car Serial Number E-48848.

Outside Door Handle Removal
Prior to Car Serial Number E-48848

Remove the door trim panel. Lift the water dam paper and remove the screw holding the front of the handle to the door outer panel.

Loosen the sealer rubber and remove the door flange to handle screw (Fig. 9).

Car Serial Number E-48848 and Higher

Remove the door trim panel and water dam paper.

Raise the door glass.

Remove the hair pin retaining spring and the lock to handle connecting link from the lock handle operating lever stud.

Remove the door flange and panel to handle screws (Fig. 9).

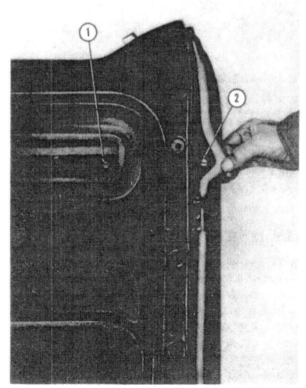

FIGURE 9—*Outside Door Handle Mounting Screws*

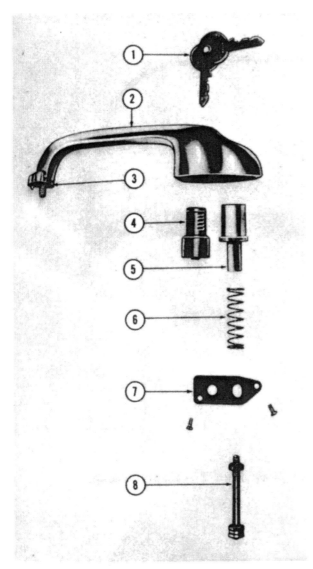

1. Door Lock Keys
2. Outside Door Handle
3. Mounting Escutcheon
4. Key Lock Cylinder
5. Lock Release Plunger
6. Lock Release Plunger Spring
7. Cylinder Lock and Release Plunger Retaining Plate
8. Lock Release Plunger Extension Shaft

FIGURE 10—Outside Door Handle and Key Lock Cylinder—1500 Series Prior to Car Serial Number E-48848

KEY LOCK

On the first type handle, the door key lock cylinder is retained in the outer door handle by the door lock release plunger retaining plate (Item 7, Fig. 10).

When in the unlocked position, a groove provided in the lock cylinder allows the door lock release plunger shoulder to pass, when depressed, thereby tripping the door lock and opening the door.

In locking the door, the key lock cylinder groove is turned out of alignment, thereby preventing the release plunger from being depressed.

On the second type door handle, the key lock cylinder is retained in the push button (Item 2, Fig. 11) by a retaining pin inserted through a hole in the body of the push button which engages a groove in the lock cylinder.

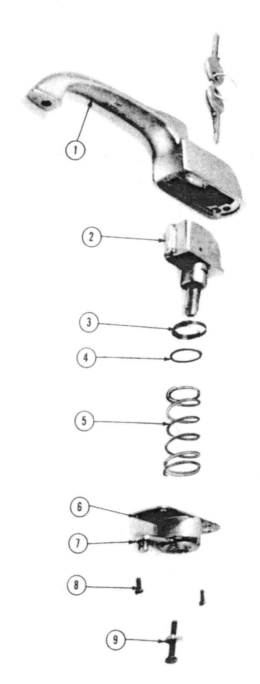

1. Handle Shell
2. Push Button and Lock Cylinder
3. Lock Cylinder Return Spring
4. Push Button Spring Washer
5. Push Button Return Spring
6. Base Plate
7. Lock Operating Lever
8. Base Plate Retaining Screw
9. Push Button Plunger Bolt

FIGURE 11—Outside Door Handle—1500 Series After Car Serial Number E-48848

REMOTE CONTROL AND WINDOW REGULATOR HANDLES

These handles are fastened to the remote control and window regulator shafts by a small pin. This pin is concealed by the rubber escutcheon and metal retaining ring in the escutcheon. The pin must be driven or pushed out before the handle can be removed (Fig. 12). Depressor Tool J-2631-A is used in this operation.

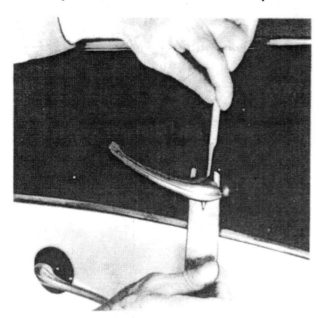

FIGURE 12—*Removing Remote Control Handle*

DOOR TRIM PANELS

The door trim panels are fastened to the sides and bottom of the doors by snap-in clips while the upper edge of the trim panel seats into a recess in the finish moulding.

To remove the door trim panel, remove the remote and window regulator handles. Use Depressor Tool J-2631-A to pry the trim panel from the door at each clip (Fig. 13).

WATER DAM PAPER

The water dam paper is taped to the door inner panel to deflect any moisture from the trim panel. Care should be exercised to avoid tearing it when handling. It must be replaced in such a manner so as to cover all large openings in the door inner panel. The flaps cut into the paper at the bottom must be "tucked" into the large openings to deflect moisture to the outside drains in the door.

DOOR LOCK AND REMOTE CONTROL

A toggle latch trigger type lock is used on all cars built prior to Serial Number E-48848. A rotary type lock is used on units starting with Serial Number E-48848.

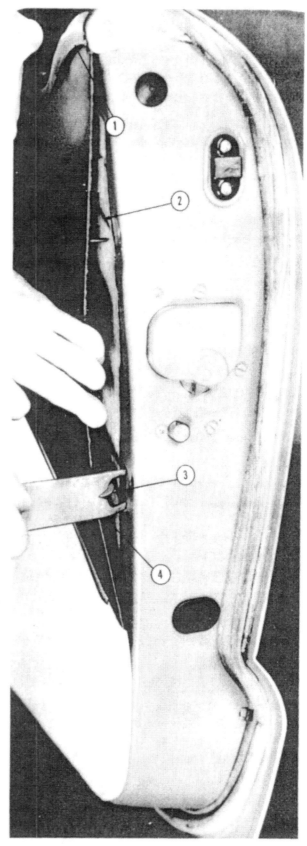

1. Recess in Finish Moulding
2. Door Trim Panel
3. Fastening Clip
4. Depressor Tool

FIGURE 13—*Removing Door Trim Panel*

DOOR AND REAR QUARTER TRIM, HARDWARE AND GLASS

The door lock and remote control are riveted to the remote control link and must be removed from the door as a unit.

Removal of Toggle Latch Type Lock

Remove the door trim panel and finish moulding.

Remove the lower glass stop upper two screws and turn stop to side.

Lower the glass and disconnect the window regulator arms (Fig. 14) from the glass bottom channel by sliding the key slotted retainers from the regulator arm studs.

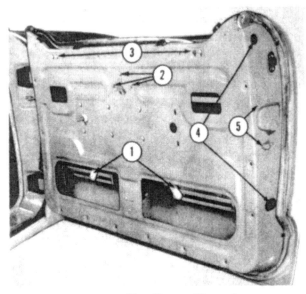

1. Regulator Arms to Glass Bottom Channel
2. Remote Control Fastening Screws
3. Upper Glass Stop
4. Location of Glass Slide Channel Fastening Nuts and Washers
5. Lock Fastening Screws

FIGURE 14—Parts to be Removed for Glass and Lock Removal—Toggle Latch Type Lock

Remove the upper glass stops (Fig. 14).

Remove the glass from the door.

Then remove the lock side glass slide channel by removing the upper and lower stud nuts and washers.

Remove the remote control and lock to door screws.

Turn the lock toggle to the vertical or locked position and remove the remote and lock assembly through the lower access hole (Fig. 15).

Rotary Type Door Lock Removal

The procedure outlined for the toggle latch type lock also applies for the second type except that the hair pin retainer and lock to handle connecting link must be removed from the lock operating lever stud on the handle (Fig. 16) before the lock assembly can be removed. For units with door ventilator, refer to Glass Removal.

FIGURE 15—Removing Door Lock and Remote Control

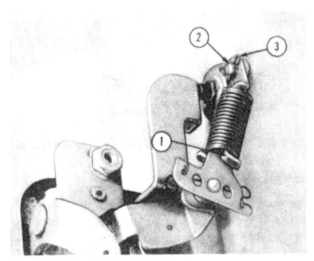

1. Lock to Handle Connecting Link
2. Handle Lock Operating Lever Stud
3. Link to Handle Hair Pin Retainer

FIGURE 16—Lock to Handle Connecting Link Fastening—Rotary Type Lock

Remove remote control and lock assembly through access hole in door (Fig. 17).

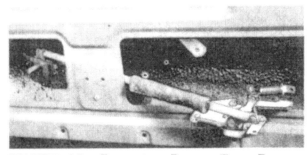

FIGURE 17—Removing Rotary Type Remote Control and Door Lock from Door

DOOR LOCK STRIKER ASSEMBLY

The door lock striker serves a dual purpose: it keeps the door lock in a latched position to the body and serves as a female dovetail preventing the door from moving up and down.

The upper wedge on the striker is tapered. It moves in and out under spring tension when closing and opening the door. This movement allows a constant bearing for the top surface of the latch without binding during movement of the door when closing and opening.

Toggle Latch Trigger Type

The latch pin engages the forked section of the lock outside latch (Fig. 18) and as the door is completely closed, the latch revolves forcing the top surface under the upper wedge on the striker.

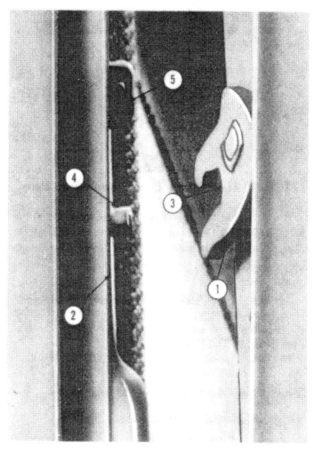

1. Lock Outside Latch
2. Lock Striker
3. Top of Forked Section of Lock Outside Latch
4. Top of Striker Latch Pin
5. Upper Wedge on Striker

FIGURE 18—Door Lock and Striker— Toggle Latch Trigger Type

When the door is completely closed and the lock latch has revolved to a vertical position, the wedge seats itself firmly against the top surface of the lock latch eliminating any up and down movement.

Adjustment of Striker Plate Toggle Latch Trigger Type Lock

The body pillars are provided with a tapped movable lock plate that is encased in the pillar which permits up and down or in and out movement.

The striker plate should be adjusted so that when closing the door the inner prong of the forked door lock latch clears the striker pin by approximately 1/16″. The striker plate should be moved toward the inside of the body far enough to compress the door sealer rubber to provide sealing and prevent door chatter or movement, yet not require excessive slamming to close the door.

After the striker plate has been located for the proper adjustment, then move the top of the striker toward the outside of the body (Fig. 19) or to a vertical position. This will insure a positive bearing surface for the top of the door latch and prevent the possibility of it becoming disengaged from the striker latch pin when the lock is in the first position or safety catch.

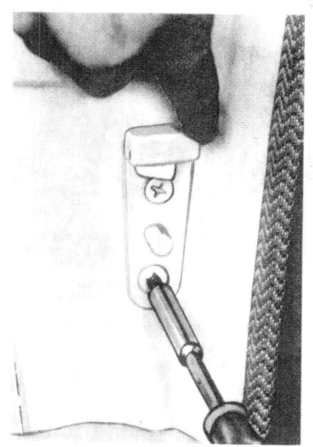

FIGURE 19—Moving Top of Lock Striker to Vertical Position—Toggle Latch Trigger Type

Rotary Type Door Lock Striker

The striker for the rotary lock can be adjusted up or down and in or out on the body pillar. It must be set on a horizontal plane with the door lock so that the lock rotor can freely engage the double toothed rack of the striker (Fig. 20). The steel stud on the lock guides the rotor into alignment with the striker teeth. A spring loaded sliding wedge incorporated in the bottom portion of the doubled toothed rack helps prevent vertical movement of the door and a plastic block at the bottom of the striker prevents a downward movement when the door is in the closed position.

1. Lock Striker Anti-Slip Lock Plate
2. Tapped Movable Plate for Adjustment
3. Door Lock Striker

FIGURE 20—*Rotary Lock Striker*

Lubrication

All moving parts of the lock and striker must be lubricated with lubriplate before assembly into the car. A few drops of a dry type lubricant similar to "Shaler Riz" applied to the rotor and key lock cylinder once every few months will keep these locks in working order.

DOOR VENTILATOR ASSEMBLY

The ventilator assembly consists of the ventilator frame and division channel unit, rubber weather strip, glass, and chrome frame assembly.

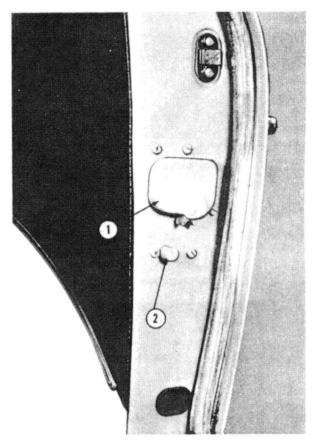

1. Lock
2. Lock Stud

FIGURE 21—*Rotary Lock Mounted in Door*

It is operated by a pivot type handle mounted to the bottom of the glass frame. The glass frame pivots at the top and the bottom. The ventilator glass frame upper pivot bracket is riveted to the pivot bracket on the outer frame.

The lower pivot shaft extends through the ventilator frame and is spring loaded to create sufficient friction by adjustment of the spring tension to hold the ventilator in any desired position.

Ventilator Assembly Removal

Remove door trim panel and finish moulding.

Move the door glass to the fully lowered position.

Remove rubber plug button and door to ventilator screw (Item 3, Fig. 23).

Remove inner panel to division channel bracket upper screw (Item 2, Fig. 23).

Remove inner door panel to division channel bottom bolt (Item 1, Fig. 23).

Lift ventilator assembly straight upward and pry upper division channel bracket past upper ledge of door (Fig. 24). The assembly can then be removed.

Care must be exercised to prevent door glass damage when prying bracket.

DOOR AND REAR QUARTER TRIM, HARDWARE AND GLASS

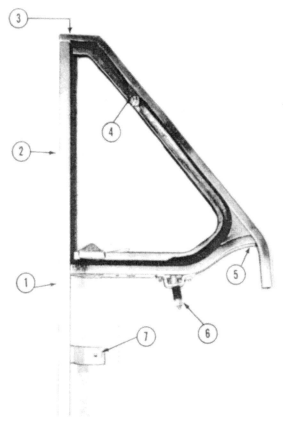

1. Center Division Bar to Frame Screws
2. Center Division Bar
3. Division Bar to Frame Upper Screws
4. Upper Pivot Rivet
5. Lower Frame to Upper Frame Screws
6. Lower Pivot, Spring, and Adjusting Nut
7. Center Division Channel Upper Mounting Bracket

FIGURE 22—*Ventilator Assembly*

1. Lower Division Bar Fastening Bolt
2. Upper Division Bar Fastening Screw
3. Door to Ventilator Frame Plug Button and Screw
4. Weather Seal Finish Plate Screws
5. Ventilator Assembly
6. Finish Moulding Screws
7. Upper Glass Stop

**FIGURE 23—*Parts to be Removed for
Ventilator Removal***

**FIGURE 24—*Prying Division Bar Upper
Bracket From Door Inner Panel***

DOOR GLASS

The door glass without ventilator assembly is encased at the top and sides by a chrome frame and set into the glass bottom channel which in turn is fastened to the frame with screws.

The door glass used with the ventilator assembly is provided with a chrome frame at the top and rear only.

Door Glass Removal Without Ventilator Assembly

Remove the door finish moulding and trim panel.

Remove the two screws in the lower glass stop and turn the glass stop to the side (Fig. 25).

DOOR AND REAR QUARTER TRIM, HARDWARE AND GLASS

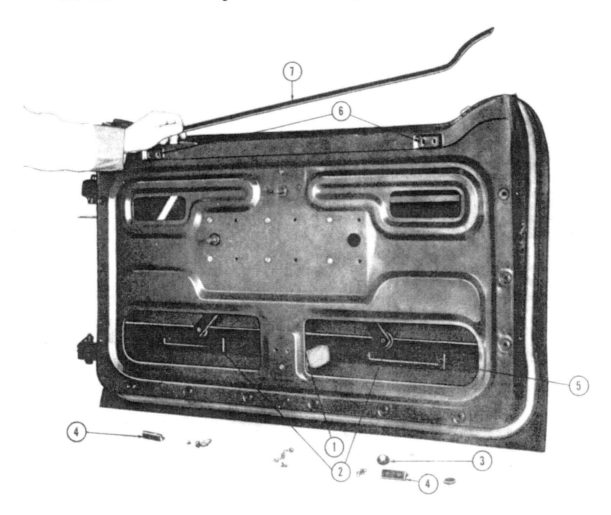

1. **Door Glass Stop**
2. **Regulator Arms**
3. **Regulator Arm to Bottom Glass Channel Retainer**
4. Upper Glass Stop
5. Bottom Glass Channel
6. Location of Upper Glass Stops
7. Weather Strip (Body Side)

FIGURE 25—*Parts to be Removed for Glass Removal—Without Ventilator*

Remove the regulator arms from the glass bottom channel by removing the regulator arm to glass channel retainers.

Lower the glass to the bottom of the door. This will permit the removal of the upper glass stops and the body side weather strip.

The glass can then be removed from the door.

Door Glass Removal With Ventilator

The ventilator assembly must be removed before the door glass can be removed (see Ventilator Removal). Then slightly spring the bottom of the window regulator assembly toward the outside of the door; at the same time, lower glass beyond lower glass stop (Fig. 26). This will facilitate door ledge weather strip and upper glass stop removal.

Remove door ledge weather strip and door glass upper stop.

FIGURE 26—*Window Regulator Pushed Out Beyond Lower Glass Stop*

Turn regulator with handle to raise glass up approximately half way and slide glass toward the hinge post approximately 2 inches (Fig. 27). This will disengage the regulator arm studs from the glass bottom channel.

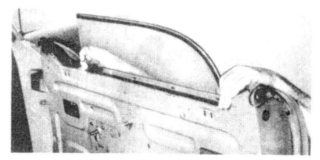

FIGURE 27—*Position of Glass for Removal From Regulator Arms*

Lift glass upward until the glass stop bracket on the bottom frame lock side contacts the inner door panel upper ledge. Spread the inner door panel slightly to allow the stop bracket to pass (Fig. 28).

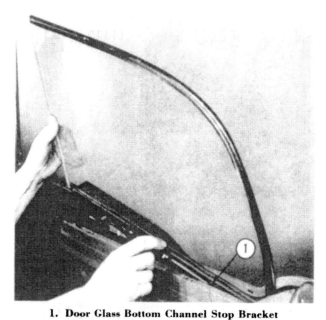

1. Door Glass Bottom Channel Stop Bracket

FIGURE 28—*Spreading Inner Door Panel Releasing Stop Bracket*

Door Glass Installation — With Ventilator

Turn the regulator to the fully raised position and set door glass bottom channel on top of regulator arm studs (Fig. 29). Align the spring loaded washers on the studs so that they do not interfere with the enlarged head of the stud entering the channel. Jolt the glass downward slightly to engage the studs into the channel.

Turn the door glass down to the stop bracket on the channel at the lock side and pry the stop past the door ledge (Fig. 28).

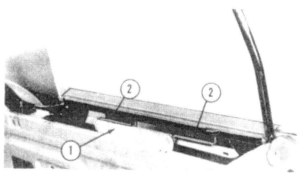

1. Regulator Raised Beyond Upper Door Ledge
2. Glass Bottom Channel Slides

FIGURE 29—*Regulator Raised and Engaging Regulator Arm Studs With Glass Bottom Channel*

Lower the glass completely and install the weather strip and upper glass stop.

Install the door ventilator.

Check the door glass operation; it must operate parallel with the ventilator division bar.

The door glass can be tilted to or away from the division bar by the adjustment shoulder bolt at the bottom of the regulator (Item 5, Fig. 30). A horizontal elongated hole in the window support plate allows for forward or back adjustment to tilt the glass after the shoulder bolt is loosened.

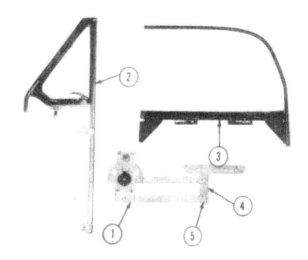

1. Regulator Assembly
2. Ventilator Assembly
3. Glass Assembly
4. Regulator Arm Window Support Plate
5. Adjusting Shoulder Bolt

FIGURE 30—*Ventilator, Window, and Regulator Assemblies*

WINDOW REGULATOR REMOVAL

Without Ventilator

Remove the trim panel.

Lower the glass and disconnect the regulator arms from the bottom glass channel.

DOOR AND REAR QUARTER TRIM, HARDWARE AND GLASS

Remove one of the finish moulding screws and raise the door glass. Insert a thin punch into the screw hole and under the glass to hold it in the raised position. Remove regulator assembly (Fig. 31).

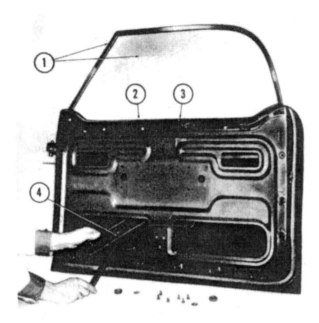

1. Door Glass and Frame
2. Door Finish Moulding
3. Punch Inserted Under Glass Assembly
4. Door Window Regulator

FIGURE 31—*Removing Window Regulator*

Window Regulator Removal With Ventilator

The regulator can only be removed after the ventilator and door glass are removed. Refer to Ventilator and Door Glass Removal.

Turn regulator arms to the half way "up" position. Then remove the door to regulator screws and remove regulator through rear opening in door inner panel.

DOOR HINGES

The door hinges are of the pin type.

They are screwed to a fixed location on the door and on the body with Phillips head screws (Fig. 32).

REAR QUARTER TRIM

The trim parts shown in Figure 33 are identical in the Hardtop and Convertible models.

The body lock pillar stormstrip is tacked to a tacking strip which is crimped into a channel of the body lock pillar. The tack heads are concealed when the trim panels are installed.

The wheelhouse trim cover is cemented to the wheelhouse panel with trim cement.

The rear seat back strainer trim panel is fastened

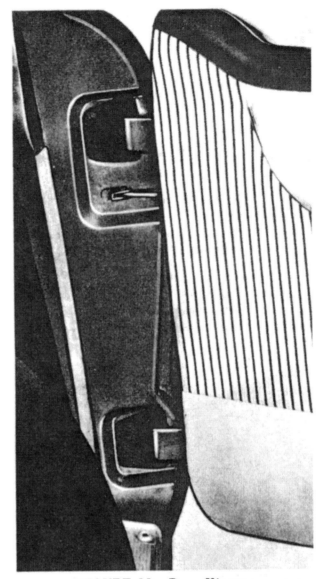

FIGURE 32—*Door Hinges*

1. Body Lock Pillar Stormstrip
2. Wheelhouse Trim Cover, Left
3. Rear Seat Back Strainer Trim Panel, Left

FIGURE 33—*Rear Quarter Trim (Hardtop Model Shown)*

to the strainer with screws. These are visible when the seat back is lowered.

The rear quarter trim panel used in the Hardtop models (Fig. 34) is one piece, while the Convertible models (Fig. 35) require two trim panels.

The trim panels in both models are fastened with screws.

The rear seat cushion riser trim panel (Item 4, Fig. 34) is cemented to the cushion riser panel with the addition of screws at the top edge. This panel is also used on the Convertible models.

1. Rear Quarter Body Lock Pillar Trim Panel, Right
2. Rear Quarter Upper Trim Panel, Right

FIGURE 35—*Rear Quarter Trim Panels (Convertible Model Shown)*

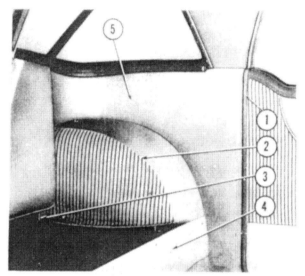

1. Body Lock Pillar Stormstrip
2. Wheelhouse Trim Cover, Left
3. Rear Seat Back Strainer Trim Panel, Left
4. Rear Seat Cushion Riser Trim Panel
5. Rear Quarter Trim Panel

FIGURE 34—*Rear Quarter Trim (Hardtop Model Shown)*

DOOR HEADER SEAL

The windshield post and door header seal retainers are fastened to the side roof rail and windshield post with sheet metal screws (Fig. 36).

Elongated holes allow for inward or outward adjustment to effect a seal above the doors.

A sealer rubber is inserted into the retainers from the belt line at the lock pillar to the front fender line.

1. Door Header Seal
2. Door Header Seal Retainer

FIGURE 36—*Door Header Weatherseal and Retainer*

TECHNICAL SERVICE LETTER REFERENCE

Date	Letter No.	Subject	Changes information on Page No.

Technical Service Manual

Windshield-Rear Window- Windshield Wiper

WINDSHIELD-REAR WINDOW-
WINDSHIELD WIPER

1. Windshield Glass Rubber Channel
2. Windshield Top and Side Reveal Moulding, Right
3. Windshield Reveal Moulding Upper Cover Clip
4. Windshield Top and Side Reveal Moulding, Left
5. Windshield Reveal Moulding Lower Corner Cover
6. Windshield Lower Reveal Moulding

FIGURE 1—*Windshield Reveal Mouldings*

WINDSHIELD ASSEMBLY

The windshield is one piece flat laminated safety glass. It has the identifying trade name of "TRIPLEX PLATE" sand blasted in the upper corner. This glass is similar to American made glasses known as "Duplate" and "L. O. F." (Libby Owen-Ford).

It is set into the body from the outside as an assembly. This assembly consists of the glass, channel rubber, reveal mouldings, and cover clips.

Reveal Mouldings

The windshield reveal mouldings are in three pieces, right and left, top and side with an expansion joint at the top center which is covered by a stainless steel cover clip that snaps on over the mouldings, and a bottom reveal moulding. Stainless steel "L" shaped clips snap over and cover the top and side mouldings at the joints of the bottom moulding (Fig. 1).

The reveal mouldings have an "L" shaped flange which extends into the rubber channel and hooks toward the inside of the glass.

This creates a bind between the outside face plate of the mouldings and the channel rubber and forces the outside lip of the channel rubber tightly against the outer surface of the glass.

When assembled in the car, it is impossible to remove these mouldings without first removing the complete windshield assembly from the car.

Windshield Removal

Place a cloth cover over top of hood and cowl for protection of paint.

Remove windshield wiper arms and blades.

Remove windshield finish mouldings (Fig. 2).

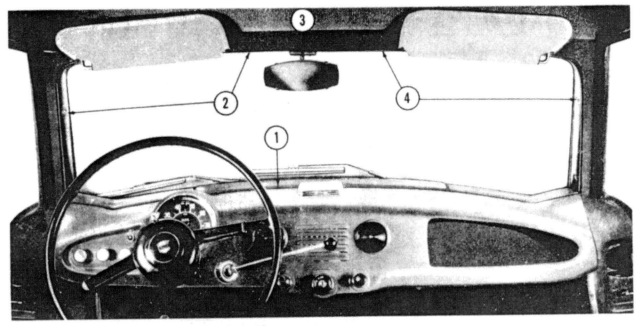

1. Windshield Finish Moulding, Lower
2. Windshield Finish Moulding Top and Side, Left
3. Rear View Mirror
4. Windshield Finish Moulding Top and Side, Right

FIGURE 2—*Parts to be Removed at Windshield*

Use fibre or hard wood wedge shaped tool to break seal of rubber lip to windshield opening flange.

Use two putty knives to lift the lip of the rubber over the flange of the windshield opening, pressing the glass assembly outward (Fig. 3).

Then from the outside, lift the glass assembly from the windshield opening and place it on a padded bench or table.

Remove or slide the moulding joint cover plates to expose the joints.

Pull channel rubber away from glass, spread lip of rubber, and carefully lift reveal moulding from groove in rubber (Fig. 4).

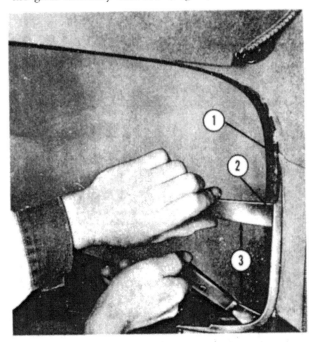

1. Channel Rubber Lip
2. Windshield Opening Flange
3. Putty Knives Between Rubber Lip and Flange

FIGURE 3—*Lifting Lip of Channel Rubber Over Windshield Opening Flange*

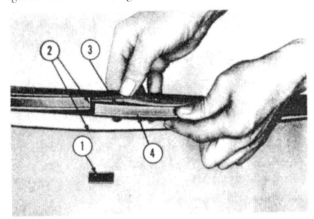

1. Moulding Cover Plates Removed
2. Rubber and Moulding Pulled off Glass
3. Spreading Lip of Rubber
4. Lifting Moulding From Rubber

FIGURE 4—*Removing Reveal Mouldings From Channel Rubber*

Remove Channel Rubber From Glass

With cloth dampened in gasoline, naphtha or cleaning fluid, remove all dried rubber cement from channel rubber and flange of windshield opening in body.

Windshield Glass Installation

Install the rubber channel over one end of the glass.

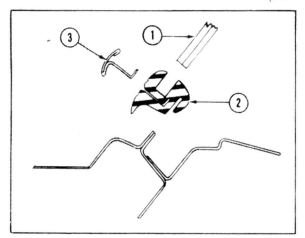

1. Glass
2. Rubber Channel
3. Reveal Moulding

FIGURE 5—*Exploded View of Windshield Assembly Parts*

Install wood "C" clamp over one end of the glass and rubber to hold rubber on glass until it is completely installed (Fig. 6).

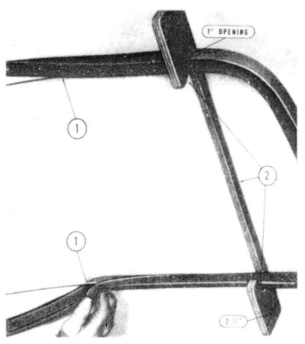

1. Installing Rubber on Glass
2. Wood "C" Clamp Made of 1/2" Plywood

FIGURE 6—*Installing Rubber Channel on Windshield Glass*

Apply liquid soap to moulding groove in channel rubber. This permits free movement of moulding into channel rubber (Fig. 7).

FIGURE 7—*Apply Liquid Soap in the Moulding Groove After Rubber is Installed on Glass*

Center the moulding on glass and rubber channel. Then start one end of the moulding in groove of rubber at top center of glass. Use a fibre or hardwood wedge shaped tool to spread the lip (Fig. 8). Open groove and push moulding flange into groove. Press moulding down into rubber channel.

Tie a cord, approximately five feet long, around the center of glass to hold rubber and reveal moulding onto glass. Continue to push the moulding flange into the groove until all mouldings are set into the rubber. Now tie another cord around center of glass to hold other end of moulding and rubber onto glass.

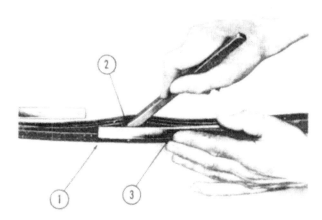

1. Top Center of Glass and Rubber
2. Spreading Lip to Open Groove in Rubber
3. Pressing Moulding Down into Rubber

FIGURE 8—*Installing Moulding into Groove of Rubber*

With wide nose pliers, TAPED TO PREVENT SCRATCHING THE MOULDINGS, lightly compress moulding into rubber. Start at end of moulding at top center of glass and work around to end. Continue the operation on the opposite moulding.

Then compress lower reveal moulding into rubber and install the clips.

This procedure moves the moulding in the rubber to the expansion joints allowing the moulding to seat properly in the rubber.

Use two cords ten feet long. Insert a cord in groove of rubber starting at top center of the glass and continuing around the other end at bottom center. Then insert the other cord in groove of rubber around the other end of glass. overlapping the ends of cords at both top and bottom center at least one foot. as shown in Figure 9.

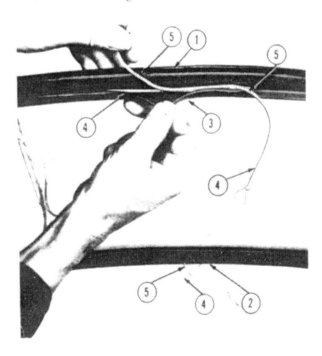

1. Top Center of Glass
2. Bottom Center of Glass
3. Groove in Rubber With Cords Overlapping at Center
4. Ends of Cord Around Left End of Windshield
5. Ends of Cord Around Right End of Windshield

FIGURE 9—*Inserting Two Cords in Groove of Channel Rubber (Used to Lift Lip of Rubber Over Flange of Windshield Opening)*

Apply Windshield Sealer to base of flange on the complete outside flange of windshield opening (Fig. 10).

> CAUTION: *Do not apply sealer to edge of body flange as it will come off when lip of rubber is lifted over windshield flange and will require considerable cleaning.*

Place the glass assembly, with rubber and mouldings installed, into windshield opening from outside of body. Center the assembly in windshield opening. Now remove the cords that were installed to hold the rubber and moulding onto glass.

From the inside of the car. pull both top cords to lift the lip of rubber over the windshield opening flange. Start at top center and lift rubber lip for a distance of six inches.

Now pull both bottom cords lifting lip of rubber over windshield opening flange at bottom center for a distance of six inches.

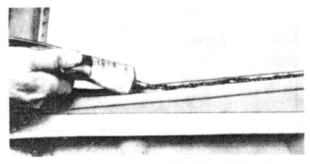

FIGURE 10—*Applying Windshield Sealer to Bottom of Flange on Outside of Windshield Opening*

Pull top and then bottom cords on right side until complete right side is in place.

Pull top and then bottom cords on left side until complete left side is in place (Fig. 11).

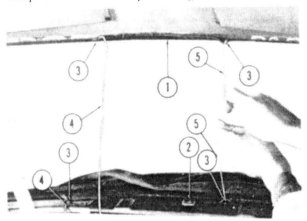

1. Top Center
2. Bottom Center
3. Lifting Lip of Rubber Over Flange of Windshield Opening
4. Left End Cord—Top and Bottom End
5. Right End Cord—Top and Bottom End

FIGURE 11—*Lifting Lip of Channel Rubber Over Flange of Windshield Opening*

With a rubber mallet. tap the windshield and reveal moulding assembly lightly so that it seats properly.

Apply windshield sealer between the windshield glass and rubber. then clean the glass.

Install finish mouldings. rear view mirror. and windshield wiper arms and blades.

Correction of Water Leakage at Windshield

Many times it is assumed windshields leak when in reality. the leakage is from another source. Possible sources are loose screws on outside of dash or insulation pad clips.

Leakage between sealer rubber and glass can be observed without removing any parts.

To locate leakage between sealer rubber and body. it is necessary to remove the finish moulding.

To correct leakage at either source, it is necessary to remove the finish moulding and reseal.

Use a pressure gun to seal between the rubber and the glass and between the rubber and the metal.

REAR WINDOW ASSEMBLY

Prior to car Serial Number E-46164, the rear window glass consists of three individual sections.

Beginning with car Serial Number E-46164, a one-piece curved rear window glass was incorporated.

The center section of the three-piece rear window glass is flat while the right and left corner sections are bent. Each of these glasses are tempered glass and have the identifying trade name of "TRIPLEX TOUGHENED" sand blasted in the corners while the one-piece rear window glass has the trade name sand blasted in the bottom center of the glass.

These glasses are similar to the American made tempered glass known as "Herculite."

They are set into a channel rubber with reveal mouldings inserted into the channel rubber.

It is impossible to remove these mouldings without first removing the complete rear window assembly.

The right and left rear quarter and rear belt mouldings are bolted and fastened to the body with lock washers and nuts on the inside under the rear window channel rubber lip.

The body belt moulding retains the rear window assembly in position at the bottom while the inside finish moulding retains it in position at the top.

Rear Window Assembly Removal

Remove the rear seat cushion and fold the back assembly forward.

Remove the rear window finish mouldings.

Remove the rear belt moulding cover clips. Remove the rear belt moulding retaining nuts and washers located under the rear window channel rubber lip (Fig. 14) and remove the belt moulding (Fig. 15).

On inside of body, insert putty knife between window opening flange and lip of rubber starting at lower corner and working upward to the other side of body (Fig. 16).

The complete assembly can then be lifted from the body.

After the complete rear window glass assembly is removed from the car, it should be placed on a clean padded bench.

Removing Reveal Moulding From Rear Window Assembly

Remove or slide the rear window reveal moulding cover clip on either of the moulding ends.

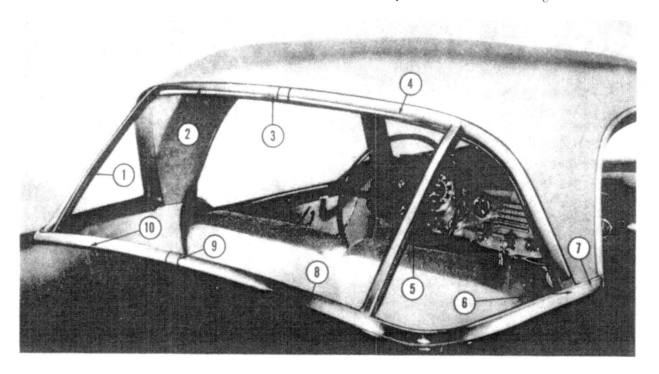

1. Left Partition Reveal Moulding
2. Left Upper Reveal Moulding
3. Upper Reveal Moulding Center Clip
4. Right Upper Reveal Moulding
5. Right Partition Reveal Moulding
6. Right Quarter Side Belt Moulding Clip
7. Right Quarter Side Belt Moulding
8. Rear Belt Moulding, Right
9. Rear Belt Moulding Clip
10. Rear Belt Moulding, Left

FIGURE 12—Three-Piece Rear Window Glass Assembly—Prior to Serial Number E-46164

FIGURE 13—*One-Piece Rear Window Assembly*
— *Serial Number E-46164 and Higher*

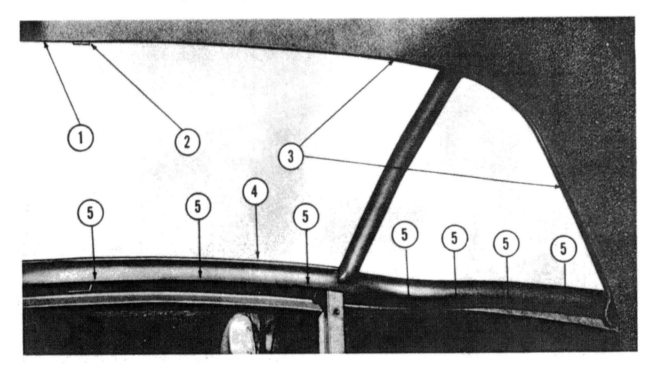

1. Rear Window Finish Moulding Top and Side, Right
2. Rear Window Finish Moulding Clip
3. Rear Window Finish Moulding Top and Side, Left
4. Rear Window Channel Rubber Bottom Section
5. Body Belt Moulding Bolt Nuts—Concealed Under
   Lip of Channel Rubber

FIGURE 14—*Rear Window Finish Mouldings
and Location of Belt Moulding Fastening Nuts*

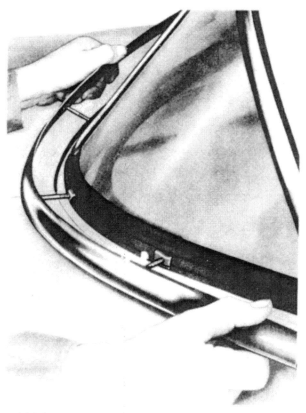

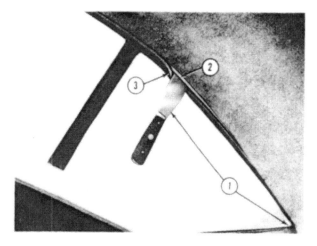

1. Lip of Rubber Removed From Flange With Use of Putty Knife
2. Flange
3. Lip of Sealer Rubber

FIGURE 16—*Releasing Lip of Rubber From Rear Window Opening Flange*

NOTE: *Either of the end glasses can be removed and replaced without removal of the center glass or the other end glass.*

Installation of Rear Window Assembly

Install the center glass into the channel rubber; then install the end glasses.

Push the end glass inward and install the partition reveal mouldings.

NOTE: *These mouldings are not interchangeable.*

FIGURE 15—*Removing Rear Belt Moulding*

Then twist upper edge of rubber and lift reveal mouldings from channel rubber.

On the three-piece rear window push end glasses inward and lift partition reveal moulding from rubber (Fig. 17). The rear window glass can then be removed from the rubber.

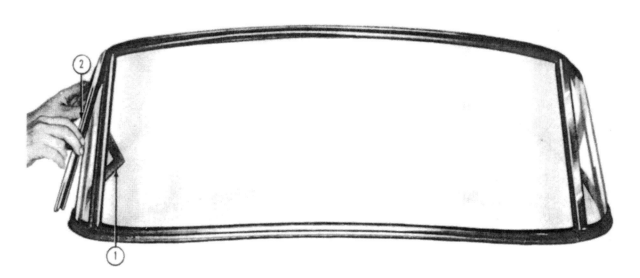

1. Push End Glasses Inward
2. Lift Partition Reveal Moulding From Rubber

FIGURE 17—*Removing Rear Window Center Partition Reveal Mouldings*

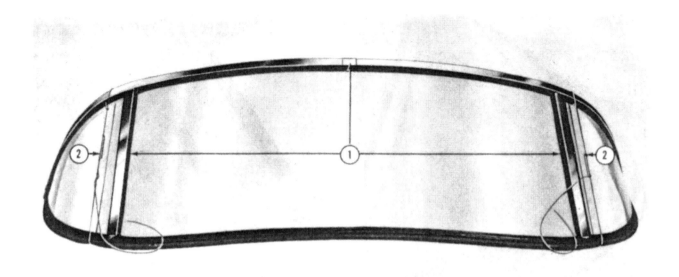

1. Reveal Mouldings Installed
2. Cord Tied to Hold Rubber and Mouldings on Glass

FIGURE 18—*Installing Glass and Reveal Mouldings in Channel Rubber*

Tie a cord around the glass and rubber (Fig. 18).

Install right and left reveal mouldings. Apply liquid soap in channel of the rubber to assist in inserting the moulding flange into the channel of the rubber. The reveal moulding must be seated properly.

To assist in lifting the lip of the rubber over the rear window opening flange when it is installed into the rear window opening, insert a cord in the groove of the rubber channel across the top and across the bottom. These cords should overlap twelve (12) inches at each end of the glass with the ends of cords left exposed (Fig. 19).

Set the complete assembly in the window opening so the bottom part of the channel rubber is on top of the flange of the window opening. Then move the glass sideways so the assembly is centered in the window opening.

Hold glass firmly against body from outside and lift bottom cord on inside which will lift the lip of rubber over flange of window opening for a distance of about ten inches. Then lift upper cord so lip of rubber is over flange about ten inches.

Perform the above operations on the other side of the glass.

Remove the cords holding the moulding and rubber to the glass (Fig. 18).

From inside of body, continue with bottom cord until lower lip of rubber is in place on body flange.

Then lift upper cord from both sides until lip of rubber is in place on flange of body.

1. Cord Inserted Into Channel of Rubber Across Bottom   2. Cord Inserted Into Channel of Rubber Across Top

FIGURE 19—*Rear Windshield Glass Assembly (Inside View)*

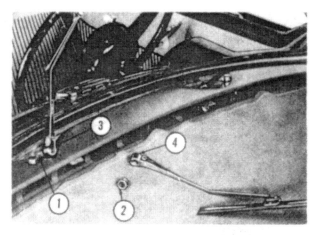

1. Wiper Arm Friction Lock Nut (On Shaft)
2. Wiper Arm Friction Lock Nut (Removed)
3. Wiper Arm on Shaft
4. Wiper Arm Removed

FIGURE 20—*Removing Windshield Wiper Arms*

From outside of body, press glass assembly toward body and lightly tap with rubber mallet on outer upper edge to permanently set the assembly into the window opening.

Seal the assembly on the outside with windshield sealer between rubber and body. Also seal between glass and rubber.

WINDSHIELD WIPER
Windshield Wiper Arms and Blades

The windshield wiper arms are fastened to the drive shafts with friction nuts which set on the shaft and screw into the arm. This tightening operation decreases the diameter of the friction nut and securely fastens the arm to the shaft.

When installing wiper arms, a final adjustment must be made so that both arms have the same limit of travel.

To remove the wiper arm from the shaft, it is only necessary to unscrew the friction nuts from the arm and lift the arm off the shaft.

WINDSHIELD WIPER MOTOR AND ATTACHING PARTS

The electric windshield wiper and attaching parts consist of a motor and transmission assembly, armor protected cable with drive shaft and housing assemblies, and the control switch assembly. This unit is the Lucas Model CRT-14.

In the event the motor should become overheated, a thermostatic switch disconnects electrical current until such time as the temperature returns to normal.

Connection of Cable to Windshield Wiper Motor and Transmission Assembly

The motor and transmission assembly is connected to the cable assembly by a connecting arm (Fig. 22). This is accessible after the transmission cover plate is removed.

Windshield Wiper Cable and Drive Shaft Assembly

The wiper cable and attaching parts consist of the drive shaft and housing assemblies, cable, and the three sections of cable armor.

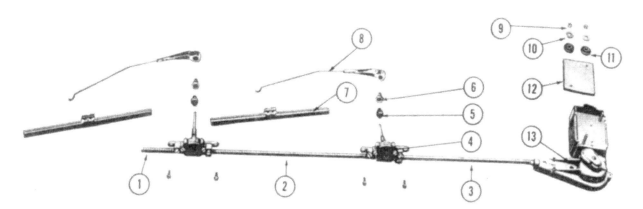

1. Windshield Wiper Cable Armor, Left
2. Windshield Wiper Cable Armor, Center
3. Windshield Wiper Cable Armor, Right
4. Windshield Wiper Drive Shaft and Housing Assembly
5. Windshield Wiper Drive Shaft to Cowl Grommet (Rubber)
6. Windshield Wiper Arm Friction Lock Nut
7. Windshield Wiper Blade
8. Windshield Wiper Arm
9. Windshield Wiper Motor to Body Nuts
10. Windshield Wiper Motor to Body Washers
11. Windshield Wiper Motor to Body Grommets (Rubber)
12. Windshield Wiper Motor to Body Insulation Pad (Rubber)
13. Windshield Wiper Motor and Transmission Assembly

FIGURE 21—*Windshield Wiper and Attaching Assemblies as Removed From Car*

WINDSHIELD—REAR WINDOW—WINDSHIELD WIPER

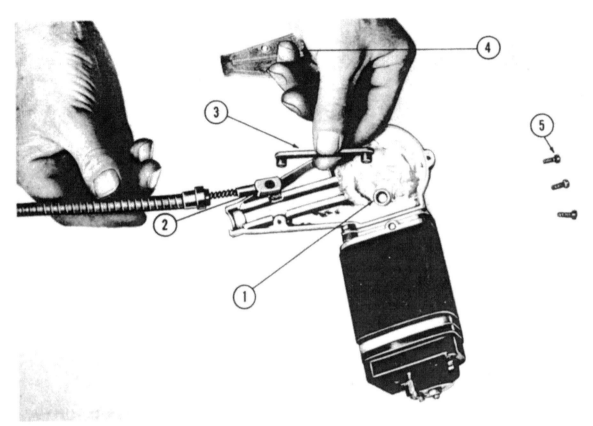

1. Windshield Wiper Transmission Drive Gear Connecting Arm Socket
2. Windshield Wiper Cable End and Connecting Arm Socket
3. Windshield Wiper Connecting Arm
4. Transmission Cover Removed
5. Transmission Cover Screws

FIGURE 22—*Connection of Cable to Transmission Drive Gear*

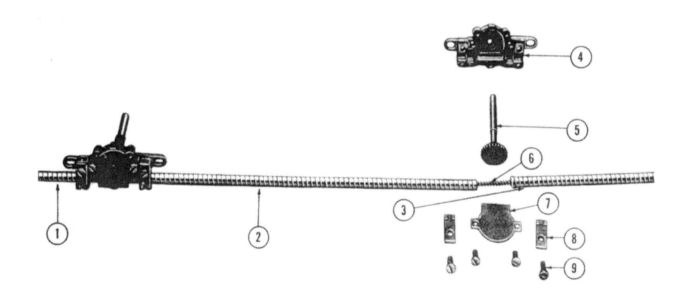

1. Windshield Wiper Cable Armor, Left
2. Windshield Wiper Cable Armor, Center
3. Windshield Wiper Cable Armor, Right
4. Windshield Wiper Drive Shaft Housing
5. Windshield Wiper Drive Shaft
6. Windshield Wiper Cable
7. Windshield Wiper Cable Shaft Housing Cover Plate
8. Windshield Wiper Cable Armor to Shaft Housing Clamp
9. Cover Plate and Clamp Screws

FIGURE 23—*Windshield Wiper Cable and Attaching Parts*

1. Right Defroster Hose and Nozzle
2. Drive Shaft and Housing Assembly
3. Motor and Transmission Assembly
4. Wires Through Dash Panel to Motor

FIGURE 24—*Location of Wiper Motor and Drive Shaft and Housing Assembly in Body on Right Side (Instrument Panel Glove Box Removed)*

Each drive shaft housing is positioned to the cable armor by two clamps which retain their proper spacing on the cable for alignment of the shaft into the holes in the cowl panel. These clamps may also be loosened while the housings are being tightened to the dash panel, then retightened. This will prevent any misalignment or binding of the cable to the sprocket end of the shaft or misalignment of the shaft in the holes of the cowl panel.

The drive shaft is packed with lubriplate when it is inserted into the housing.

The right side drive shaft and housing assembly is visible when the glove box is removed.

Both sides are accessible for removal after the defroster nozzles are removed.

NOTE: *Disconnect the battery before performing any service operation to either the switch, motor, or cable assemblies.*

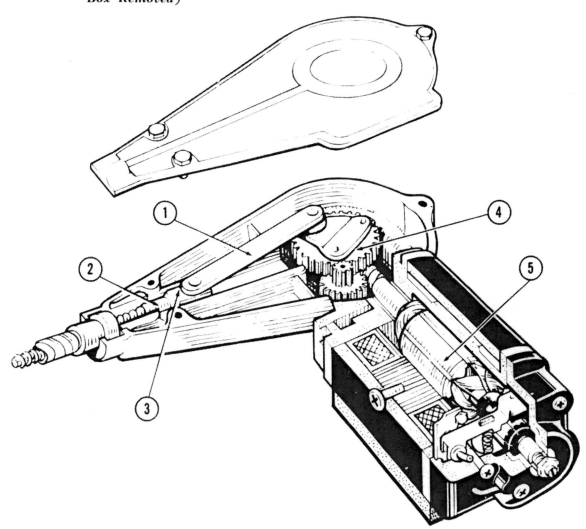

1. Connecting Arm   4. Final Gear
2. Inner Cable   5. Armature
3. Trunnion

FIGURE 25—*Sectional View of Windshield Wiper Motor*

1. Top Mounting Nut

FIGURE 26—_Location of Inside Mounting Nut for Windshield Wiper Motor on Right Front Wheelhouse Panel Under Hood_

1. Lower Mounting Nut

FIGURE 27—_Location of Outside Mounting Nut for Windshield Wiper Motor on Top Ledge of Right Front Wheelhouse Panel Under Right Front Fender_

Windshield Wiper Motor and Transmission Assembly

The motor and transmission assembly is mounted to the dash and front wheelhouse panel from the inside behind the instrument panel. Two studs from the motor housing are inserted through the dash and front wheelhouse panels and fastened by washers, lock washers and nuts on the outside. One of these is visible when the hood is raised (Fig. 26). The other is not visible but is accessible for removal. It is located on the top ledge of the right front wheelhouse panel, under the right front fender as shown in Figure 27.

It is not necessary to remove the windshield wiper motor and transmission assembly to disconnect the cable or wires.

The transmission cover plate is exposed and accessible for removal to disconnect the cable as shown in Figure 28.

After the cable is disconnected from the transmission, either the motor and transmission assembly or the cable and drive shaft assembly can be removed individually without disturbing the other.

The wires enter the dash panel from the engine compartment below the wiper motor and are mounted to the motor end as shown in Figure 28.

Windshield Wiper Control and Switch Assembly

The windshield wiper control and switch assembly are mounted to the instrument panel to the left side of the steering column.

The switch is retained to the instrument panel by a nut accessible after the knob is removed. The knob is fastened to the switch shaft by a set screw (Fig. 29).

WINDSHIELD WIPER MOTOR TEST DATA

Normal Current Consumption (Motor Cold and Driving Both Blades on a Wet Windshield)	2.0—3.25 Amperes
Stall Current (Motor Cold)	7.5—8.5 Amperes
Armature Resistance (Between Adjacent Commutator Segments)	0.8—1.0 Ohms
Field Coil Resistance	8.4—9.0 Ohms

Protective thermostat opens circuit at 194°F. to 203°F. and recloses the circuit at or just before temperature is reduced to 140°F.

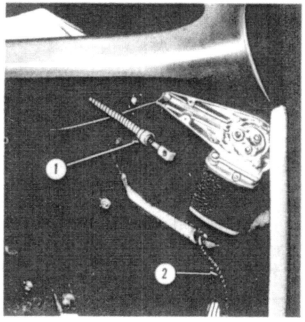

1. Cable End Removed from Transmission
2. Wires Through Dash Panel to End of Motor

FIGURE 28—*Removing Wiper Cable from Transmission Without Removing Motor and Transmission Assembly from Car*

1. Wiper Control Knob
2. Nut

FIGURE 29—*Windshield Wiper Control and Switch*

TECHNICAL SERVICE LETTER REFERENCE

Date	Letter No.	Subject	Changes information on Page No.

Technical Service Manual

HEADLINING — INSTRUMENT PANEL AND MOUNTED ASSEMBLIES

Headlining–Instrument Panel and Mounted Assemblies

HEADLINING — INSTRUMENT PANEL and MOUNTED ASSEMBLIES

HEADLINING

The headlining is tailored to conform with the contour of the roof panel and provides an interior trim surface for the car ceiling.

At the seam of each of the fitted panels, a tubular cloth strip or listing is sewed. Listing wires are inserted through these listings. The ends of the wires are fastened to the side roof rails with screws. This serves as a support for the headlining from the windshield header to the rear window frame.

It is retained along the side roof rail by a saw tooth metal retainer strip which extends along the door opening from the windshield header down to the belt line.

On first type units, it was cemented to the side roof rail under the door glass header sealer rubber.

The rear edge of the headlining is cemented to the rear window frame and concealed by the rear window sealer rubber and the finish moulding frame.

The front edge of the headlining is cemented to the windshield header; then held in place by a steel trim rail fastened with screws, all concealed by the headlining.

Headlining Removal

Remove rear window finish moulding.
   Remove rear quarter trim panel.
   Loosen and remove headlining from under top edge of rear window sealer rubber.

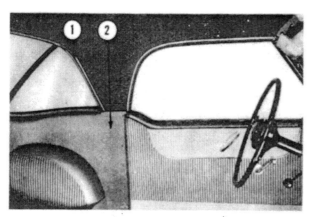

1. **Rear Window Finish Moulding**
2. **Rear Quarter Trim Panel**

FIGURE 1—*Trim Parts to be Removed for Headlining Removal*

Then with a dull putty knife, unhook the headlining from the saw teeth of the retainer along the side roof rail (Fig. 2). On units where the headlining is cemented to the side roof rail, the sealer rubber and retainer must be removed first.

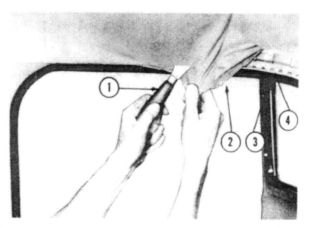

1. **Lifting Headlining Off Saw Teeth of Retainer**
2. **Pulling Headlining Down as It is Released from Retainer**
3. **Headlining Retainer**
4. **Saw Teeth on Inside of Retainer (Next to Body)**

FIGURE 2—*Removing Headlining from Retainer*

Remove screws holding headlining listing wires to side roof rails (Fig. 3); start at the rear listing wire and continue toward the windshield.

With the headlining lowered in this manner, the inside front edge trim rail at the windshield header will be visible and accessible for removal to completely free the headlining from the body.

> NOTE: *The headlining listing wires are of different lengths and should be left in the headlining at the time of removal. When a new headlining is to be installed, the listing wires can be transferred to their correct location.*

INSTRUMENT PANEL

The top edge of the instrument panel is fastened to the top of the dash panel with sheet metal screws. These screws are visible when the windshield lower finish moulding is removed. Each end of the instrument panel is also fastened to the front body pillar with a sheet metal screw. The bottom flange of the instrument panel is supported by two instrument panel to dash braces (Fig. 6).

HEADLINING — INSTRUMENT PANEL AND MOUNTED ASSEMBLIES

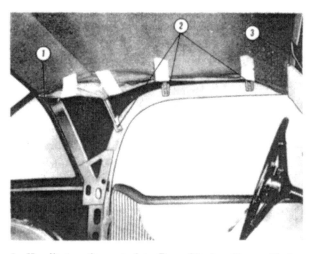

1. Headlining Cemented to Rear Window Frame Under Sealer Rubber Lip
2. Headlining Listing Wires Screwed to Side Roof Rails
3. Headlining Folded Over Concealing Edge of Trim Rail at Windshield Header

FIGURE 3—*Removing Headlining from Body*

GLOVE BOX

The glove box is fastened to the flange of the glove box opening in the instrument panel with sheet metal screws. These are visible and accessible for removal through the opening in the instrument panel (Fig. 6).

On cars equipped with a glove box door, the hinges are riveted to the door while the hinge base is welded to the instrument panel. The hinge pins can be removed after the glove box is removed.

Glove Box Lock

The glove box lock cylinder housing is inserted through the door from the outside and retained to the door by a lock nut. The latch assembly is set into the lock housing from the inside of the door and retained to the housing with a set screw. The lock striker is spot welded to the glove box upper opening flange.

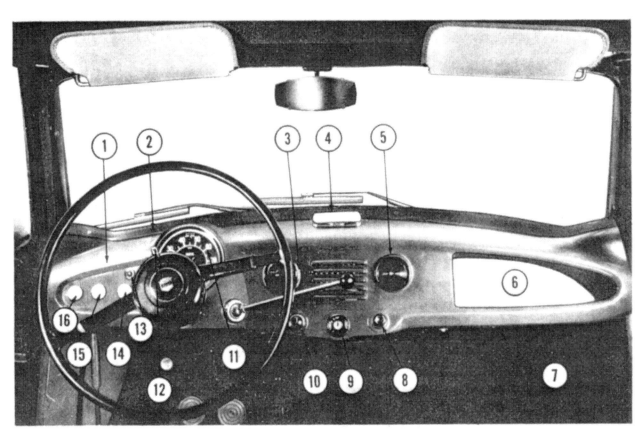

1. Instrument Panel
2. Windshield Lower Finish Moulding
3. Radio Station Selector Knob
4. Ash Receiver
5. Radio Switch and Volume Control Knob
6. Glove Box
7. Instrument Panel to Body Pillar Fastening Screw
8. Cigar Lighter
9. Ignition Key Lock and Light Switch Assembly
10. Starter Button (Pull-Out)
11. Instrument Cluster and Speedometer
12. Directional Signal Control Lever
13. Directional Signal Flasher Light
14. Windshield Wiper Control Switch
15. Weather Eye Water Valve and Defroster Fan Switch Control Knob
16. Choke

FIGURE 4—*Instrument Panel*

HEADLINING — INSTRUMENT PANEL AND MOUNTED ASSEMBLIES

1. Courtesy Light Switch (Late Type)
2. Glove Box Door

FIGURE 5—_Instrument Panel With Glove Box Door_

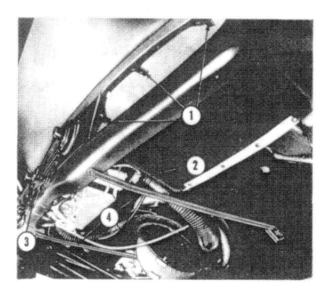

1. Glove Box Mounting to Instrument Panel
2. Courtesy Light
3. Courtesy Light Switch
4. Instrument Panel to Dash Braces

FIGURE 6—_Glove Box, Courtesy Light, Switch, and Instrument Panel to Dash Braces_

1. Glove Box Cylinder Housing	3. Latch Assembly
2. Lock Nut	4. Rubber Bumpers
	5. Lock Striker

FIGURE 7—_Glove Box Lock Mounting_

Cylinder Lock and Latch Removal

Remove the set screw from the housing (Fig. 8).

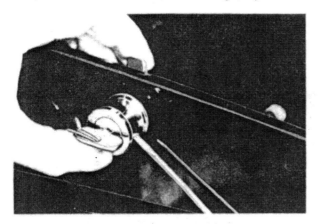

FIGURE 8—*Removing Lock Housing Set Screw*

Lift the latch assembly from the lock housing and then lift out the cylinder (Fig. 9).

When reassembling the lock and latch to the housing, the hole in the latch assembly must index with the screw hole in the cylinder lock housing.

INSTRUMENT PANEL COURTESY LIGHT

The instrument panel courtesy light bulb and socket are located under the instrument panel on the right instrument panel to dash brace.

On first type units, the courtesy light switch is combined with the headlamp switch which is also a part of the ignition key lock and switch assembly.

On later units, the courtesy light switch is located on the instrument panel lower flange to the right of the cigar lighter (Fig. 5).

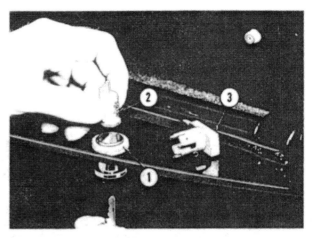

1. Cylinder Lock Housing
2. Lock Cylinder
3. Latch Assembly

FIGURE 9—*Removing Lock Cylinder*

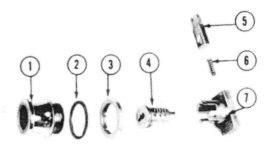

1. Cylinder Lock Housing	5. Latch Bolt
2. Spacer	6. Spring
3. Nut	7. Latch Housing
4. Lock Cylinder	

FIGURE 10—*Complete Lock Parts*

TECHNICAL SERVICE LETTER REFERENCE

Date	Letter No.	Subject	Changes information on Page No.

TECHNICAL SERVICE LETTER REFERENCE

Date	Letter No.	Subject	Changes information on Page No.

Technical Service Manual

SEAT ASSEMBLIES AND ADJUSTERS

Seat Assemblies and Adjusters

SEAT ASSEMBLIES and ADJUSTERS

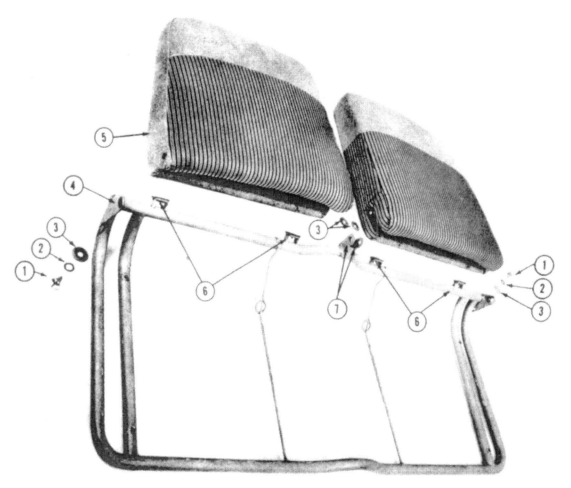

1. Shoulder Screw
2. Spring Washer
3. Fibre Washer
4. Threaded Bushing in Seat Base
5. Socket in Seat Back Outer Hinge Bracket
6. Seat Back Stop Rubber Bumpers and Screws
7. Seat Base Center Hinge Brackets
8. Seat Back Center Hinge Pin Welded to Seat Back Frame

FIGURE 1—Seat Bottom Frame and Folding Back Assemblies

FRONT SEAT ASSEMBLY

The front seat has split backs which fold forward. This assembly prior to trim installation, consists of a tubular seat bottom frame, and a right and left tubular seat back frame, each hinged to the seat base at the center and at each end.

A hinge pin and bracket assembly is welded to the inside lower edge of the back tubular frame to hinge the seat back at the center of the seat bottom frame (Fig. 1). When the seat back is mounted to the seat bottom frame, this hinge pin is inserted into the seat bottom panel center hinge bracket.

A bushing assembly is welded to the outside lower edge of the seat back frame. A threaded bushing is provided on the outside edge of the seat bottom frame. This permits the use of a threaded shoulder screw which can be tightened into the bushing of the bottom frame end bracket after the smooth pin section of the shoulder screw is inserted into the bushing of the seat back.

Fibre washers are used on the seat back pins at the center hinge and between the upholstery and the seat bottom frame end brackets. They serve as spacer washers and to prevent damage to the seat back upholstery. Spring washers are used on each end between the seat base bracket and the fibre washers. They serve as tension and spacer washers.

When the seat backs are to be removed from the seat bottom frame, it is only necessary to remove the shoulder screw and lift the seat back up on the outside edge and pull it away from the center hinge.

The seat bottom frame is mounted to studs on the seat adjuster slides. Concave washers are used to fit the contour of the tubular frame at the top and bottom; lock washers and nuts hold it securely (Fig. 2).

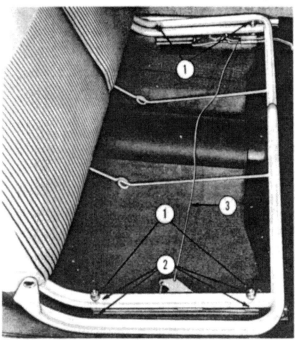

1. **Seat Bottom Frame to Adjuster Nuts and Lock Washer**
2. **Concave Washers**
3. **Latch Wire**

FIGURE 2—*Front Seat Bottom Frame Mounted to Seat Adjuster Slides—First Type*

A coil spring fastened to the seat base and body floor is under tension when the seat assembly is pushed to the rear position. This spring tension assists in moving the seat to the forward positions.

Each seat adjuster is provided with a latch to hold the adjusted position selected. Two types of latch wires have been used.

The first type (Fig. 2) is adjustable at one end with a nut and lock nut. It must be adjusted so both latches will release simultaneously when the control handle is operated. This latch wire is placed on top of the seat base cross supports (Fig. 3).

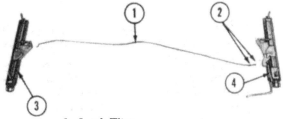

1. **Latch Wire**
2. **Latch Wire Adjustable Nuts**
3. **Adjuster Slide, Right**
4. **Adjuster Slide, Left**

FIGURE 3—*Seat Adjuster Slides and Latch Wire—First Type*

The second type latch wire is placed under the seat base cross supports. It is coupled to the latches by a coil spring sleeve and anchored to the front cross tube with a clip which allows the wire to slide in it when operating the handle (Fig. 4).

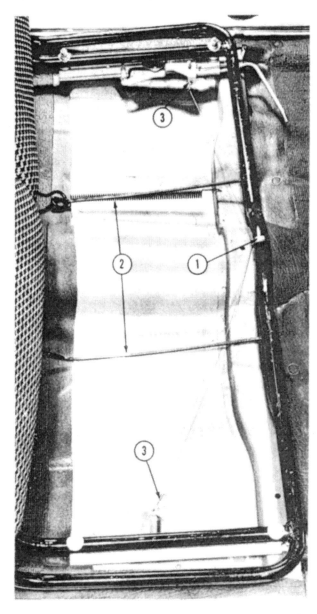

1. **Latch Wire Mounting to Front Tube**
2. **Seat Base Cross Supports**
3. **Latch Wire Anchored to Latch**

FIGURE 4—*Front Seat Bottom Frame With Second Type Latch Wire Mounting*

FRONT SEAT BACK UPHOLSTERY ASSEMBLY AND SPRING

Front Seat Back Upholstery Assembly

The upholstery on the back of the front seat back is referred to as the front seat kickpad (Fig. 5).

The upholstery on the ends of the seat back, which is sewed to the kickpad and front seat back, is in two sections:

Front seat back outside facing
Front seat back inside facing

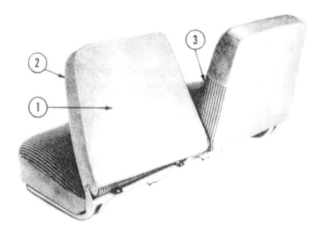

1. Front Seat Back Kickpad
2. Front Seat Back Outside Facing
3. Front Seat Back Inside Facing

FIGURE 5—*Front Seat Cushion and Folding Back Assembly (Rear View)*

The upholstery on the front of the front seat back is referred to as the front seat back upholstery (Fig. 6).

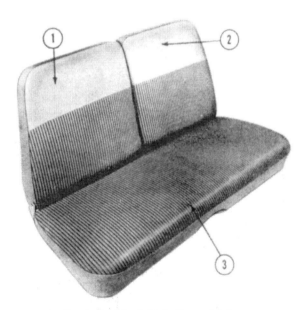

1. Front Seat Back Upholstery, Right
2. Front Seat Back Upholstery, Left
3. Front Seat Cushion Assembly

FIGURE 6—*Front Seat Cushion and Folding Backs (Front View)*

The front seat back upholstery kickpad and facings are sewed together to form the front seat back upholstery assembly.

This assembly is removed from and installed on the seat back frame and spring assembly as one unit after the seat backs are removed from the seat bottom frame.

Each seat back has two listing wires which are fastened to the spring at the bottom with hog rings (Fig. 7).

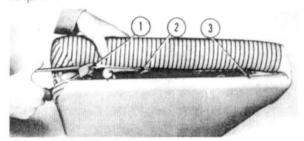

1. Hog Rings Holding Listing Wires to Springs
2. Listing Wire in Listing Front Seat Back Upholstery Section
3. Listing Wire in Listing Kickpad Upholstery Section

FIGURE 7—*Fastening Seat Back Upholstery to Seat Back and Springs*

Removal Procedure

Remove front seat back assembly from front seat bottom frame.

Remove hog rings from listings wires at bottom of seat back (Fig. 7).

Remove listing wires from upholstery.

Lift upholstery over seat back inside pivot pin.

Fold upholstery assembly and remove as a unit from top of front seat back frame and spring assembly holding cotton pad to prevent tearing pad (Fig. 8).

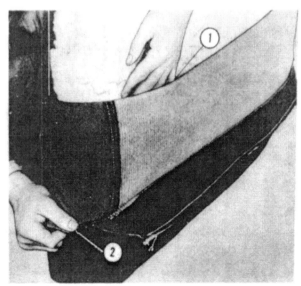

1. Holding Pad Assembly
2. Folding Upholstery Assembly From Front Seat Back Frame and Spring Assembly

FIGURE 8—*Removing Upholstery Assembly from Front Seat Back Frame, Spring and Pad Assembly*

Removing Front Seat Spring and Pad Assembly from Seat Back Frame

Remove the seat back upholstery and lift seat back spring supports from hooks in top and inside tubing of seat back frame.

Lift spring assembly from bottom of seat back tubing, releasing spring bottom supports (Fig. 9).

Front Seat Back Spring, Pad, and Insulation Assembly

As shown in Figure 9, the combination spring and topper pad is fastened to the spring assembly with hog rings.

These parts may be removed and reinstalled in the event of spring replacement after the upholstery and the spring and pad assembly have been removed from the seat back frame.

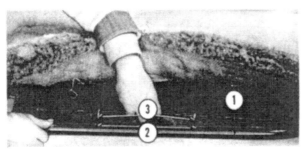

1. Seat Back Top Rail
2. Holes in Seat Back Top Rail for Spring Supports
3. Spring Supports

FIGURE 9—Removing Front Seat Back Spring and Pad Assembly from Front Seat Back Frame

FRONT SEAT CUSHION

The front seat cushion assembly, as shown in Figure 6, consists of springs, spring pad support, foam pad, and upholstery. The first type is fastened to the spring assembly as shown in Figure 10 while later models use hog rings.

Spring Pad Support

The spring pad support is a series of spring steel wire interwoven into a burlap covering. It is fastened to the top border wire of the springs with hog rings. This forms a support for the foam pad and prevents possible sagging of the cushion pad between the spring coils.

Front Seat Cushion Upholstery Removal

Remove cushion from car and place on clean cloth or bench. Unhook upholstery cover from springs and remove.

Cushion Spring Removal Procedure— After Upholstery Removal

Cut hog rings from pad skirt to spring.

Cut hog rings and remove spring border wire pad.

Cut hog rings and remove spring pad support.

NOTE: *When installing new springs, inspect and tighten all coil and diagonal brace wire clips. If necessary, install "C" clips over diagonal brace wire ends and border wires. Rough handling of springs in shipment for service replacement often loosens the clips causing failure.*

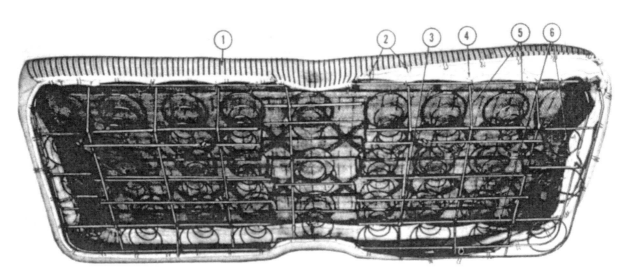

1. Front Seat Cushion Assembly (Rear of Cushion)
2. Front Seat Cushion Upholstery with Hook on Listing
3. Front of Foam Pad Skirt Fastened to Spring Top Border Wire at Front Edge
4. Rear of Foam Pad Skirt Fastened to Spring Lower Border Wire at Rear Edge
5. Spring Pad Support (Burlap with Spring Steel Wire Supports
6. Spring Pad Support Fastened to Spring Top Border Wire with Hog Rings

FIGURE 10—Front Seat Cushion Assembly

REAR SEAT BACK

The rear seat back assembly is one unit for the complete width of the body. It consists of a wood base panel, pad, and upholstery which is tacked to the inside edge of the wood base panel.

This assembly is hinged at the bottom to the lower flat surface of the shock absorber towers. When it is in the raised position, it serves as a seat back rest.

The seat back is retained in the raised position by a lock and striker assembly mounted at the top center of the seat back and belt rail.

REAR SEAT BACK LOCKS

The A Series locking arrangement consists of a rear seat back catch mounted to the top center of the seat back rest.

This catch assembly engages an adjustable spring tension friction type striker assembly mounted to the body belt rail. The seat back is lowered by pulling the seat back forward which disengages the catch assembly.

On the B and 1500 Series, a key lock assembly is used whereby the lock bolt is actuated with the key to engage the lock bolt arm with the striker.

1. Rear Seat Back Assembly (Front View)
2. Rear Seat Back Hinges
3. Rear Seat Back Key Lock

FIGURE 11—*Rear Seat Back Assembly Latched —Raised Position—B and 1500 Series Shown*

1. Rear Seat Back Assembly (Rear View)
2. Rear Seat Back Hinges
3. Rear Seat Back Lock Striker
4. Rear Seat Back Key Lock Bolt
5. Trunk Compartment Rubber Mat

FIGURE 12—*Rear Seat Back Folded Forward—A Series Shown*

7

SEAT ASSEMBLIES AND ADJUSTERS

1. Locking Cam Arm Retaining Bolt
2. Lock Washer
3. Locking Cam Arm
4. Spacer Washer
5. Lock Retaining Nut
6. Locating Washer
7. Cylinder Lock and Lock Housing

FIGURE 13—Rear Seat Back Key Lock Assembly—B and 1500 Series

A push button release type key lock assembly has been incorporated in the rear seat back on 1500 Series cars. The lock catch engages the adjustable lock striker under spring tension to retain the seat back in the raised position.

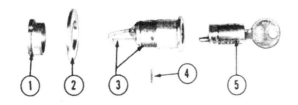

1. Lock Retaining Nut
2. Lock Escutcheon
3. Locking Catch and Cylinder Housing
4. Cylinder to Housing Retaining Pin
5. Key Lock Cylinder

FIGURE 14—Rear Seat Back Lock Assembly Push Button Type

The lock assemblies are inserted through the seat back and retained in position by either a locking nut or collar.

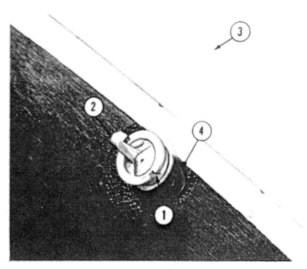

1. Locking Collar
2. Lock Catch
3. Front of Seat Back
4. Rear of Seat Back

FIGURE 15—Seat Back Lock Mounting— Push Button Type Shown

REAR SEAT CUSHION

The rear seat cushion consists of a completely upholstered pillow type pad made up into one unit extending the full width of the seat. It is retained in its proper position by two hold down straps sewed to the cushion front edge.

The first type is fastened to the front of the cushion riser with glove type snap fasteners (Fig. 16) while the second type is fastened to the top of the cushion riser under the cushion.

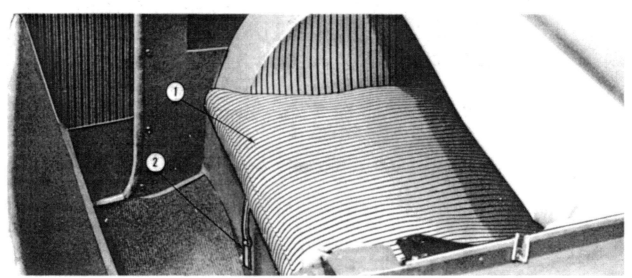

1. Rear Seat Cushion Assembly
2. Rear Seat Cushion Assembly Hold Down Straps

FIGURE 16—Rear Seat Cushion

TECHNICAL SERVICE LETTER REFERENCE

Date	Letter No.	Subject	Changes information on Page No.

Technical Service Manual

Convertible Top— Deck Cover

CONVERTIBLE TOP— DECK COVER

FIGURE 1—*Convertible Top in Raised Position—Model A and B Series Shown*

TOP OPERATION

The convertible top is raised and lowered manually. The folding frame assembly is fastened to and pivots at the body lock pillar. The back curtain with its three vinylite windows is sewed to the top cover. The front of the top is located on the windshield header by two dowels and locked into position by toggle clamps. It is retained along the belt rail by glove type snap fasteners.

On early production units, the top was retained along the belt rail permanently with bolts and nuts which also include the male studs for the top boot cover.

To Lower the Top

Release snap fasteners holding the rear curtain to the sides and across the back of the belt rail.

Push rear curtain to inside so it will fold into the rear seat compartment when the top is lowered.

Release toggle clamps above the windshield.

Lift front top bow and as the complete top is lowered, step into the rear seat compartment.

Disengage the front side rails from the rear side rails.

Then lift the front top bow and front side rail assemblies toward the front of the car. This will permit the side rail connecting links to pivot and allow the front section of the top to fold forward to a full lowered position.

CAUTION: *To prevent chafing or cutting the top cover at the front top bow, do not permit the front top bow to slide on the belt rail or front end of the rear side rail when raising or lowering the top.*

Care must also be exercised to fold the top material in such a manner that it is not pinched between any of the folding bows.

To Raise the Top

With the door open, tilt the front seat back forward and step into the rear seat compartment.

Holding the front bow in the center, lift up and push backward to bring the side rails into alignment and insert the ends of the front rails into the rear rails on both sides.

Holding the front bow, lift the complete top up and push forward, stepping out of the car as the top is being raised.

Align the front bow over the dowel pins in the windshield header and fasten the toggle clamps.

Fasten snap fasteners holding rear curtain to belt rail.

FRONT TOP BOW WEATHER SEAL

The weather seal (Fig. 2) is fastened to the front top bow with sheet metal screws.

CONVERTIBLE TOP— DECK COVER

SIDE RAIL WEATHER STRIPS

The side rail weather strips are set into "U" shaped metal retainers which in turn are screwed to the side rail (Fig. 2). These are adjustable in or out to provide a positive seal of the door glass.

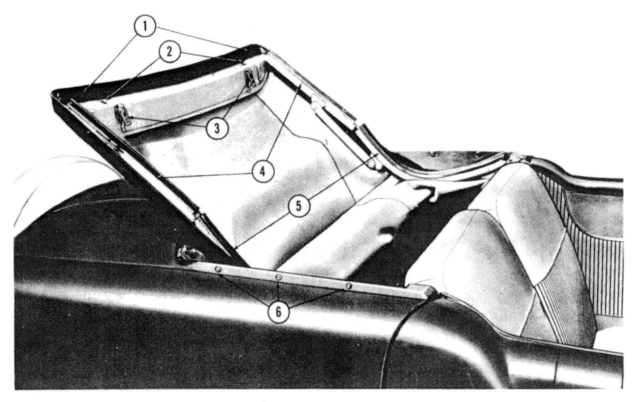

1. Front Top Bow Weather Seal
2. Windshield Header Dowel Locating Sockets
3. Toggle Clamps
4. Front Side Rails
5. Rear Side Rails
6. Snap Fastener Studs

FIGURE 2—*Front Side Rail Interlocking With Rear Side Rail*

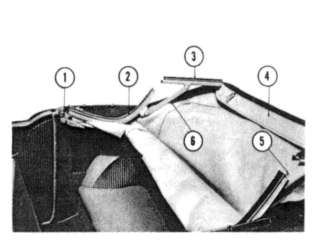

1. Pivot Fastening to Body Lock Pillar
2. Rear Side Rail
3. Front Side Rail
4. Front Top Bow
5. Location Tongue Front Side Rail to Rear Side Rail
6. Front to Rear Side Rail Connecting Link

FIGURE 3—*Front Top Bow and Side Rail Assembly Disengaged from Rear Side Rails*

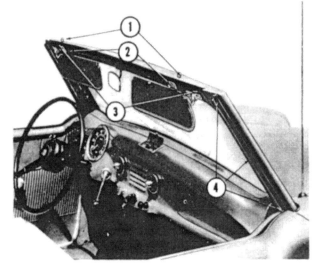

1. Dowels on Windshield Header
2. Toggle Clamp Catch
3. Sponge Rubber Sealer
4. Windshield Post Door Weather Seal

FIGURE 4—*Convertible Top Locating Dowels and Sealers*

1. Top Covering to Rear Side Rail Screw
2. Rear Side Rail Weather Strip
3. Front Top Bow Weather Seal
4. Top Support Strap
5. Rear Bow Pivot Shoulder Bolt

FIGURE 5—*Parts to be Removed for Replacement of Top Covering*

TOP COVERING REMOVAL

Remove the screws located at the top seams to rear bow which hold the top support straps.

Remove screws at the bottom of the rear side rail.

Release the back curtain to belt rail snap fasteners.

Remove the rear bow pivot shoulder bolts.

Slide support straps off the rear bow. Then pull the weather seals from the side rail retainers and remove the retainer screws.

Pull the top material loose at the side rails.

Fold the top assembly to the down position resting the front top bow on the rear deck.

Remove the front top bow weather seal retaining screws and metal strip.

The top is cemented to the front top bow; loosen the top material and remove covering and rear bow from car.

Apply a small amount of Silicone to one end of the bow to facilitate sliding it in or out of the tube sewed onto the top covering.

DECK COVER

An exterior deck cover (trunk lid) has been incorporated on 1500 Series cars.

It consists of inner and outer panels which are flanged and welded together. It is hinged to the front of the deck opening with two die cast chromed hinges and locked at the rear of the opening by a chrome handle and lock assembly (Fig. 6).

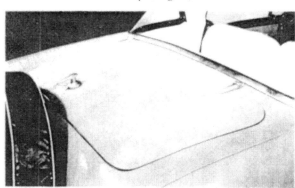

FIGURE 6—*Rear Deck Cover*

REAR DECK DRAIN TROUGH AND SEALER RUBBER

A "U" shaped channel surrounding the trunk opening acts as a drain trough. A drain hose is connected to a drain tube at each rear corner of the drain trough.

A one piece sealer rubber is cemented into a "U" shaped channel welded to the inside of the drain trough opening to provide a seal against the **deck cover**.

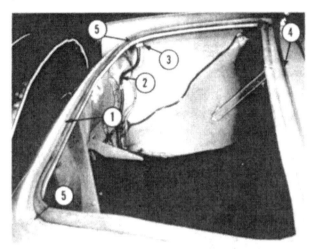

1. Trunk Sealer Rubber
2. Drain Hose
3. Drain Hose to Drain Tube Clamp
4. Drain Trough
5. Drain Tube

FIGURE 7—*Rear Deck Drain Trough Hose and Sealer Rubber*

DECK COVER HINGES

Die cast chrome hinges are fastened to the upper deck panel and deck cover by threaded studs, washers, and nuts.

The cover is retained in the open position by a telescope type stay hinge. When the deck cover is raised, the stay hinge mechanism locks itself in the extended position to hold the deck cover open. To lower the deck cover, it must be raised slightly to trip the latch which will allow the stay hinge to telescope.

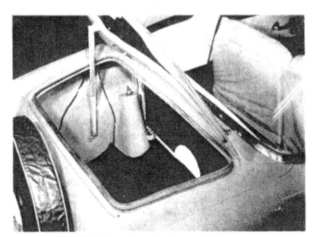

FIGURE 8—*Deck Cover Stay Hinge*

DECK COVER HANDLE AND LOCK

The handle and key lock cylinder are assembled into one permanent unit. This unit is removable from the deck cover only after the deck cover lock is removed.

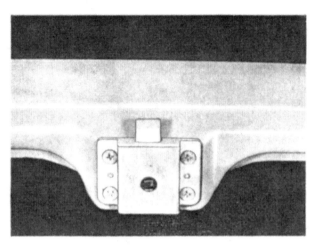

FIGURE 9—*Rear Deck Cover Lock Mounting*

FIGURE 10—*Rear Deck Cover Lock Handle Mounting (Lock Removed)*

DECK COVER LOCK STRIKER

Elongated holes in the lock striker mounting plate allow for up and down adjustment. Serrations on the back of the striker provide a positive anchoring in the desired position.

Metropolitan Lubrication Service Chart

LUBRICATE AT EACH ARROW POINT EVERY 1,000 MILES EXCEPT AS NOTED

ENGINE COMPARTMENT

Water Pump (1 plug) . . . . **EO**
Oil Bath Air Cleaner —
  every 2,000 miles . . . . **EO**
  Clean and refill
    Above +32°F. — SAE 50
    Below +32°F. — SAE 20
Throttle Linkage . . . . **EO**
Gear Shift Lever (fitting) —
  every 5,000 miles . . . . **CL**
Steering Gear (plug) —
  every 3,000 miles . . . . SAE 80 **EPL**
Drag Link (fitting on
  each side) . . . . **CL**
Spark Plugs—3000 miles, clean
  and adjust. Replace at 10,000
  miles. See pages 22, 23.

UNDER CHASSIS

Control Arms (2 fittings on
  each side) . . . . **CL**
Spindle (3 fittings on each
  side) . . . . **CL**
Tie Rod End (fitting on
  each side) . . . . **CL**
Shifting Linkage Grommet
  Bushings . . . . **EO**
Pedal Shaft (fitting) . . . . . **CL**
Master Brake and Clutch
  Cylinders . . . . **HBF**
  Check level — Accessible through
    hole in floor

Wheel Bearings (Repack) . . . **WBL**
  Front — Every 5,000 miles fill
    wheel cup
  Every 10,000 miles Repack
  Rear — Repack only when disassem-
    bled for other service operations

Universal Joints (2 fittings) . . . . **EPL**
  Every 10,000 miles — Use hand gun
  only — SAE 140

Hand Brake Balance Lever
  Assembly — (fitting) . . . . . . **CL**
Hand Brake Controls . . . . **EO**

COOLING SYSTEM DRAIN
  Radiator—Right side, bottom.
  Engine Block—Right side, rear.

Generator (1 oil hole) —
  every 6,000 miles . . . . **EO**
Oil Filter — if so equipped —
  Replace element every 5,000 miles.
CRANKCASE (check level) . . . . **EO**
  Every 2,000 miles drain and refill
  Above +32°F. . . . . SAE 30
  Above +20°F. . . . . . . SAE 20 20W
  Above +10°F. . . . . SAE 10W
  Below +10°F. . . . . SAE 5W
  For sustained high speeds during
  extremely hot weather use SAE 40
Distributor —
  Cam and pivot . . . . **PJ**
  Cam bearings and automatic
    advance . . . . **EO**
Tie Rod End (fitting on
  each side) . . . . **CL**
Idler Assembly (fitting) . . . . . . **CL**

DO NOT LUBRICATE
Rear Springs, Rear Spring Bolts and
Shackles, Shock Absorbers
Clutch Throwout Lever (Clevis) . . . . **EO**
TRANSMISSION (check level) . . . . **EO**
  Dip stick through floor pan
  Summer (Above +32°F.) SAE 40
  Winter (+32° to −10°F.) SAE 30
  Below −10°F. . . . . SAE 20
Every 5,000 miles drain and refill

TIRE PRESSURE (COLD)
Front . . . . 24 lbs.
Rear . . . . 22 lbs.

DIFFERENTIAL (check level) . . . . **HGL**
SAE 90
  Drain, flush, and refill 500 miles on
  new unit. Every 5,000 miles thereafter.

BATTERY—Check water level.
  Do not overfill.

LUBRICANT SYMBOLS
CL Chassis Lubricant
EPL Extreme Pressure Gear Lubricant
HBF Hydraulic Brake Fluid Heavy Duty
  (SAE-70-R-1)
HGL Hypoid Gear Lubricant—Suitable Type
EO Engine Oil
WBL Wheel Bearing Lubricant
PJ Petroleum Jelly

CAPACITIES

MEASURE SYSTEM	CRANKCASE Quarts	TRANSMISSION Pints	DIFFERENTIAL Pints	COOLING SYSTEM With Heater Quarts	Without Heater Quarts	GAS TANK Gallons
U.S.A.	4	5.5	2	8	7	10.5
British Imperial	3.3	4.6	1.6	6.6	5.8	8.7

A SAMPLE LIST OF OTHER BOOKS AVAILABLE FROM

www.VelocePress.com

PLEASE CHECK OUR WEBSITE FOR THE MOST UP-TO-DATE INFORMATION

AUTOBOOKS SERIES OF WORKSHOP MANUALS

ALFA ROMEO GIULIA 1750, 2000 1962-1978 WORKSHOP MANUAL
AUSTIN HEALEY SPRITE, MG MIDGET 1958-1980 WORKSHOP MANUAL
BMW 1600 1966-1973 WORKSHOP MANUAL
FIAT 1100, 1100D, 1100R & 1200 1957-1969 WORKSHOP MANUAL
FIAT 124 1966-1974 WORKSHOP MANUAL
FIAT 124 SPORT 1966-1975 WORKSHOP MANUAL
FIAT 125 & 125 SPECIAL 1967-1973 WORKSHOP MANUAL
FIAT 126, 126L, 126DV, 126/650 & 126/650DV 1972-1982 WORKSHOP MANUAL
FIAT 127 SALOON, SPECIAL & SPORT, 900, 1050 1971-1981 WORKSHOP MANUAL
FIAT 128 1969-1982 WORKSHOP MANUAL
FIAT 1300, 1500 1961-1967 WORKSHOP MANUAL
FIAT 131 MIRAFIORI 1975-1982 WORKSHOP MANUAL
FIAT 132 1972-1982 WORKSHOP MANUAL
FIAT 500 1957-1973 WORKSHOP MANUAL
FIAT 600, 600D & MULTIPLA 1955-1969 WORKSHOP MANUAL
FIAT 850 1964-1972 WORKSHOP MANUAL
JAGUAR E-TYPE 1961-1972 WORKSHOP MANUAL
JAGUAR MK 1, 2 1955-1969 WORKSHOP MANUAL
JAGUAR S TYPE, 420 1963-1968 WORKSHOP MANUAL
JAGUAR XK 120, 140, 150 MK 7, 8, 9 1948-1961 WORKSHOP MANUAL
LAND ROVER 1, 2 1948-1961 WORKSHOP MANUAL
MERCEDES-BENZ 190 1959-1968 WORKSHOP MANUAL
MERCDEDS-BENZ 220/8 1968-1972 WORKSHOP MANUAL
MERCEDES-BENZ 230 1963-1968 WORKSHOP MANUAL
MERCEDES-BENZ 250 1968-1972 WORKSHOP MANUAL
MG MIDGET TA-TF 1936-1955 WORKSHOP MANUAL
MINI 1959-1980 WORKSHOP MANUAL
MORRIS MINOR 1952-1971 WORKSHOP MANUAL
PEUGEOT 404 1960-1975 WORKSHOP MANUAL
PORSCHE 911 1964-1969 WORKSHOP MANUAL
PORSCHE 911 1970-1977 WORKSHOP MANUAL
RENAULT 8, 10, 1100 1962-1971 WORKSHOP MANUAL
RENAULT 16 1965-1979 WORKSHOP MANUAL
ROVER 3500, 3500S 1968-1976 WORKSHOP MANUAL
SUNBEAM RAPIER, ALPINE 1955-1965 WORKSHOP MANUAL
TRIUMPH SPITFIRE, GT6, VITESSE 1962-1968 WORKSHOP MANUAL
TRIUMPH TR2, TR3, TR3A 1952-1962 WORKSHOP MANUAL
TRIUMPH TR4, TR4A 1961-1967 WORKSHOP MANUAL
VOLKSWAGEN BEETLE 1968-1977 WORKSHOP MANUAL

All VelocePress titles are available through your local independent bookseller, Amazon.com, or they may be purchased directly through our website at www.VelocePress.com. Wholesale customers may also purchase directly from us or from the Ingram Book Group.

MOTORCYCLE WORKSHOP MANUALS, MAINTENANCE & TECHNICAL TITLES

ARIEL WORKSHOP MANUAL 1933-1951
BMW FACTORY WORKSHOP MANUAL R26 R27 (1956-1967)
BMW FACTORY WSM R50 R50S R60 R69S R50US R60US R69US (1955-1969)
BSA SERVICE & REPAIR ALL PRE-WAR MODELS TO 1939, SV & OHV 150cc TO 1,000cc
DUCATI FACTORY WORKSHOP MANUAL SINGLE CYLINDER NARROW CASE OHC ENGINES 160cc, 250cc, 350cc - MONZA JUNIOR, MONZA, 250GT, MARK 3, MACH 1, MOTOCROSS & SEBRING
HONDA FACTORY WORKSHOP MANUAL 250cc TO 305cc C/CS/CB 72 & 77 SERIES 1960-1969
HONDA FACTORY WORKSHOP MANUAL 125cc TO 150cc C/CS/CB/CA 92 & 95 SERIES 1959-1966
HONDA FACTORY WORKSHOP MANUAL 50cc C110 SPORT CUB (1962-1969)
HONDA FACTORY WORKSHOP MANUAL 50cc C100 SUPER CUB
HONDA SERVICE & REPAIR 50cc TO 305cc C100, C102, MONKEY BIKE, CE 105H TRIALS BIKE, C110, C114, C92, CB92, BENLEY, C72, CB72, C77 & CB77
NORTON FACTORY WORKSHOP MANUAL 1957-1970
NORTON WORKSHOP MANUAL 1932-1939
ROYAL ENFIELD 736cc INTERCEPTOR & ENFIELD INDIAN CHIEF
SUZUKI T10 FACTORY WORKSHOP MANUAL 250cc 1963-1967
SUZUKI T20 & T200 FACTORY WORKSHOP MANUAL 200cc X-5 INVADER & STING RAY SCRAMBLER, 250cc X-6 HUSTLER 1965-1969
TRIUMPH FACTORY WORKSHOP MANUAL NO. 11 (1945-1955)
TRIUMPH WORKSHOP MANUAL 1935-1939
TRIUMPH WORKSHOP MANUAL 1937-1951
VESPA SERVICE & REPAIR ALL MODELS 125cc & 150cc 1951-1961
VINCENT SERVICE & REPAIR 1935-1955

CLASSIC AUTO TITLES & REFERENCE BOOKS

ABARTH BUYERS GUIDE
CARRERA PANAMERICANA 1950 ~ THE STORY OF THE 1950 MEXICAN ROAD RACE
DIALED IN ~ THE JAN OPPERMAN STORY
FERRARI 308 SERIES BUYER'S AND OWNER'S GUIDE
FERRARI BERLINETTA LUSSO
FERRARI BROCHURES & SALES LITERATURE 1946-1967
FERRARI SERIAL NUMBERS PART I ~ STREET CARS TO SERIAL # 21399 (1948-1977)
FERRARI SERIAL NUMBERS PART II ~ RACE CARS TO SERIAL # 1050 (1948-1973)
FERRARI SPYDER CALIFORNIA
IF HEMINGWAY HAD WRITTEN A RACING NOVEL ~ THE BEST OF MOTOR RACING FICTION 1950-2000
LE MANS 24 ~ WHAT THE MOVIE COULD HAVE BEEN
MASERATI BROCHURES AND SALES LITERATURE ~ POSTWAR THROUGH INLINE 6 CYLINDER CARS

All VelocePress titles are available through your local independent bookseller, Amazon.com, or they may be purchased directly through our website at www.VelocePress.com. Wholesale customers may also purchase directly from us or from the Ingram Book Group.

OTHER WORKSHOP MANUALS, MAINTENANCE & TECHNICAL TITLES

AUSTIN HEALEY SIX CYLINDER CARS 1956-1968
BMW ISETTA FACTORY REPAIR MANUAL
FERRARI 250/GT SERVICE AND MAINTENANCE
FERRARI GUIDE TO PERFORMANCE
FERRARI OPERATING, MAINTENANCE & SERVICE HANDBOOKS 1948-1963
FERRARI OWNER'S HANDBOOK
FERRARI TUNING TIPS & MAINTENANCE TECHNIQUES
METROPOLITAN WORKSHOP MANUAL
MASERATI OWNER'S HANDBOOK
OBERT'S FIAT GUIDE
PERFORMANCE TUNING THE SUNBEAM TIGER
PORSCHE 356 SERVICE AND MAINTENANCE MANUAL 1948-1965
PORSCHE 912 WORKSHOP MANUAL
SOUPING THE VOLKSWAGEN IMPROVING THE PERFORMANCE OF YOUR VW
TRIUMPH TR2, TR3 & TR4 WORKSHOP MANUAL
VOLVO ALL MODELS 1944-1968 WORKSHOP MANUAL

BROOKLANDS ROAD TEST PORTFOLIOS

FIAT DINO 1968-1973
MV AGUSTA F4 750 & 1000 1997-2007
JAGUAR MK1 & MK2 1955-1969
LOTUS CORTINA 1963-1970
FIAT 500 1936-1972
FERRARI ROAD CARS 1946-1956

CPSIA information can be obtained at www.ICGtesting.com
Printed in the USA
LVOW12s2323230814

400616LV00001B/68/P